PRAISE FOR
SOMETHING BETWEEN US

"A piercing account of the fortress mindset that has gripped American culture, hardening not only our politics but also our homes, roads, bodies, and minds. Pandian pulls off the great anthropological trick of making the familiar seem strange and disturbing. An important book."

—**ERIC KLINENBERG**, author of *Palaces for the People: How Social Infrastructure Can Help Fight Inequality, Polarization, and the Decline of Civic Life* and *2020: One City, Seven People, and the Year Everything Changed*

"A brave book tackling some of our most contentious political issues through, at times, harrowing fieldwork. It accomplishes the rare feat of balancing the intellectual acuity of ethnographic study with the wit and urgency of journalism. I was left both unnerved and inspired to action."

—**BRADLEY GARRETT**, author of *Bunker: What It Takes to Survive the Apocalypse*

"In *Something Between Us*, Anand Pandian offers a profound interrogation of the walls—literal and figurative—that divide American life. Through sharp and considerate ethnography, Pandian reveals the insidious ways fear and exclusion shape the divisions of our daily interactions. This essential work invites readers to dismantle these barriers, envisioning new structures for humanity built on mutuality, openness, and repair."

—**JOVAN SCOTT LEWIS**, author of *Violent Utopia: Dispossession and Black Restoration in Tulsa*

"This is not a book, to start with, but an experience. I would rank it as some of the best writing by just about anyone lately about the ways our environments, our infrastructure, and our politics keep us divided, topics that are not easy to write about well or at all. I am glad he did that work; he created something truly wonderful as a result."

—JOSHUA RENO, co-author of *Imagining the Heartland: White Supremacy and the American Midwest*

"*Something Between Us* is a profound and fascinating exploration of the fortresses we've built around ourselves in America—in our communities and in our minds—and a rousing call to a more hopeful vision of collective life."

—ELI PARISER, author of *The Filter Bubble: What the Internet Is Hiding from You*

SOMETHING BETWEEN US

SOMETHING BETWEEN US

REDWOOD PRESS

An Imprint of Stanford University Press

STANFORD, CALIFORNIA

The Everyday Walls
of American Life,
and How
to Take Them Down

ANAND PANDIAN

Stanford University Press
Stanford, California

Library of Congress Cataloging-in-Publication Data
Names: Pandian, Anand, author.
Title: Something between us : the everyday walls of American life, and how to take them down / Anand Pandian.
Description: Stanford, California : Redwood Press, an imprint of Stanford University Press, 2025. | Includes index.
Identifiers: LCCN 2024029464 | ISBN 9781503637870 (cloth) | ISBN 9781503642324 (ebook)
Subjects: LCSH: Polarization (Social sciences) — United States. | Social conflict — United States. | Political culture — United States. | Group identity — Political aspects — United States. | United States — Social conditions — 21st century.
Classification: LCC HN90.P57 P37 2025 | DDC 306.0973 — dc23/eng/20240809
LC record available at https://lccn.loc.gov/2024029464

Cover design: Martyn Schmoll
Cover art: iStock

For neighbors near and far

CONTENTS

PREFACE

I spent a few weeks driving across the United States in the summer of 2017, not long after Donald Trump's first inauguration as president of the country. One afternoon during a stopover in a small town in southern Michigan, I went out to a park on the edge of that town to catch up on some notes and phone calls. After some time, a white man in his sixties sat down on the bench beside me, and we fell into conversation. He was slightly drunk, a little red in the eye, and keen to talk. He had recently retired from work as a mechanic at a nearby plant. His wife was ailing, mostly bedridden at home, and he was worried about her medical care.

I can't remember how the subject of politics came up, but he told me that he'd voted for Trump the previous year. He also wanted me to understand that this didn't change what he owed me as a newcomer to his town. No, he didn't know me from Adam, but our meeting was the Lord's blessing, he told me, and I ought to have someone around there to call on in case of trouble. He scribbled down his number and address on a scrap of paper and insisted that I take it. "I don't care if you're brown or red or whatever," he told me, and I believed him.

I was heading out the next morning, but I kept thinking about that unexpected gesture of kindness. It was like a flash of some other solidarity that still remained possible. I picked up a pie at a market nearby, meaning to drop it off for that man and his family. When I pulled up at the address he'd shared, the shades were drawn, and no one seemed to be home. I left the pie and a note on the concrete landing of that small tract house clad in blue vinyl siding. I felt a bit nervous and exposed, walking back to my car. I was, after all, a stranger. But it felt like the right thing to do. He had treated me like a neighbor, and I wanted to reciprocate.

This encounter has been much on my mind in the fall of 2024, as I strive to make sense, like so many others, of an election that returns Trump to the White House, despite all that we'd seen in his first term as president. Time and again, the rival presidential candidates talked about strangers and neighbors, but in different ways. In her final weeks on the campaign trail, Kamala Harris spoke regularly about the need to take strangers *as* neighbors, vowing in her concession address at Howard University on November 6 to continue heeding "how we live our lives, by treating one another with kindness and respect, by looking in the face of a stranger and seeing a neighbor, by always using our strength to lift people up."[1]

Donald Trump often mocked this idea of neighborliness. At a rally in Ohio in March 2024, he described undocumented migrants to the United States as criminals and animals. He parodied the idea of welcoming such people into the country. "Hi neighbor, how are you doing neighbor?" you might say naïvely to such people, he suggested. But then, he added, "they punch you in the face and whack you."[2] Trump was speaking that day in Vandalia, Ohio, just about twenty miles west of the city of Springfield, which was needled relentlessly by his campaign a few months later. And indeed, the false claims he made about Haitian residents in Springfield took just this form: they were less neighbors than aggressors, preying even on the pets of others nearby.

So much of the 2024 election seemed to turn on this question: were Americans willing to meet others in the world as possible neighbors, as people who deserved their attention and concern? To be sure, countless voters saw through the rhetoric of both campaigns. There were deep contradictions between the humanitarian language of the Harris campaign and the unfathomable toll of the ongoing violence inflicted on Palestinian people with American weapons and support, not to mention the campaign's promise to clamp down further on asylum claims at the southern border,[3] or the widespread sense that the Democratic Party had lost sight of its working-class base.[4] Meanwhile, there were many who cast ballots for Trump not because they believed his demonizing and misleading stories, but because they wanted to signal their rejection of the political establishment in the United States. Nevertheless, the fraught question of how we meet others unlike ourselves has to do with much more than who wins or loses in such political campaigns. For all of us have much to lose in the erosion of neighborly concern, the waning impetus to look out for others we don't know that well.

Recent years have seen many important efforts to grapple with the consequences of social isolation and mistrust in the United States, beginning with Robert Putnam's classic 2000 study *Bowling Alone*.[5] This book seeks to complement such work by paying closer attention to the infrastructure of everyday life in the contemporary United States. I try to show how various everyday forms of distance have worked their way into the basic texture of American life in recent years, from the homes and neighborhoods where people live and the cars and trucks they drive, to the ways that people imagine their individual bodies and the ideas they're willing to keep in mind. These everyday structures of division and suspicion magnify the social and political divides that have become so intractable in the country. To overcome these divides, we have to work to transform the circumstances of daily life.

The neighbor is a powerful image of collective belonging, especially in a world where the consequences of how we live extend to many distant and unseen places, where kinship and relationships can be meaningful on both local and planetary scales. In saying this, I don't mean to idealize American neighbors and neighborhoods. As I seek to show throughout this book, contemporary patterns of isolation draw on deep histories of racial segregation and systemic neglect in the United States, lines that have long been drawn between lives that matter and lives that don't. At the same time, neighborliness has also long been practiced as a more expansive form of conviviality, equipping people to live with the reality of social difference and disagreement. "It provides a ground, a place to stand, when consciously organized aspects of democratic public life are fragile or broken entirely," philosopher Nancy Rosenblum writes.[6]

On the evening of the election this year, I tuned into our local conservative talk radio station for a little while, as I do now and then. The host addressed himself to all the males that might be listening, telling them to get out and vote. He reported that this was happening in Arizona, where you could see "pickup trucks lined up as far you can see" at polling places. I tried to imagine the scene that he described, a line of men each framed by a massive vehicle of their own, as the host went on to share speculations rife that day that even Jill Biden—wearing a red suit to a polling station—might be defecting from the Democratic Party.[7] Distance is what makes such conspiratorial thinking plausible, the physical and mental bubbles we occupy so much these days. I felt it myself the day before the election, when I volunteered for a vote drive in York, Pennsylvania, not far from where my family and I live in Baltimore. Knocking on doors that evening, I encountered far more video doorbells than people. I couldn't tell if the residents were truly out, or whether they'd decided to wait out the stranger on the doorstep.

The energy was different at the union office where the vote drive was headquartered, a few miles away. Volunteers from other places along the East Coast had camped out in York for days. One had come all the way from Hawaii. They were working with a more encompassing sense of place and community. The same was true of the community organizers I knew back home in Baltimore. I was struck by the spirit of resolve with which so many of them met the outcome of the votes cast in the election. Naadiya Hutchinson, a young environmental justice organizer I knew in the city called a meeting of social and environmental activists soon after the election to parse what would change at federal, state, and local levels—and to plan accordingly. "If anything has become clear over the past few weeks, it is that our communities stand united and ready to act," she insisted. The possibility of a more just and hopeful future for our country remains anchored in such commitments to collective solidarity.

The United States is at a crossroads, I argue in this book, poised between a politics of suspicion and retreat, and another founded on more expansive relationships of mutual aid and communal caretaking. The work of the latter is difficult in practice and generational in scope, and it will demand looking beyond the tides of events like presidential elections. At the same time, such moments can help to clarify what it will take to achieve genuine social change.

One lesson of this era is that many of our institutions—political parties and economic enterprises, infrastructures for social welfare, media and educational institutions—need serious rethinking. Contradictions between the inclusionary promises they make and the exclusionary ways in which they often operate—the role they often play in deepening patterns of inequality—have become impossible to ignore. The public trust these institutions rely upon must be rebuilt.

As a professor, I think about places like colleges and universities. "The professors are the enemy," J. D. Vance has said in an echo of Richard Nixon, and such attacks will no doubt mount.[8] We will have to defend our schools from ideological strictures imposed in the name of freedom of thought, as we've seen most particularly in states like Florida in recent years.[9] But we can also think about ways to defuse the tensions that fuel such polarized charges. Many of the elite universities lodged in American cities appear to be more keen on amassing real estate and revenue than being responsive neighbors, sociologist Davarian Baldwin argues.[10] And it doesn't help that our learning is often expressed in inaccessible ways and confined to restricted publication venues. What if we committed to expressing ourselves in a manner that more people found meaningful, in relation to the terms they use to make sense of their own lives?

As an anthropologist, I've pursued this commitment as a practical necessity. To converse effectively with others about their lives, I've had to make sense of my own ideas in countless everyday settings far from the universities where I've worked. This book grows out of such conversations and encounters in more than a dozen states around the country. I went to south Texas and Arizona in the wake of the 2016 election, wanting to understand the appeal of the border wall as an idea and how migrant advocates have grappled with its effects. But the trail of the argument that began to take shape led me much further: to homebuilders in North Dakota and activists for housing justice in north Texas, to diesel truck enthusiasts in Iowa and pedestrian safety planners in Florida, to white nationalist demonstrators in Tennessee and environmental justice organizers in the Hudson River Valley. This book grows out of years of listening and striving to think beyond the walls of mind that have stifled our national discourse. These exchanges haven't always resulted in agreements about how to see the world. But I've come away with a much better understanding of why things are as stuck as they are, and what it would take to really change them.[11]

That small town in southern Michigan: I was there to visit someone other than the retired factory worker I met by chance. This was also the hometown of a small businessman I met at a libertarian conference in Las Vegas earlier that summer in 2017. I call him Frank in the book, and I write about the avid discussions and debates we kept up for many years, until the eventual collapse of our relationship in the wake of the 2020 presidential election. Frank even paid a visit to see me in Baltimore, and it was interesting to imagine my own life through his eyes. We spent an afternoon walking around my campus at Johns Hopkins University. He expressed his sense that conservative voices and writers were routinely suppressed and censored on campuses like mine. I tried to object, offering examples of recent events here, and picking up the copy of Adam Smith's *Theory of Moral Sentiments* that happened to lying on my office desk that day. We went around in circles, as we often did, unable to agree on the most basic facts.

The topic of immigration came up later that afternoon, when we sat talking on my front porch. Frank leaned over to rap his knuckles on my front door. "This is your house," he said. "How many people do you want in here?" I've thought about his question for years. Like many others I've met while researching this book, Frank imagined the country's borders in everyday terms. As he saw it, our safety and well-being came down to whether or not we could enforce stark lines, between those on the inside and those on the outside. But I couldn't help but think about all the spaces neither in nor out, like the very porch we were sitting on, looking out at others passing by on the sidewalk, the wider world that enveloped us as we talked. Such spaces in between sustain the possibility of a more inclusive practice of community.[12]

I experienced this myself a couple of days after the 2024 election. Bleary-eyed after staying up too late absorbing the returns and their implications, I stumbled outside that Thursday morning to learn that I'd left a light on in our car overnight. The battery was dead, our kids were going to be late for school, and my wife and I were debating what to do when a neighbor who lived up the street walked by. "Do you need a jump?" he asked, and we gratefully accepted his offer. We recognized each other vaguely, though we'd never had the chance to meet or talk. And the more I thought about that moment, the more meaningful it seemed. Our neighbor overheard us talking as he walked by. He identified a problem and offered to help. None of this would have happened if he'd been wearing headphones that morning, or driving up the road instead, or if he'd simply decided to keep going without stopping to get involved. It mattered that there was a space to share, the chance to pay attention, and an inclination to do so.

We need to ensure that such gestures have a place in the situations of daily life. Whether it's everyday challenges, like dead batteries or lost keys, or moments of far more encompassing need, like the two hurricanes that devastated the southeastern United States a few weeks before the 2024 election, taking on the travails of others can have a transformative impact on the quality of personal and collective life.[13] As organizers Astra Taylor and Leah Hunt-Hendrix have observed, "solidarity weaves us into a larger and more resilient 'we' through the precious and powerful sense that even though we are different, our lives and our fates are connected."[14] We need to pay more attention to the circumstances that nurture the development of such solidarity, and ensure its expression in more open and inclusive terms. Much of the activism and organizing that followed the 2016 election and the coronavirus pandemic was founded on this conviction, which seems to be even more urgent and crucial now.[15]

These aspirations will face serious tests in the years to come. How will people respond to the deportation of families who have lived beside them for decades, or the gutting of hard-won protections for clean water and air, or the removal of books meaningful to the most marginal members of their communities from local school curricula, or the deepening of media foxholes that celebrate masculine aggression and disdain for the struggles of others elsewhere? In this book, I try to show how everyday infrastructures of defense and retreat have made it difficult to give such concerns the attention they deserve. These everyday walls encourage us to think of safety and security in individual and antagonistic terms. But the spaces of our homes and roadways, the places we occupy in body and mind, can also be remade to better support the need for collective caretaking, as those who continue to organize for justice and well-being in a broader sense have shown. The shape of the country will depend on the choices we make.

Xenophobic and authoritarian politics draw their power from a fear of foreigners and strangers, an idea that the dangers they pose are already around us, needing to be identified and rooted out. But as Toni Morrison observed, such ideas often reflect "an uneasy relationship with our own foreignness, our own rapidly disintegrating sense of belonging."[6] The problem lies less with the strangers among us than the strangeness within, the consequences of a feeling of radical estrangement from the world.

So much turns on the edges between the familiar and the foreign, these lines we've come to live with on a daily basis. Can we learn once again to take these edges as spaces of encounter, rather than hard divides between ourselves and the world beyond? It may be daunting, the idea of making a common life—in public space, in the pursuit of well-being on an imperiled earth, even in the unpredictable span of a conversation—with others unlike ourselves. But we need to find our way back to the communion we may share with those beyond our bounds.

We need to rekindle that open spirit of kinship once again.

Notes to the Preface

1. "Remarks: Kamala Harris Delivers Her Concession Speech in Washington—November 6, 2024," *Rollcall.* https://rollcall.com/factbase/harris/transcript/kamala-harris-remarks-concession-speech-november-6-2024/

2. "Speech: Donald Trump Holds a Political Rally in Vandalia, Ohio—March 16, 2024," *Rollcall.* https://rollcall.com/factbase/trump/transcript/donald-trump-speech-political-rally-vandalia-ohio-march-16-2024/

3. Myah Ward and Irie Sentner. "Harris in Arizona Visit Vows to Outdo Biden on Border Security," *Politico*, September 27, 2024. https://www.politico.com/news/2024/09/27/harris-border-asylum-policy-biden-00181473

4. Senator Bernie Sanders opened his November 6, 2024, "Statement on the Results of the 2024 Presidential Election" with these words: "It should come as no great surprise that a Democratic Party which has abandoned working class people would find that the working class has abandoned them," *Instagram*. https://www.instagram.com/berniesanders/p/DCC3TFUBbkO/?hl=en&img_index=1

5. Robert D. Putnam, *Bowling Alone: The Collapse and Revival of American Community* (New York: Simon & Schuster, 2000).

6. Nancy L. Rosenblum, *Good Neighbors: The Democracy of Everyday Life in America* (Princeton: Princeton University Press, 2016), 247.

7. Brian Flood, "Seeing Red? Social Media Erupts over First Lady Jill Biden's Election Day Outfit," *Fox News*, November 5, 2024. https://www.foxnews.com/media/seeing-red-social-media-erupts-over-first-lady-jill-bidens-election-day-outfit

8. Henry Reichman, "'The Professors Are the Enemy': Right-Wing Attacks on Academic Freedom Have Real Repercussions," *The Chronicle of Higher Education*, December 14, 2021. https://www.chronicle.com/article/the-professors-are-the-enemy

9. See Carrie N. Baker, "From the Frontlines of the MAGA War on Higher Education: The Ms. Q&A with New College of Florida Professor Amy Reid," *Ms Magazine*, August 16, 2024. https://msmagazine.com/2024/08/16/new-college-florida-ron-desantis-gender-studies-edi-woke-critical-race-theory/

10. Davarian L. Baldwin, *In the Shadow of the Ivory Tower: How Universities Are Plundering Our Cities* (New York: Bold Type Books, 2021).

11. An exemplary instance of such engagement is Arlie Russell Hochschild, *Strangers in Their Own Land: Anger and Mourning on the American Right* (New York: New Press, 2016).

12. This interstitial approach can be practiced in social as well as spatial terms in highly consequential ways. Consider, for example, one way of addressing the challenges posed by the arrival of large numbers of refugees and asylum seekers to American cities during the years of the Biden presidency, as proposed by migration scholar Karen Jacobsen: "By working with diaspora individuals and families to support new arrivals, federal and state governments could redirect funds that are now going to hotels and shelters. . . . Diaspora households can offer information about navigating city bureaucracies, finding jobs and accessing banking services, in addition to the comfort of familiar food and company. These communities can be an enormous help to new immigrants as they become established and begin to contribute to the city." See Karen Jacobsen, "Many Immigrants to the US Are Fleeing Violence and Persecution—Here's How the Federal Government Can Help Cities Absorb Them," *The Conversation*, May 3, 2024. https://theconversation.com/many-immigrants-to-the-us-are-fleeing-violence-and-persecution-heres-how-the-federal-government-can-help-cities-absorb-them-220575

13. Adria R. Walker, "'We Look After Our Neighbors': How Mutual-Aid Groups Are Filling the Gaps After Hurricane Helene," *The Guardian*, October 6, 2024. https://www.theguardian.com/us-news/2024/oct/06/hurricane-helene-mutual-aid

14. Astra Taylor and Leah Hunt-Hendrix, "The One Idea That Could Save Amer-

ican Democracy," *New York Times*, March 21, 2024. https://www.nytimes.com/2024/03/21/opinion/democracy-solidarity-trump.html

15. "One of the greatest struggles of our time will be to cultivate a life-affirming political culture that can be enacted in the everyday, a counterculture of rebellious care," Kelly Hayes and Mariame Kaba write in *Let This Radicalize You: Organizing and the Revolution of Reciprocal Care* (Chicago: Haymarket Books, 2023). And as organizations like New_ Public are demonstrating, this can be done through online as well as physical communities.

16. Toni Morrison, *The Origin of Others* (Cambridge, MA: Harvard University Press, 2017), 94–95.

SOMETHING BETWEEN US

INTRODUCTION
BUILDING WALLS

World of Concrete, I quickly learned, was a space for genuine enthusiasts. "Concrete is My Addiction," declared T-shirts for sale in the lobby gift shop. You could take home an acrylic painting of a cement mixer pouring out a sidewalk. The expo floor at this annual trade show in Las Vegas presented acres and acres of concrete mixes, tools, and technologies, interspersed with gleaming machines and hulking construction vehicles.

Anthropologists often wind up in unusual places. That January of 2017, I'd come to this construction industry trade show for a specific reason. Throughout his election campaign the previous year, Donald Trump had promised to build "an impenetrable physical wall" between the United States and Mexico, made from "hardened concrete." Wherever he campaigned, massive crowds would loudly chant "Build the Wall," calling for the construction of what would have to be the biggest concrete structure in the history of the United States. I wondered how industry professionals felt about this. There seemed no better place to go than their annual convention.[1]

Walk through these corridors, and you could easily imagine why the idea of securing the nation's borders with concrete might appeal. "Rip open a bag of confidence," Sakrete promised on the expo's complimentary bag for attendees. "Count on Concrete," the American Concrete Pavement Association declared. The mottos were all like this. Build Trust. Build with Strength. Concrete to the Core. "Imagine if he'd said that he was going to build a tall wooden fence," a young contractor from Denver suggested; "what would people think of that?" Concrete, though, the very idea of it, "impenetrable." As one industry leader from Texas quipped, "It's the one thing you want between yourself and the zombie apocalypse."

It was the third week of January, leading up to the presidential inauguration. One company was selling circular saw blades embossed with Trump's smiling face, an inaugural special and a magnet for tickled observers. "Made in the US?" I asked, curious.

"China," like so much else on view here, a salesperson quietly admitted.

On the morning of the inauguration, here and there on the expo floor, people had pulled up the event on their mobile phones. I caught the final minutes of the new president's address with a few representatives from a small concrete coatings company in western Ohio. Cheers and claps broke the still air of the convention center at the conclusion of that ominous speech.

The team from western Ohio didn't think the border wall would ever be built. It would cost too much and supplies of portland cement were already low. All the same, a young man named Chris told me, the border had to be secured somehow. It was like spending $1,000 on a home security system but failing to close the door itself. "The border's like our back door," he said. "You go and leave it open, and anyone can walk right in."

"It's not even a door," he added with a laugh. "More like a screen door."

Like most of the other reps from the company, Chris was a millennial. With a trim beard and short, sandy hair, he projected an air of casual self-sufficiency. He spoke with a dose of wry humor about how far he lived from other people. "I don't really like neighbors," he remarked.

I was struck by the mismatch between the salesman's genial manner and the suspicions that he voiced, his sense of anyone beyond his home or country as a potential threat. I wondered, as we talked amidst that sea of construction equipment, what it would take to build genuine warmth and concern for outsiders in this country, rather than such walls.

Over the last eight years, I've crisscrossed the United States as an anthropologist, pursuing conversation and debate between the coasts and heartland. I set out in 2016 to grasp the appeal of the border wall that Trump had promised, the fantasy of wrapping the country in a stark, symbolic barrier. I wanted to understand the power of that campaign slogan, "Build the Wall," which, to me, felt willfully cruel.[2] What I learned is that the idea appealed to many Americans because it resonated with the burgeoning walls of their daily lives. Time and again, I encountered people who thought of the country's borders in relation to the more familiar barriers they lived with and took for granted: household doors and fences, everyday safety and security devices, even the body's reliance on the protection of skin.

"I don't leave my doors unlocked," a patrol officer I met in North Dakota told me. "I don't think the nation should leave its doors unlocked either."

We are accustomed to thinking of polarization as a matter of politics and social identity, as a kind of modern-day tribalism.[3] This book argues that we need to pay more attention instead to the everyday walls and divides that Americans have come to rely on in their daily lives. Insider versus outsider, familiar versus stranger, safety versus threat: these stark distinctions are anchored and sustained by the physical makeup of so much of contemporary American life—from fortified homes and neighborhoods to bulked-up cars and trucks, from visions of the body as an armored fortress to media that shut out contrary perspectives. These interlocking divides make it more difficult to take unfamiliar people and perspectives seriously; harder to acknowledge the needs of strangers, to trust their motives and empathize with their struggles. To grasp the hardening of American views about others, we have to look at the hardening of daily life.[4]

Indifference is a kind of personal insulation. Something happens in the world, but it makes no difference to how you feel, what you think. James Baldwin described it as a "death of the heart," the price America paid for racial segregation: "You don't know what's happening on the other side of the wall."[5] The everyday walls of American life make for cascading lines between inside and out: between the inner worlds that people care most about, and the places beyond neglected at their expense; between those who can afford to shield themselves from the outside world, and others left beyond to fend for themselves as best they can. This book pursues these many walls, and the collective life we may yet build beyond them.

———————

Early in 2017, I attended a gun show in Fort Lauderdale, Florida. My hand was stamped with the word "KNIFE" when I paid the entrance fee. Inside, there were thousands of handguns, rifles, and other weapons packed onto the tables of a crowded hall. Many of the vendors had holsters and other rigs designed for concealed-carry weapons. I spent some time talking to a man representing a brand called Thunderwear. A woman in jeans walking her dog down the street; a man running shirtless at the beach; another in hospital scrubs, sporting a confident smile and a stethoscope around his neck: all of them, their poster implied, could be wearing a snug spandex holster without anyone knowing. Some people buy Thunderwear, the salesman told me, because it's the most comfortable way to wear your gun to bed at night.

I came away from the gun show with a sense of how complicated feelings of threat and danger could be. What mattered most when it came to safety? There were two-dollar faux Terrorist Hunting Permit stickers available for each of fifty states, as if they were lurking everywhere unseen: "No bag limit, tagging not required." There was the man who told me how exposed he'd felt driving through a major snowstorm in Baltimore a few years back: it wasn't the snow that left him anxious; it was the fact that he had to drive the city with all his guns stowed in a locker that day. Then there were the bumper stickers on the Land Cruiser beside my rental car out front: "Smoking is safer than liberalism" and "I ♥ MY CARBON FOOTPRINT."[6]

As American schools convulse with regular shootings, calls abound in conservative circles for a "fortification of soft targets."[7] Measures proposed for the "hardening" of schools include bulletproof doors and windows, metal detectors, armed teachers and administrators, even ballistic blankets and whiteboards. School security alone has already become a multibillion-dollar industry, even as the effectiveness of such measures remains unclear.[8] "To embrace a fortress mentality is to reject liberal democracy itself," Sarah

Jones writes in a reflection on the appeal of hardened spaces to American conservatives and liberals alike.[9] And indeed, the troubling logic of hardening can be found in much of contemporary American life.

Consider this well-known motto and promise from the home security company ADT: "a line in the sand between your family and an uncertain world." Americans are bunkering now in increasingly isolated homes and secured compounds, without regular exposure to people they don't know. Nearly one out of five American homes in a residential community is secured today by community walls or fences, a development that builds on a century of intentional segregation and suburban white flight. But the retreat of everyday life and leisure into more secluded spaces has also unfolded at a more intimate scale. The front porch sessions with neighbors and passersby that once epitomized American social life have given way to more private gatherings on the backyard deck, or time with the television and other screens indoors. Such changes lessen the chance for happenstance conversation with neighbors and strangers, and the trust in social difference that such interactions can build.[10]

The spaces in which we shelter change our sense of the world beyond. Stepping outside can feel daunting in a society of cascading walls. It's little wonder that when Americans leave their homes, they do so more and more in automobiles styled as armored enclosures. In recent years, imposing vehicles like SUVs and trucks have come to dominate the American car market, far outpacing sales for smaller sedans. These are automobiles designed with aggressive profiles and built as defensive steel cocoons, often marketed as ways to survive an uncertain and even hostile world. As an automotive designer in Los Angeles told me, such vehicles appeal in a society that is "suffering a case of insecurity." When people on foot and bicycle have to share their streets with drivers in such armored cockpits, the consequences can be deadly; pedestrian deaths on American roadways have soared by more than 50 percent over the last decade.

The fortress mindset thrives on feelings of suspicion, and the urge to protect oneself can make shared spaces and resources more dangerous than they already are. Americans are often encouraged to buy what they can to fortify and even seal off their own individual bodies, as shared public infrastructure is allowed to decay. Think of bottled sports drinks like *BodyArmor* or *BioSteel*. The coronavirus pandemic supercharged such ideas, setting off a boom in personal disinfectant products and touchless technology, making it easier to deny the truth that we depend on one another for our well-being, as seen too in the deep resistance to face masks and vaccination in the United States. I think of a middle-aged white businessman from Michigan with whom I debated the pandemic for many months. A staunch libertarian, he rejects compulsory public health precautions on the grounds that they deny "my feelings, my rights, my personal body."

Regular exposure to other points of view could complicate such die-hard convictions. But our fractured media have helped propel these social and spatial divisions. Partisan networks and social media are deepening the existing fissures of American society, raising invisible walls of mind over the physical divides that people live with already. Facebook is like "the 21st century equivalent to the suburban tract developments of Levittown," designer Cliff Kuang has written, a digital space in which "the only voices we hear are those of virtual neighbors who think exactly like us."[11] Take a walk with your eyes glued to such feeds, and the world begins to approximate an open-air cell, with each of us locked into a world of our own.

A few years ago, I had the chance to visit one of William Levitt's massive "Levittown" developments, not far from where I live now in Baltimore. Built on 22 square miles of farmland in the 1950s, the Pennsylvania development eventually totaled more than 17,000 homes, each of which was laid out in one of four basic prototypes. Intended as a white community, Levittown was infamous for the violent reaction to a Black couple who tried to settle there in 1957, which stifled its racial integration.[12] It was a beautiful spring day when I visited, and people were surprisingly willing to chat with a brown stranger walking down the street. The houses and porches had a warm face, reflecting many personal touches that had been added to the original uniform designs. But all of this was within one of the subdivisions, on one of its quiet residential streets. On the outside, along the parkway, the feeling was profoundly different, with high fences and hedges lining the road and few walkers on streets laid out for speeding cars. Like so many American communities, the space was open on the inside but closed to the outside.

Walls at home and on the road, walls for the body and the mind: this long archipelago of ordinary divides extends into the smallest arenas of daily worlds, shielding many Americans from the possible unease of foreign people and ideas, propelling skepticism about the collective good. Longstanding patterns of neighborhood racial segregation have fueled prejudice against social outgroups in the United States, as many scholars have shown.[13] The proliferating walls of contemporary American life bring such divides down to a more intimate and everyday level, deepening the gulf between self and other, insider and outsider.[14]

The easy give and take of neighbors has long been a "compass for maintaining our democratic bearings," political philosopher Nancy Rosenblum observes, a reminder of how to coexist with people we don't know that well.[15] But in an atomized society, others become phantoms all too easily, grist for the mill of resentment and mistrust. Societies built around hardened boundaries—gates and walls, seals and armor, containers and dividers—tend to produce exclusionary viewpoints. And this is a problem that implicates all of us in varying ways, whether liberal or conservative, immigrant or native-born, white or Black or brown, a problem we have to find our way around.

———

My own parents emigrated to the United States from India in 1972, and my siblings and I were born and raised in this country. We spent a lot of time in India as children. But the United States was home, even if there was somewhere else in the world where we also belonged. As with so many other immigrant families here, however, this basic faith of ours was shaken in 2016, when the question of whether we truly belonged snapped into sharper focus than at any other moment in my lifetime. Again and again, people we knew—even my own father—were accosted with that taunt, *Go back to your own country.* The idea of the border wall was a magnet for such expressions of a harsh nativist politics, and I felt compelled to grapple with its appeal, as an anthropologist but also as an Indian American with children of my own.

I began to think about this book project on the morning of November 9th in 2016. Like so many others, I was thrown by the outcome of the presidential election held the previous day. I could count on one hand the number of people I knew who had voted for Trump. Most people I knew seemed somehow crushed and numb with disbelief that day and in the days that followed.

What President Obama said in his farewell address in Chicago a couple of months later was as true of me as anyone else:

> For too many of us it's become safer to retreat into our own bubbles, whether in our neighborhoods, or on college campuses, or places of worship, or especially our social media feeds, surrounded by people who look like us and share the same political outlook and never challenge our assumptions.[16]

I had to acknowledge that even as an anthropologist, I knew very little about this country where I was born and raised, where I lived and worked. I began to strike up conversations with people I might pass but never stop to talk with: others sitting at nearby café tables, staff on my university campus, clerks at local stores. A few weeks after the election results became clear, I attended a victory rally for Trump in Hershey, Pennsylvania, a charged and unsettling experience.[17] And over the months and years that followed, I traveled to many places in the United States where I had never been, trying to make sense of a circumstance I found deeply troubling but completely opaque.

I was far from alone in doing such things. Sitting one night over a plate of fried rice at a Chinese American diner in Rock Springs, Wyoming, I caught glimpses of a Fox News segment about another East Coast professor with a research agenda similar to mine. The chyrons across the bottom of the screen seemed to revel in this tide of newfound liberal attention, with glosses like "PROFESSOR TO STUDY THE MYSTERY OF TRUMP VOTERS" and "ELITES STRUGGLE TO MAKE SENSE OF TRUMP VICTORY." The truck driver sitting further down the counter scoffed, making it clear that he wasn't impressed. "There ain't no mystery to Trump voters," he blurted out, talking back to the pundits on the screen. "Just gettin' tired of being pushed around and shit on."

I didn't agree with what that truck driver said, but everything seemed to conspire to make any possibility of mutual understanding between us laughable, even problematic. Such narratives of legitimate grievance and rightful vengeance were rife, and I wanted to find a way to write against them. But to do this effectively as an ethnographer, I had to take seriously the chance of connection, even sympathy, in highly fraught circumstances. I had to entertain the possibility of what James Baldwin recalled feeling among other Americans abroad, even those bent on "denying the only kin they have" for reasons of race and prejudice. "These are my countrymen and I do care about them and even if I didn't, there is something between us," Baldwin movingly observed in his 1965 debate with William F. Buckley at Cambridge University.[18] That profound phrase — "something between us" — evokes possible relationships as well as the barriers that can make them impossible. Such is the texture of this book, and the idea that has shaped its title.

I rely in this book on stories and travels across the United States, vivid and challenging encounters with salesmen and truck drivers, police officers and urban planners, activists for social and environmental justice. Over the last eight years, I've wandered into trade shows for homebuilders and medical suppliers. I've talked to organizers for migrant rights at rallies before the national Capitol and to white nationalists at a White Lives Matter rally in Tennessee. I've visited GMC dealerships in Los Angeles and a truck festival in Iowa, a bottled water convention in Texas and small towns in the Hudson River Valley reeling from water pollution. I attended a glitzy libertarian festival in Las Vegas, and in Georgia I pursued intense discussions with one of the country's leading conservative cartoonists. I've logged many thousands of miles on local highways and country roads, striking up conversations with strangers on park benches and in derelict shopping malls. This investigation of everyday walls has demanded openness, often vulnerability, from an Indian American domestic traveler. But I've come to see that people are far more complicated than they may seem from a distance.[19]

Take social life in India, for example, still imagined all too easily by foreign observers as a land of fixed ideas and stubborn social boundaries. Years of sustained fieldwork as an anthropologist in India have taught me otherwise, helping me to see the deeply diverse and creative ways in which people often engage the divide between self and other. Such dynamics are social but also spatial, I came to understand, shaped by the architecture of homes and communities, by traditional structures like verandas and courtyards that have long supported a fundamentally open relationship between the inside and outside of people's lives, and by modern efforts to build on these legacies, such as Bengali poet Rabindranath Tagore's effort to imagine a future "Where the mind is without fear and the head is held high / Where knowledge is free /

Where the world has not been broken up into fragments / By narrow domestic walls."[20]

As an anthropologist, I've learned that it takes patience and imagination to unravel what people truly care about. We try to meet people with as much empathy and understanding as we can muster, even in the face of profound disagreement. An ethnography, the kind of book that anthropologists tend to write—literally, a written account of a community or people—seeks to convey the lived experience of a place through intimate stories of encounter. And these details matter especially when it comes to situations that people tend to interpret in starkly different ways. Ethnography is a uniquely effective means to relate both the power of structural forms and forces, as well as the resistance and ambivalence they occasion in the thickets of daily life.[21]

This book seeks to convey both the difficulties posed by a society of pervasive walls and the unexpected openings they nevertheless allow. Working as an anthropologist, I show how these overlapping divides orchestrate American life as a patterned reality, one that still carries the potential for novel forms of solidarity and critique. I pursue the challenge of thinking beyond the twists and turns of our immediate present, seeking to outline the larger cultural fabric that frames these difficulties, but also makes alternatives possible. For while our impasses draw from deep American histories of segregation and suspicion, they also surface more radical visions for a life in common with others.

The narrative is organized into four sections, each focusing on a different kind of hardening of American life: walls for the home and road, body and mind. Each section unfolds as a series of stories or dispatches from different places around the country. In each of these sections, I try to show how everyday commitments to hard lines surface in different milieus, but I also come around to describing in each of these sections, in the company of activists and social critics, how to imagine and pursue a dismantling of these ordinary barriers.

The first section explores the changing nature of the American home, its reconfiguration as a space organized to lock out strangers and other threats, and what it would mean to live instead with a wider sense of collective belonging. I examine the trajectory of the house as bastion in contemporary America, tracking a waning of social space around and beyond the home that turns potential neighbors into strangers. I trace legacies of residential segregation and suburbanization that continue to propel these developments and show how activist movements for desegregation articulate a more expansive vision of neighborliness.

Americans spend as much time within cars, trucks, and other motor vehicles as they do in open environments beyond their homes and workplaces. It is therefore essential to consider how our experience of vehicles and roadways shapes our understanding of the wider world. The chapters in the second section examine recent developments in American automotive culture that conceive of the world as a space of danger and aggression, demanding defensive measures of protection rather than openness and exposure. Why are Americans so drawn to armored vehicles that promise insulation, that render us insensible to the welfare of those beyond these shells? What will it take to develop streetscapes more suitable for pedestrians, cyclists, and others?

Protection comes down to the body, that fragile vessel of flesh and bone in which we pass through the world, weather its storms. The body is home to the most visceral sensations of vulnerability and danger. Here, too, walls proliferate and demand fortification, from the skin and its boundaries, to clothing and other layers of armor, to the many environmental barriers designed to secure what we absorb and ingest. The third section examines a series of imperatives to armor the body of the American nation—and the individual bodies of white citizens in particular—with defensive walls. I ask what it means to live instead with the vulnerability of a greater state of exposure, most especially for racial others left beyond the span of such care.

Some of the hardest and most stubborn walls are intangible in form. As the events of recent years have shown, Americans hold profoundly different ideas about what is simply *real*, ideas fed by social media and partisan news platforms that often verge on the irreconcilable. These walls of the mind may seem fleeting and ephemeral, yet they are just as powerful as anything made of brick or concrete. In the fourth section, I turn to the intangible walls that frame ideas and imagination in the contemporary United States, lines that mark out the space of the plausible from what remains unbelievable. I also engage with efforts to think beyond such isolating perspectives and the media portals and devices that carry them.

Walls at home and on the road, for the body and the mind: the lines running through this book are different faces of a more basic line between self
and other, one also complicated and confounded in many important ways.
Each of the four sections of the book moves toward such openings, and these
threads are drawn together in a conclusion that strikes a more hopeful note.
I try to show, through these particular chapters, how more recent endeavors
in mutual aid and collective caretaking can help us see the real crossroads of
this moment: the hardening of divisions and suspicions, but also the chance
we have to move beyond them.

It was a gorgeous winter day in southern Arizona, sunlight breaking through
the clouds to catch the red earth and high grasses, an occasional saguaro
cactus keeping watch from some high promontory. I'd gone out into the
Sonora desert that day with a volunteer crew from the Tucson Samaritans,
an organization that maintains water stations for migrants finding their way
through that forbidding landscape. We walked along seasonal streambeds
full of tattered backpacks, their polyester threads coming apart and mingling
with the leaves and pebbles underfoot. "There are so many stories," one of the
volunteers told me as we picked our way through thickets of scrub, leaving
jugs of water and packets of food in places where people were known to rest.

The volunteer was a retired schoolteacher in her late seventies. Week
after week, she came out onto these trails, carrying as much as her shoulders
could handle, tending to the needs of people she almost never saw. As we
headed back to Tucson that afternoon, I wondered about the yellow toy car
she was holding in her hands. Then we pulled over beside a wooden cross,
marking the place where a young woman was found stumbling down that
road some years ago, a stillborn baby in her arms. Every time they passed
this way, the former teacher explained, she would leave something here for
that stillborn boy.

"All of us could have been someone else," she told me. "What if I was walking in the desert, and I delivered this child? I'm taking care of him. I don't
want him forgotten."[22]

The next day, I returned to the spot to pay my respects. A Border Patrol
officer flagged me down at a checkpoint further down the road, and we fell

into conversation. The young officer told me that he'd sympathized at first with the people traversing these hills. Then it began to nag at him, the feeling they were lying about who they were, why they'd come. He knew the roadside cross, he'd driven past it many times, but never stopped to take a look. "You get desensitized," he told me. "You hear it often enough and something in you shuts off."[23]

The border guard cupped his fingers as he spoke these words, turning them in the air as if he was switching off a dial or turning the lock of an invisible door. A pair of sunglasses hid his eyes from view, mirroring the road back at me. We weren't that far from the line of concrete and steel that marked the border between the United States and Mexico. But the guard was speaking of another kind of border, a different kind of wall, one built not with mortar but mistrust.

Whether the plight of refugees or the recent pandemic, the climate crisis or systemic racism, so much turns on the care and concern we can muster for lives and circumstances beyond our own. And yet the deep divides of our national life in the United States have made effective action on such matters a serious and sometimes intractable challenge. Why is it so difficult to acknowledge and address the intertwining of our lives with others elsewhere?

It may be tempting to take such difficulties as a sign of moral or personal failure. But our feelings for others are structural realities as much as personal qualities. Ordinary environments and circumstances of life shape the possibility or impossibility of meaningful relationships, what we feel or can't feel for others. Every means of isolation, whether grand or minuscule in scale, has a role to play in these dynamics. When others are experienced as distant abstractions, it's easy to dismiss what they might say or need.[24] At the same time, commitments to real relationships with others in a spirit of social solidarity and mutual aid—"where we choose to help each other out, share things, and put time and resources into caring for the most vulnerable," as Dean Spade puts it—can change these difficult dynamics in profound ways.[25]

Across the country in 2020, the pandemic spurred a return to socializing with neighbors on front yards and porches.[26] Countless cities and towns carved out new places for walking, biking, and outdoor life—new ways of sharing public space with people both known and unknown.[27] And movements for racial justice and solidarity with the vulnerable brought millions of Americans together that year and beyond, spurring more radical commitments to collective caretaking, redrawing the line between stranger and kin.[28]

On the one hand, the pandemic had supercharged an idea of the body as an armored enclosure, to seal off against the dangers of the world beyond. On the other hand, calls abounded to redesign personal and public space for conviviality rather than isolation, for coming back into new ways of living more intentionally and meaningfully in the company of others. Even as the enduring strife of those years underscored the tenacity of political and social polarization in the United States, these small experiments in belonging suggested the genesis of something very different: "a vision of a different society," as the abolitionist organizer Mariame Kaba put it, "built on cooperation instead of individualism, on mutual aid instead of self-preservation."[29] Such efforts anchor the vision of an alternative collective life that animates this book.

Conviviality is a kind of "radical openness" in the social sphere, cultural theorist Paul Gilroy has argued, a rejection of the categorical divides that sustain racism, an ability instead "to live with alterity without becoming anxious, fearful, or violent."[30] Less a fantasy of social harmony under fraught circumstances, conviviality brings into focus ways of dealing with conflict and living at ease with difference, through everyday circumstances of encounter and infrastructures of connection.[31] Commons, parks, and open streetscapes; living quarters and resources arranged to encourage social awareness instead of solipsism; communication platforms to nurture contrary lines of thought: such spaces can nurture the capacity to live and thrive alongside others unlike oneself, working against the tendency to reject and retreat.[32]

These are possibilities with global significance. In recent decades, dozens of countries around the world have met aspiring migrants and refugees in need with fortified borders and imposing walls, marking continent after continent with lines that often reach hundreds of miles in length.[33] Such gestures extend, to the largest scale, histories and patterns of enclosure that have accompanied the development of capitalist economies and individualistic societies over many centuries in Europe, the United States, and beyond.[34] In the face of such histories and their contemporary echoes, there is much at stake in learning to ask what kinds of boundaries are truly necessary and sustaining. As Todd Miller puts it in *Build Bridges, Not Walls: A Journey to a World Without Borders,* "what kind of raw and beautiful world lies beyond the fences and walls that confine not just our bodies, but also our imagination, our speech, our very humanity?"[35]

The promise of such vision comes through with so many of the people and stories I've encountered through this research. I think, for example, of the Black and white women of the Denton Women's Interracial Fellowship who led a local struggle for desegregation in Texas in the 1960s, coming together in a north Texas town that had exiled its entire Black population just a few decades earlier. I think of a Providence-based writer and activist who set out in 2016 to walk barefoot across the United States to protest the looming climate catastrophe; he perished in a tragic collision with an SUV in the Florida Panhandle, and yet his story invites a serious rethinking of our American streetscapes with his vision of a roadway hospitable to all living beings. And I think of a young woman I met in Ohio who grew up on a daily diet of conservative talk radio, caught in the crossfire between a "liberal wahoo" mother and a father who'd condemn even the free pencils from elementary school as "government handouts." She eventually left college to become a menstrual equity activist and coined one of the most popular slogans of the 2017 Women's Marches: "Shed Walls, Don't Build Them."

"Some of the most difficult tasks of our lives are the claiming of differences, and learning to use those differences for bridges rather than as barriers between us," Audre Lorde observed.[36] These words remind us of a dissident heritage essential to the United States that we know now, the critical vision of those who have understood the occupation of this continent and its capitalist logic otherwise, those who have given voice to the possibility of more radical forms of American collective life. In this spirit, throughout this book, I pay heed to the work of activists of many kinds—migrant and refugee advocates, feminist organizers, agitators for shared space, clean water, and safe roads—in order to consider what a more just and open American society could look and feel like. Such work can help us imagine and cultivate social alternatives and unexpected forms of connection across the rigid lines we take so easily for granted.[37]

There is no better way to learn once again how to meet strangers in this land as potential kin. We need to confront the many walls we've come to live with, and what it could mean to take them down. The pages that follow take some steps in that direction.

PART I
SPACE TO SHELTER

ONE

FORTRESS HOMES

TREASURE COAST, FLORIDA

To get there, you have to drive past a long line of other gated communities, places with names like Sandy Ridge and Seminole Bluffs. The development is one of the most exclusive on Florida's Treasure Coast, with houses that list for up to $20 million. But you wouldn't know this from what you can see on the coastal highway, everything hidden from view by a high wall blanketed with shrubs and palms. I pull into the guardhouse, styled like a gazebo. My credentials are confirmed, and the railway-style gate goes up. The director of security Timothy Rowe is waiting for me inside.

The place is a haven for corporate America, Rowe explains: not merely CEOs or COOs but the company owners themselves, those who wouldn't flinch at the thought of a $200,000 membership to the development's residential club. For most these are second or third homes, alongside places in Vail, the Hamptons, Martha's Vineyard.

Why retreat each winter to a place with dozens of armed guards on duty? "It's a sense of security these people want," Rowe says. "You could walk out of your home and not lock your door, that sense of comfort. With us here, the outside world can't get to them."

He offers to drive me around, take me on a tour of the community. "How you doin' chief?" one of his officers asks as we leave his office.

"Livin' the dream," Rowe replies as we head out to the parking lot.

He clears the clutter in the front seat of his Chevy Tahoe, apologizing for the age of the vehicle. A tall man with cropped white hair and mournful eyes, he's been going through a divorce, with his children just through college; money has been tight at home.

Like many in private security, Rowe started out as a police officer. He tells me that he's thought of writing a book himself, something along the lines of *You Won't Believe the Shit I've Seen.* "They're ten times more paranoid than you and me," he remarks as we roll slowly through the curving streets. "They think everybody's after their money."

Then again, all the security seems to leave these residents strangely, excessively, off guard. Every so often, Rowe explains, he gets a call from someone complaining that a garage door isn't working. It turns out they'd driven the wrong car home from the club that night—so many here seem to favor the same gray model of Lexus, and they often leave their keys just dangling for anyone to take.

How to work with a population so primed for disaster, so desperate for repose? With all the news of terrorist attacks, active shooters, and burglary rings, "Americans are in fear," Rowe observes. "It's only a matter of time, a question of when and where it's going to happen." The walls and gates that circle this community cannot truly protect against all these threats, he admits. What they provide instead is psychological solace, an illusion of peace and security. "They like people smiling and waving at them," he says.[1]

One colleague of Rowe's put it to me this way: "It's like Mayberry, and I'm Andy Taylor." Indeed, it feels like the "Whitopia" sketched by writer Rich Benjamin, a "white-bread world" with "ineffable social charisma, a pleasant look and feel."[2] There are dozens of people of color among the staff, Rowe tells me, but hardly any among the residents. There are only a handful of Jewish households in this community of well over a thousand homes.[3]

Rowe had grown up in New York state. His uncle had a dairy farm, and others in the family worked for GM or Sylvania. "I can recall walking down the streets in Buffalo with my father. To every person who came by, he'd say, *Hey, how are you doing?* When I was a kid, nobody ever locked their doors. It's sad to think that I could have done that."

I try to think about what it must be like for him now, looking after the security needs of an exclusive gated community in Florida, wrestling with their paranoia, hanging on to these recollections of a bygone faith and generosity. "Can you imagine a way for us to get back to that more trusting relationship with the outside world?" I ask.

"I don't see us getting back to those days of leaving your door unlocked without worrying what might happen," Rowe replies. "Everything on the news is bad. *Watch out for this guy, watch out for that guy.* They pound fear into us, because then we buy things."

"Fear," he adds, "there's such a market for it. They can sell a hell of a lot more crap to people who are scared than to those who are not. If you trust your neighbors, feel you're safe, are you going to go out and buy a doorbell camera or a deadbolt?"

I find it unsettling, what I can see of these sprawling, gabled homes on roads with names like Porpoise Lane and Palm Frond Cove. Construction and remodeling are ceaseless endeavors here, but this is impossible to grasp from the look of these houses. Everything seems to have appeared all at once, no blemishes or signs of age evident on these walls and roofs, everything old remade to look new, and everything new made to look as though it was always there. It's a pleasant evening in early January, a time of peak occupancy, but the streets are quiet and still, hardly anyone visible outside.

"They flock each winter to this heaven on earth," declares an exultant flyer that Rowe lends me. Year by year, residents come and go, expecting that what is theirs will remain as they left it. It's as though the gates are guarding against the passage of time, protecting a vision of domestic life that may never have been, yet must always be.

These measures may seem extreme. But pervasive concerns for security are now built into the physical form of countless American homes: their walls and windows, gates and alarms, even the prevailing colors of household paint palettes. Ideals of enclosure and protection shape the imagination of American domestic space, construing closed doors as a necessary refuge from the anxiety and uncertainty of the outside world—ideas that have intensified in the recent years of the coronavirus pandemic.

————————

The wealthy of American society have long walled themselves off in exclusive enclaves. The history of residential development in the United States is a history of economic and racial segregation, those with privilege freeing themselves from having to confront the deprivation and distress of others. Gated communities build on the exclusionary heritage of the American suburb— their mortared walls and railway gates lending a tangible concreteness to the implicit logic of restrictive covenants and zoning codes.[4] As Edward J. Blakely and Mary Gail Snyder observe, the proliferation of these insular communities can dissolve the fabric of urban social life, thwarting connection and contact in a manner that weakens "the bonds of mutual responsibility and the social contract."[5]

It was only in the later decades of the twentieth century that the gated community became a middle-class aspiration in the United States, first in planned retirement communities and then as a prevailing form of residential development, especially in the Sunbelt states. "It is the American dream with a twist," the anthropologist Setha Low writes, "one that intentionally restricts access and emphasizes social control and security over other community values."[6] Gated communities now include apartment complexes as well as independently owned homes, and their security appeals for different reasons. Many minority, low-income, and immigrant families, for example, look to gated complexes to seek refuge from conditions of urban scarcity and episodic violence.[7]

For affluent homeowners, whether gated communities truly afford significant protection remains an open question.[8] On the other hand, decades of research have documented the serious effects of such arrangements on the quality of urban society, in their insistence on the divide between inside and out. "I am deeply concerned that they are shifting our sense of whom we are responsible to and whom we share problems with," urban planner Gary Pivo observed in a 1997 forum on gated communities sponsored by the Fannie Mae

Foundation. "These associations probably do enhance community, a certain kind of community, one that turns its back on outsiders."[9]

I think of another gated community I visited in Arizona, a few weeks after I had toured the Florida complex with Timothy Rowe. "It's almost like a cocoon," a security officer said of this exclusive space in the hills east of Scottsdale. And indeed, you could hardly see the hundreds of sprawling bungalows nestled into the compound, each of them painted in earthy tones and surrounded by desert vegetation. He took me to the club house, where these residents—mostly CEOs and other executives who like to vacation in Arizona—would take their meals together after rounds of golf on their signature green. Phoenix was a distant sight through the plate glass windows, hundreds of feet below the ridge. "Nobody gets in here that doesn't belong," the security officer mused softly. "That's why they feel safe, once they're inside the walls."

Planted into the brushlands a few miles away was another colony of multimillion-dollar getaways. Here again, manned gates and sentry posts restricted access to the development. But then too, I learned, each cul-de-sac in this colony had its own individual railway gate, and many of the owners had installed gates across their driveways as well, meaning that anyone coming in or out of these homes would have to clear three separate gates. I was astonished, but the security director here saw nothing unusual in such arrangements. "Security comes in layers," he suggested: front doors and alarm systems, railway gates and armed patrols; even the Border Patrol, further south, was doing exactly the same for the country as a whole.

"People shouldn't be able to just walk into where you live," the security director at this second complex told me. "You should be able to defend yourself against the rest of the world."

I was struck by what he said, this highly defensive view of the relationship between one's own life and others beyond it. It was all the more remarkable given the nature of the walls around this development. These barriers were so low—I could see as we drove together through the gated community in his Ford Explorer that afternoon—that the perimeter walls almost disappeared against the horizon. The community was lodged beside a national forest, and residents would find javelinas poking into their garbage now and then, the occasional bobcat sunning itself on the putting green. Was this not a source of anxiety, the evident limitations of these borders, their inability to keep out the rest of the world? The security director let out a gruff laugh when I asked him this question. "It's mostly psychological," he said.

The burgeoning walls of contemporary Western society "inadvertently produce a collective ethos and subjectivity that is defensive, parochial, nationalistic, and militarized," political theorist Wendy Brown has observed. "They generate an increasingly closed and policed collective identity in place of the open society they would defend."[10]

———————

Nearly one out of five American homes in a residential community is secured now by community walls or fences, according to the US Census Bureau.[11] Those of us whose homes don't lie within sentry posts and railway gates may likely question the safety they promise. All the same, it's worth asking where such boundaries and their effects truly end when it comes to American domestic life. Is a gated community fundamentally different from other kinds of neighborhoods, or instead is it the most obvious manifestation of more prevalent patterns and tendencies?

Take the looped roads and cul-de-sacs of a typical suburban subdivision; the isolating doors and fences that enclose and define an individual home and its various spaces; or the more minor and invisible barriers—impervious coatings and sealants—that shield inside from out in countless ways. Such nested and enveloping layers of protection are like "Matryoshka wooden dolls," Rich Benjamin writes, "staggered forms of security and comfort."[12] Tallying up such insulating walls in America is like trying to take a census in a bewildering hall of mirrors.

I had come to Florida that winter of 2017 for the International Builders' Show, a construction expo in nearby Orlando. Tens of thousands of architects, developers, designers, and contractors attend the event each year, the largest of its kind in the world. I had no official business being there, but it seemed as good a place as any to begin to unravel how the home in America had been constructed as a private refuge from the danger and insecurity of the world beyond.

Well over a thousand exhibitors displayed their wares in the cavernous

halls of the Orlando convention center. Crack the spine of the official show guide and the first thing you'd see was an ad for water-resistant wall and roof panels from Zip System: "ARMOR UP AGAINST THE STORM," declared a steel plate shaped like a police badge, defying the ominous clouds and lightning of a dark gray sky. It was almost as though nature itself harbored criminal tendencies that needed to be repelled.

Other companies, meanwhile, promised relief from other threats. There was Formica laminate for a "worry-free" shield against the mess of kids and pets. NuTone had just introduced a video doorbell system that made it impossible to tell whether you were away or not. Set up against one wall was a massive black steel box called the BombNado, a shelter from nuclear and chemical disaster to hide below the floor of your garage, one that could also double as gun vault, wine cellar, and all-around panic room.

Vendors would insist that such assurances were necessary, but that they could remain consistent with the good cheer that a good home should possess. After all, bunkers like the BombNado were there for retreat in case of necessity, not as models of ordinary life. At a high-profile session called "60 Design Ideas in 60 Minutes," speakers described new trends—sliding door systems, collapsible walls, outdoor kitchens and living rooms—to "really open up the house," as one architect put it. "The lines are blurred. Where's the backyard? Where does the house end?"

Such developments did confound the divide between indoor and outdoor space, offering new visions of where to relax with a drink at the end of the day, but always in a manner that would continue to enclose or protect in some other way: by opening, say, out into a hedged yard or roof deck. You could have the feeling of exposure, without the risk.

To give another example, Sierra Pacific had just released for the trade show a new line of windows called FeelSafe, promising all the transparency of glass while remaining shatterproof and resistant to hurricanes and intruders alike. "Anything a wall can do, we can do better," declared one fixture mounted above their elaborate showcase near the center of the exhibition hall. The bravado in this particular slogan was irresistible, and I approached the sales desk for a conversation about what this could mean.

"Let's build a wall of windows on the border instead of concrete," I joked with one of their sales representatives, pointing out the promise hanging on the display above our heads. "At least that way people could see each other from the opposite side."

She laughed and rolled her eyes at the mention of that other wall. "This is just marketing. Don't get me started on politics."

The show was sponsored by the National Association of Home Builders (NAHB), one of the largest and most influential construction trade associations in the United States. For a new study of American home buyers, the organization had recently surveyed more than 4,000 individuals of different generations to sketch what Americans wanted from their homes. At the top of their lists, they found, were features like laundry rooms and energy-efficient appliances, not home security systems. But most home buyers were still looking for distance between themselves and others: single-family detached homes in suburban settings, and on cul-de-sacs instead of open streets. Among baby boomers, in particular, 40 percent of the respondents described access control gates as a desirable or essential feature.[13]

In one marquee session, prominent speakers from the NAHB described the Trump administration as "a railroad car going full speed," threatening a collision between a pro-growth agenda and an immigration policy likely to further contract an already tight labor market in construction. Sitting next to me was an older man in a plaid shirt, a real estate developer from Tallahassee, quite angry about these contradictions. "He sold fear," the developer said, eyeing the crowd. "I can guarantee that 80 percent of the people in this room voted for Trump."

"What about gated communities?" I asked. Weren't some people here also in the business of selling fear?

He replied with a terse yet highly suggestive formula, one he would not elaborate on any further. "Security, thus fear."

The paradox is well-known: the proliferation of means to secure and protect can bring fear instead of assurance. People drift beyond lines laid down, or carry on their bodies the mark of being out of place. The unsettling tension between expectation and reality can have deadly effects, as the killing of Trayvon Martin by George Zimmerman showed in 2012.

Zimmerman had pursued Martin through the streets of a gated community in Sanford, Florida, a couple of hours from the place that Timothy Rowe managed on the Treasure Coast. Amid the national outcry, a debate ensued about the role of neighborhood design in the killing, the wrongful suspicion that an unarmed Black teenager walking home from a convenience store was instead a burglar. Urbanist Robert Steuteville called attention to the "corrosive effect of creating a landscape of exclusion and segmentation," the way that milieus of isolation and retreat can turn against the life of their streets, making suspect those who simply appeared on foot.[14]

As with fortified neighborhoods, so with the fortress homes they enclose. Social life in the modern West is organized increasingly around an "archipelago of domestic fortresses," sociologists Rowland Atkinson and Sarah Blandy argue, one that begins with the individual home and its defenses, extending outward into neighborhoods, cities, and even the borders of national homelands. "The dream of a completely cocooned home," they write, "is not a dream of escape from danger, but its reverse: a gilded form of internment, accompanied by the background threat of crime and disorder and metaphysical insecurity."[15]

These dreams feed on the rampant individualism of everyday life in market societies, and the commercial interests that continually infuse these lives with new occasions for fear, fresh opportunities to purchase some additional degree of protection. This is the work of the "dread merchants," as Bradley Garrett has termed them, the "doomsday capitalists" like Atlas

Survival Shelters—makers of the BombNado—who peddle the possibility of bunkering ever more fully against the dangers of an uncertain world.[16] They were a limited presence at the International Builders' Show, a scattering of dark notes amidst this sunny festival of commerce. Pay closer heed, however, and you could find the shadow of that uncertainty tingeing so much of what was on view, reminders that sublime indifference was a tenuous and hard-won state of mind.

One morning at the trade show, I took an official tour of custom homes in the Orlando area. This was the American dream scaled up to gargantuan proportions, the majority more than 7,000 square feet in size, with one, still under construction, sketched out in our tour booklets with an astounding 22,457 square feet of interior space. Most participants were builders and developers themselves, examining and appraising what they saw in relation to their own construction projects back home. I had to set aside my instinctive sense of terror at the size of these residences and to focus instead, like they did, on smaller details: the quality of the crown molding around a corner, the texture of a particular kind of stone slab, the layout of a future bathroom marked out only by piping now.

As we trundled on the tour bus through the suburbs of Orlando, I fell in with a few guys from a small town in western Minnesota. They were part of a family construction firm that built a handful of houses each year; the farmers they worked with always made their deals by handshake, they said, never by contract. As they saw it, families on the Northern Plains wanted homes with a warmer feel than most of what we were looking at here. Kevin, who ran the company with his brother and father, described one white bungalow we visited as "sterile," bemused by its contemporary design features.

"Don't fall," he joked as a colleague of his peered into a long window cut like a vertical slit into a wall, a transparent gap extending to the edge of this second floor.

"What'd you think of this place?" I asked him.

"Not like we have back home," he said with a shrug.

The minor drama of such distaste played out each day on the expo floor, a blaring riot of household objects with clashing style and sensibility, all clamoring for attention from passersby. Somewhere in the midst of it all was the pulse of a market, a collective sense of desire and taste that could be tapped with reliability. Was there consistency and predictability to what Americans felt and wanted from their homes? "You can see currents and pick up on it," a marketing director for Sherwin-Williams told me. "You walk around, see what people are making. You try to be an oracle for what is happening."

Her company had a standing inventory of more than 1,500 colors. Each year, they issued a Colormix, a small selection of colors and palettes that seemed to capture prevailing moods and feelings. For 2017, I learned, their breakout palette was a set of dark and brooding shades like Marea Baja, Mature Grape, and Black Swan, an ensemble they decided to call Noir.

"With all that's going on in the world, it's not a very confident place right now," the marketing director explained. People seemed to be cocooning, wanting to withdraw from the strife in the news, and these darker shades on a wall would give the semblance of a cave or retreat. "You want safe walls that you can live in," she said. "A stillness. Some quiet. A little rest, that feeling of safety."

The marketer admitted this feeling was an illusion, an impression forged by the psychological magic of color. All the same, she knew that it would gradually become real, that as their dark hues were circulated and echoed in the days to come — as they began to define the products that would fill future store displays, catalogues, and trade shows like this one — the moods carried by these tones would find their way into countless homes. I was struck by her conviction that such minor things could actually change our experience of the world. Could something as prosaic as paint become a vehicle of "security, thus fear"?

These questions were on my mind as I wandered once more through the expo floor later that day. It was the final day of the show. I walked past a display of synthetic countertop surfaces branded "Eternal." A company called Integrity was offering "Virtually Indestructible" windows and doors. At the back of the hall was an exhibition of weather-resistant Typar building wrap, "The Ultimate Barrier of Defense. For Whatever Comes Your Way." A salesman was at the demonstration counter, showing how the fabric could defy the most powerful jets of water. You could wall off your house with the stuff to ward off thunderstorms. But this was the same plastic material in a host of more modest daily barriers, from waterproof envelopes to surgical gowns — even disposable diapers.

"Is all this really necessary?" I wondered aloud. Did a baby's leaky privates need to be swaddled each night with disposable versions of the same indestructible stuff that shielded homes from hurricane-force winds and rain? Why adopt such a defensive posture with regard to what might happen in the world?

"The company actually has a motto for this," the salesman said, explaining the common assurance that ran through their construction, healthcare, and personal hygiene products alike. "We call it *A World of Protection*."

A world of protection. It sounded good and captured so much of what was on view at the International Builders' Show. But how livable was this idea, this vision of domestic life?

Safe housing is a profoundly unequal privilege in the United States, rather than a right to which anyone might lay claim. Far more Black, Latinx, and low-income households live in substandard housing than white Americans, and many of the problems prevalent in such homes — excessive heat and cold, exposure to lead and other contaminants, mold and other pathogens — are associated with both disease and death.[17] The ideal of investing in household safety and protection must be measured against the fact that white American households possess eight to ten times as much wealth as Black and Latinx households.[18]

Such inequalities must be understood as well in international terms, where we find worlds of both protection and alarming exposure. Those who have fled their homelands in Central America for the United States in recent years, for example, often pursue migration as a "survival strategy," as the anthropologist Emily Yates-Doerr has observed, a means of escaping malnutrition, economic exploitation, and sexual and political violence at home.[19] Many undocumented migrants to the United States find employment in the construction industry, where more than 20 percent of laborers and more than 30 percent of roofers are undocumented.[20]

Charged with securing the homes of others, many of these essential workers experience a tremendous degree of anxiety and uncertainty in their own homes. I was reminded of this truth at a national rally in support of the DREAM Act in Washington, DC, later that year. "They call us dreamers, but we are the ones who cannot sleep," read a sign held up by a Central American migrant rights activist. "There's no rest," she later told me, explaining what it was like to fear deportation. "You don't know what's going to happen, you can't say what will happen in the future. How can you sleep?"

––––––––––

In early 2021, I reconnected with Tim Rowe in Florida, as I did now and then. "Livin' the dream," he said when I asked how he was doing, replying as he always did. Even now, despite the chaos of the last year? "Well, nightmares are also dreams," he added with a chuckle.

They had some coronavirus cases in the gated community he helped to manage, Rowe recounted, but they'd also put many strict measures into place. Temperatures were taken at the gates, anti-bacterial soap dispensers had been placed everywhere, and weddings and other special events were suspended. As a community with many older people, they took the virus seriously. But still, "the natives were restless," as Rowe put it, eager to return to a life of easy socializing. With the quarantines in effect the previous summer of 2020, most of these wealthy individuals had stayed on in Florida instead of traveling to other places where they also had homes.

"Why are you making our houses more visible?" the residents kept asking the staff that summer, as workers pruned back trees in annual maintenance routines that homeowners were hardly ever around to see.

Meanwhile, the demand for homes here was booming, Rowe told me. There was the pandemic itself, but also the Black Lives Matter protests around the country in 2020, that specter of urban violence. "We feel a little more protected from the outside world," he said. "You can walk around your neighborhood without having to worry about a riot, knowing that the pandemic was being controlled." The gates promised residents a fullness of life without ever having to leave. Sales had sped up, and people were paying premium prices to buy their way in.

"It's that false sense of security," Rowe told me. "What's happening in downtown Chicago is not going to happen here."

What Tim Rowe observed in Florida was true around the country. "After years of slow sales and stagnant prices, homes in residential golf club communities across the country are seeing a surge in demand amid the pandemic," the *Wall Street Journal* reported in December 2020. The newspaper had spoken with many who had made the move, including a corporate executive who had relocated his family to a lakefront gated property in central Georgia. "The people that are running this place certainly have kind of insulated us in a little bubble," he told a reporter. "You feel very safe."[21]

The riddle of what Americans would want henceforth from their homes was a central theme in the 2021 edition of the NAHB International Builders' Show. Like most everything else at the time, the trade show had reconstituted as an online event. And there was much to reckon with here, in the wake of the pandemic's work-at-home conditions and stay-at-home orders that had focused attention on domestic space like never before. What did it mean now for the home to serve as refuge from the world beyond? What among these new arrangements would pass, and what would remain as a more enduring blueprint?

This being a trade show, new accessories came into focus. Speakers introduced new products for personal health like hands-free hardware, HEPA air filters and other purifiers, even anti-viral polymers to incorporate into flooring and paneling. Homes had become everything for people — offices, gyms, bars, movie theaters — and these diverse needs had to be accommodated. Builders had begun to integrate designs for a soundproof "Zoom room" into new houses. And there was the renewed importance of "delivery accommodation," where and how people would get their packages from Amazon, Grubhub, and so on.

Despite all the tumult that the country had seen, speakers from the housing industry were bullish on its future. In spite of the pandemic, home sales had boomed in 2020 — so much so, analysts reported, that stocks in home-building companies were soaring, and vacant lots to build on were very hard to come by. Mortgage rates were at historic lows, and families had been forced to save. Sales were highest in smaller metros and the outlying regions of metropolitan counties: in suburban and exurban areas. "Suburb life will continue to grow," an analyst for one leading consultancy noted.[22] In fact, as others noted during the trade show, it was in the suburbs where home prices were rising most steeply. People were getting further from one another.

Some of these were changes already underway, speakers emphasized. Millennials, for example, had been getting older, wanting more space for their kids, cars, and dogs.[23] At the same time, data from the NAHB showed, they also wanted more security. The 2021 edition of their regular survey of *What*

Home Buyers Really Want found that well over 50 percent of respondents under the age of fifty-four identified access-control gates as desirable or essential features of a new home. The study, which surveyed over 3,000 recent and prospective homebuyers in the summer of 2020, actually found that such gates appealed most to those between the ages of thirty-five and forty-four.[24]

Because of the pandemic, the survey found, more people than ever were looking for walking and jogging trails nearby, as well as parks and other walkable amenities. As means of socializing with others outdoors, porches and patios were among the most sought-after features of new homes. But it was also the case, however, that this deeper interest in life out-of-doors remained shaped by an abiding concern for safety and security. Three of the top five household technology features identified in the NAHB survey were in fact home security devices: cameras, wireless security systems, and video doorbells. More than 70 percent of survey respondents described such devices as either desirable or "essential/must have" features.[25]

Evidently, this was a way of being in the world that America was still growing into, not growing beyond.[26] The truth of this situation came through in a session on home technologies at the 2021 International Builders' Show, hosted by a popular home improvement podcaster. "Smart home technology is going to make us safer and more secure, no matter where you're living," the show host suggested.

The host was a genial-looking Gen Xer with a bushy beard and colorful tattoos running down the length of his arms. He looked friendly, and said this quite casually, which made the remarks all the more stark and troubling. He had conjured, once again, a sharp divide between the inside and outside of a home, as though everyone beyond those walls was a potential threat. Even neighbors in this scenario were just people someplace else.

Imagine, he mused, "someone coming up to scope your house out," when a camera picked up movement and the lights came on automatically. "Most likely they're going to bail on out of there and head down the street someplace. Now it's not your problem. I know that sounds cold, but you want to keep the people away as best you can."

TWO
NEIGHBORS AND OTHERS

FARGO, NORTH DAKOTA

It was a gorgeous July day in Fargo, North Dakota—puffy white clouds sailing through the mild blue skies of a Sunday afternoon, a perfect day to be out and about, ducking into open houses. Rolling from one neighborhood to another, a sheaf of real estate listings in hand, I was trying to get a sense of what made for an appealing idea of home in this place. The roofs were all pitched sharply with months of snow in mind. I stepped inside to find walls painted in warm, earthy tones and bedrooms carpeted with furry brown shag.

Coming from a compact coastal city, what struck me more than anything else was the sheer volume of space occupied by the multi-car garages fronting each of these houses. Their polished floors gleamed, as did most everything in these fresh homes. The garages were meant to stow trucks, boats, tools, and other things, but they also afforded little space for windows and other apertures onto the streets and front lawns. Wouldn't people miss this?

"What do we do in our front yards anyway?" one friendly young realtor mused. "It's a space where we water our grass, a showcase. Besides," she added, "it's so cold here half the year you're not gonna wanna be outside."

Fargo has a charming central district with beautiful Victorian houses, many boasting wraparound porches shaded by stately elms and oaks. A real estate firm founded by North Dakota Governor Doug Burgum recently began a high-profile effort to revitalize the city's downtown with both commercial and condominium developments. And yet the booming real estate market in Fargo is anchored somewhere else altogether, in the vast expanse of farmland to the south and west of the city proper. It is here, among scattered fields still plowed with wheat and sugar beets, that one may find most houses for sale.

That Sunday afternoon in 2017 my tour of open houses took me to areas so newly developed that the GPS on my phone was completely thrown off, advising me to stop the car and walk through blank green space rather than to use the broad asphalt roads laid out clearly in every direction. One of these houses was especially hard to locate because the metal numerals for the street address still lay wrapped on a shelf inside, waiting to be installed beside the door. I found it difficult to believe that such a home, however large and well-appointed, could be pitched to the market at $820,000, when it was surrounded by grassy lots and giant heaps of dirt.

To my eyes, the area looked empty and uninhabited. But realtor Paul Krabbenhoft assured me that such areas would be filled in completely within three years. "North Dakota is still a frontier state," he told me. "It's Midwest culture. There's always more land."[1]

Recent years have seen a construction boom in Fargo and other nearby cities, fueled by energy development and a growing technology sector, and drawing in settlers from around the United States and many other countries. The image of an open frontier is a powerful one in this expansive state with less than a million inhabitants, one of the least densely populated in the country. This vision is also one of the founding myths of the United States.

Lodged in the historical momentum of westward expansion was an imagination of the frontier as a "civilizational struggle" and a "way of life," historian Greg Grandin observes, one that condoned "the terror and bloodshed that went along with settler expansion."[2] The most influential articulation of this idea came in an 1893 address by Frederick Jackson Turner to the American Historical Association in Chicago. Turner celebrated the way that fractious states and settlers came together in opposition to a "common danger," the native peoples they dispossessed. But there was another side to these dynamics of national unification, the historian emphasized. The wilderness didn't just disappear, but seeped instead into the character of those who settled it. This was the foundation of American individualism, as Turner saw it: a pronounced antipathy to control, a complex society that tended to break down into small and scattered units.

"The tendency," Turner wrote, "is anti-social."[3]

A society shaped with scattered individuals: there has long been something paradoxical about the form of American social life, its uneasy resolution of the tension between a fervent commitment to personal liberty and the reality of collective need. The myth of the frontier was one way to resolve this tension, with the idea of a society—propertied and white—spreading outward together, finding common purpose in the domestication of a rugged landscape.

The grandness of this image, however, has always sat uneasily with the truth of how the West was settled. For even now, as we see in Fargo and so much of the Midwest, the prairies have been settled and occupied not simply as open range, but as a proliferation of cities and roadways, tract homes and commercial centers. "Any adequate explanation of the contemporary New West," as Robert Bennett writes, "must account for its rapidly sprawling suburban landscape and culture."[4] What can the suburban frontier teach us about how we've come to live with those beside us?

The isolation of American homes affects the texture of neighborliness, the possibility of striking up relationships with others beyond the bounds of one's own network of family and friends. In the Fargo metropolitan area, where housing development is booming most rapidly in low-density suburban fringes, the basic layout of homes has changed over time in ways that make conversations with neighbors more fraught and unlikely, intensifying the divide between known and unknown people. In particular, such patterns of residential interaction have complicated relationships between white residents of Fargo and the many refugees who have settled there in recent years.

When I look back at the real estate listings and brochures that I collected that July day in Fargo in 2017, I am struck by the visual representation of these houses: each fully occupying the frame of a photograph as a solitary structure, as though there was nothing relevant to see beside it. There may be nothing unusual in this photographic convention. Still, it's worth pondering what it means to imagine a domestic future in this manner. The brochures linger at length on the features and amenities a homebuyer would find *within* these spaces, and what family and friends might say when they come inside. But details on the space beyond these homes are hazy at best. And in such photographs of available houses, you never see other people at all.

———

American suburbia is a defensive formation, a nesting ground for *Bourgeois Nightmares*, as urban historian Robert Fogelson argues, animated by vexations of racial others, burdensome neighbors, market machinations, "the deep-seated fears of unwanted change that have plagued Americans since the mid-nineteenth century."[5] These deep currents of sentiment have a great deal to do with the tactics that President Trump employed in his failed re-election campaign in 2020, his warnings to the "Suburban Housewives of America . . . [that] Biden will destroy your neighborhood and your American Dream," the threat that crime and violence would land in the suburbs in the name of affordable housing.[6]

The charge was widely panned as a racist dog whistle, and it didn't work. Trump didn't just lose that election; he lost it because of suburban voters, who turned decisively toward Democratic candidates in many key states.[7] American suburbs are far more diverse now in terms of race, class, and culture than they were as postwar refuges for urban white flight. And yet there remains that basic structure of escape, and its political implications: if not by vote, then by lifestyle. "Before celebrating suburbs as havens of diversity . . . we should keep in mind their central role in the politics of normalization and containment," historian Andrea Vesentini urges. "Exclusion is still inscribed in suburbia's design, which either removes social life from everyday experience or brings it under social control."[8]

Paul Krabbenhoft and I first met at the International Builders' Show in Orlando in early 2017. A well-groomed man with a runner's build and a genial smile, he sat down beside me on a daylong bus tour of custom homes in the Orlando area. At the time, he was a board member of the National Association of Home Builders and had worked in real estate and residential development in the Fargo Moorhead metro area for more than twenty-five years. He seemed equally passionate about his conservative values and his public service work in soil and water conservation, a juxtaposition I found intriguing. My only exposure to Fargo was the dark 1996 film by the Coen brothers, which began in the city but drifted mostly through Minnesota. Paul and I made plans to meet up once again in the Midwest later that year.

As Paul and I drove together through Fargo's subdivisions one afternoon that July, he told me how he'd found in real estate a way of reinventing himself in the wake of a troubled youth. As a young man he'd studied finance at the University of Montana, before returning to the Fargo Moorhead area to take over the family farm. The family had money, but with the crisis in the agricultural and financial sectors in the 1980s, Paul had to file for bankruptcy at the age of thirty-five. "Rich folks and poor folks put their pants on the same way," he was forced to accept, and he found a new vocation assisting some friends in the homebuilding industry with the design and sale of new homes.

Eventually, in the boom times of the 2000s, Paul and a partner were developing and marketing a hundred homes a year on the southwestern periphery of Fargo, the same area where he had had his final and most difficult days as a farmer. "I was literally the last guy to have wheat here," he marveled as we drove one day down 17th Avenue South, subdivisions and strip malls on all sides. "I've been part of the change."

I went back that evening to one of the subdivisions that Paul had helped develop, two lengthy rows of "twin homes" clad in vinyl siding, set back from the street behind broad concrete driveways and small patches of grass. It was a beautiful summer evening, but hardly anyone was outside. I struck up a conversation with two older men lounging beside a grill on a pair of lawn chairs, planted within a largely empty garage. "What I like about living here is that there's very little traffic," one of them told me. "The only ones who come down this road are people who live here." He pointed out an Amazon box lying on the front stoop of the place next door. The family was out of town, and the box had been there for three days; no one had touched it, he told me proudly.

The next morning, Paul took me to a new development he was representing in nearby Moorhead, across the Red River from Fargo. We stepped into a brand-new home, the smell of fresh paint lingering in the cool air inside. The compact house was constructed on an open plan, with interior walls and doors to shut off only the bedrooms and baths. Stand in the heart of the living area, and the house felt profoundly different whether you faced toward the front or the back. Look to the street, and the space felt enclosed, almost hemmed in; the house was fronted by a three-car garage, with nothing more than a narrow window in the den and a fanlight aperture set in the front door to look out onto the street and sidewalk. Turn to the back, though, and you'd find yourself flooded with light from many angles and directions, for most of the glass panes on the walls were concentrated back here.

"Doesn't it bother people that there aren't many windows in the front?" I asked Paul. "You can hardly see what's happening on the street."

"What the house is like on the inside is what they care about," he replied. "And," he added, gesturing toward the sunroom built with windows on all sides at the rear of the house, "living on the back."

The sunroom was indeed bright and cheerful. Its glass doors led to a small, paved patio and a grassy space shared with surrounding homes, looking out into other private decks and yards. "This is where we engage socially with our neighbors," Paul explained, talking about the backyard barbecues he and his wife often hosted.

"It's a bit selfish," he acknowledged, the idea that "this is my space, I'll engage with who I want, when I want." But this was an orientation that had slowly developed over the years. "My generation, we grew up with a wealth explosion. Everything was about making a buck. We were paying more attention to ourselves than to the community."

What Paul observed with regard to socializing in Fargo speaks to larger patterns of change in the social life of American neighborhoods. The development of the suburb as a residential form involved turning inward as much as spreading outward, Andrea Vesentini argues in his book, *Indoor America*. Suburbs rejected the "porosity" of the city, proposing the family home as a bulwark against the many threats of the world beyond, its uncertainty and discomforts. New ways of organizing interior space in the suburbs, Vesentini shows, focused domestic space away from the life of the street, neighborhood, and community, in pursuit of an ideal of introversion and containment. "Interiors were devised as interconnected escape capsules to enable their independence from the outside world."[9]

Take, for example, the fate of the front porch. An iconic feature of the American home, a porch was altogether absent from that new home in Moorhead, as with many houses built in the United States since the Second World War. "Emblem of an open society," as historian Michael Dolan has put it, the porch has long made a place for Americans to encounter and commune with neighbors and strangers alike.[10] Take this sketch by James Agee of a casual summer's evening in Knoxville in 1915, a scene viewed from the rockers on a middle-class porch front:

> People go by; things go by. A horse, drawing a buggy, breaks his hollow iron music on the asphalt; a loud auto; a quiet auto; people in pairs, not in a hurry, scuffling, switching their weight of aestival body, talking casually, the taste hovering over them of vanilla, strawberry, pasteboard and starched milk.[11]

As liminal spaces between the inside and outside of American homes, porches made social interchange possible even in the face of harsh realities like racial and class division.[12] It was on a porch one evening in southern New York, for example, that household cook Mary Ann Cord, formerly enslaved, told Mark Twain the gripping story that would set him on the path to writing *The Adventures of Huckleberry Finn*. But over the course of the twentieth century, front porches slowly gave way to interior living rooms and backyard decks as places to gather.

There were many reasons for this decline. With the development of air conditioning, families no longer had to bide their time waiting for the temperature to drop on summer days. The television could pick up from front porch storytellers and the spectacle of the street. With the explosion of mass-produced housing in the postwar era, builders cut costs by eliminating accessory spaces like porches and vestibules. There was also the crowning of the automobile as the chief means of transport and king of the roads, which lent noise and dust to the experience of the porch, giving another reason to take shelter inside. As new residential roads and developments were laid out with vehicles rather than pedestrians in mind, the basic aperture of the American home shifted from the front door to the garage.[13]

"It's not that the vestibule disappeared," Fargo builder Jason Eid noted when we met: "it actually grew big enough for a car." Eid's family business,

Eid-Co Homes, had built over 5,000 houses in Fargo over the course of nearly seventy years. The company was responsible for the new home that Paul and I visited in Moorhead. Like many of their houses, Eid explained, its design was informed by a commitment to utility and efficiency. Front porches were more of a "ponytail" idea, he said, appealing to professors and designers with a certain kind of vision, but ultimately costs that the market wouldn't support.

In recent years, porches have made a bit of a comeback as typical features of new homes, in Fargo as elsewhere around the country. The impulse to retreat, however, continues to manifest in many structural features of the suburban home. I could see this in the new houses that Paul Krabbenhoft showed me as we circled back that day from Moorhead to south Fargo, all constructed by another major local builder.

With names like The Woods and Pine Lake Grove (both pseudonyms), these sprawling new developments evoked the bygone days of an open frontier, promising big lots with homes set at a distance from one another and good views of the landscape. Later, I asked the developer who had started the company why such a layout would appeal to local homebuyers. "People here don't want to be congested," he told me. "I don't want to open my window and pass over some sugar by hand to the neighbor next door."

Echoes of the frontier in such developments are a reminder of the instability in what they promise. People are encouraged to cocoon and look inward, while perched on the edge of an urban formation expanding continually outward. What does this imply for the texture of the urban life to come? This particular development's subdivisions lay on the southern edge of Fargo, on land that was planted with wheat and soy even just a decade ago. Cul-de-sacs for luxury homes adjoin streets lined with more modest tract developments as well as apartment buildings. In 2019, one of these streets was caught up in a fierce debate about development, about the degree of proximity with which homeowners were willing to live.

A local developer filed a request with the city to permit the rezoning of one particular block, to allow the building of duplexes on land slated for seven single-family homes: in other words, to allow up to fourteen families to live on this 1.67-acre parcel of land, instead of the originally planned seven families. In his remarks to the Fargo City Commission, the developer described the measure as a chance to "infill" the development and its underutilized infrastructure, observing that Portland, Minneapolis, and many other cities around the country had changed their zoning laws to accommodate more affordable housing. A city commissioner agreed, speaking of the housing crisis across the country, the need "to open up avenues for homeownership for more families."[14]

The city's planning commission had already approved the measure, but it had met with vocal resistance from many of the homeowners adjacent to the tract.[15] At the hearing before the Fargo City Commission that November, residents talked about the many cars already parked along that street, the traffic and congestion they faced, and where they would pile up the snow they shoveled. They were also concerned, in particular, about rental properties, and those who might rent them. People had built and bought homes there with the expectation that they would be surrounded by other owners of "middle-range homes." But rentals, many protestors said, brought uncertainty: the possibility of crime, the loss of home value, and simply doubts about who your neighbors might be. "You never really know who's going to be living across the street from you," a middle-aged resident suggested.[16]

One young mother came up to the podium to speak eloquently of the "dream" that had brought her family to settle in this corner of the city, "to raise our kids on a neighborhood street that is safe and quiet." She talked about the many ways that neighbors on the street pitched in for each other: holding mail, digging cars out of the snow, welcoming new homeowners with treats. All of this would be threatened, as she saw it, by that proposal to rezone the lots across the street, most especially for children on the block. "Our neighborhood is their world," she said, talking about how they walked to the school bus stop, and already had to cross too many driveways to get to the park. "I'm asking for it to be kept as a safe, quiet, and neighborly community."[17]

Without a doubt, this was a vision of collective life, turned outward to the shared space of the neighborhood as much as inward to its individual homes. And yet the precarious character of this vision is striking, the sense of how easily it might be tainted by the presence of a handful of additional families in this space.[18] Requisite distance was needed to secure the dream. The Fargo City Commission ultimately bowed to this idea, rejecting the rezoning proposal and reserving the tract solely for the construction of single-family homes.[19]

When people hold so doggedly to individual interests, the meeting of collective needs can be a serious challenge. Affordable housing and urban sprawl are familiar and long-known problems. The "2007 Growth Plan" for the City of Fargo acknowledges that "urban sprawl and leapfrog development" are deterrents to the development of a sustainable and livable city.[20] The plan outlines various measures to promote a more appealing and walkable urban environment, such as the creation of mixed residential developments of precisely the kind that was contested so bitterly in 2019. Still, the city's growth plan sets out a goal of designating 40 percent of its urban land as "low to medium density residential areas."[21] And it isn't simply a desire for space that drives the proliferation of such areas.

Intolerance for higher densities of urban life has as much to do with who those others are, as with the question of how close they might be. In Fargo, the conversion of all that prairie farmland into residential subdivisions has been fueled in part by intangible impressions of a changing city, an urban planner in the municipal office explained to me: a sense of being thrown by the traffic and the homeless downtown and the new racial demographics of Fargo. "You *see* these differences at the bank, the grocery store, the cleaners," the planner said: a newly visible minority population in a city famous for its Scandinavian and German heritage. As one Fargo builder suggested to me, "with all the different people coming in at such a fast rate, West Fargo is a powder keg waiting to blow."

Most of these "new Americans," as people here identify them, have been drawn by the booming economy in North Dakota, while a smaller proportion have come as refugees. A faith-based agency, Lutheran Social Services, had been resettling refugees in Fargo since the late 1940s: Germans and Baltic peoples at first, then Southeast Asians and Kurds in the 1970s, Bosnians in the 1990s, and a few hundred individuals more recently each year from Bhutan, Iraq, Somalia, and elsewhere. This population has become a flashpoint in recent debates over the changing face of Fargo's local communities and schools.[22]

The idea of "North Dakota nice" remains a powerful one for many Fargo residents, as the anthropologist Jennifer Erickson has noted: the notion that people here are "nicer, friendlier, and harder working than people in other parts of the country."[23] And yet, as Erickson observes, this self-image that many local residents carry is also anchored in the conception of "a homogeneous local culture in Fargo based on an imagined, whitewashed past."[24]

In the summer of 2015, thousands signed a petition posted to change.org, calling for a halt to refugee resettlement in Fargo.[25] Most of those who added comments online expressed a sense of frustration that Americans in need had been overlooked in the zeal to help these foreigners. Many also said that their neighborhoods had become undesirable and unsafe. "We are getting way too many immigrants in my neighborhood!!" one woman wrote in exasperation:

> We want to move away on account of it. The smell from their apartments is so strong & floods the neighborhood. That's all I smell when sitting in my back yard or when my kids and I go for a walk. It's over powering! Crime & vandalism has increased. I have purchased a hand gun to protect my family & plan to get my concealed weapons permit in the next month so I feel safe when we go for walks.

The Fargo Police Department had appointed a cultural liaison officer to manage such tensions, and we met one afternoon for a chat at a local high school. Was it true that people were moving out on account of these others moving in? "They would leave anyway," Officer Kempf told me. "When people think of success around here, they think of a three-car garage, a nice big yard, three-and-a-half baths. Once I make enough money, I don't want to share a wall with anybody. Everybody does that, it's the American way."

Vince Kempf, a twenty-five-year veteran of the Fargo Police Department, was teaching himself Nepali to better communicate with Bhutanese refugees, and he kept a stash of Himalayan yak cheese to chew on in his office. In his time on the police force, he told me, the rate of violent crimes had doubled, but property crimes had dropped by half; both of these rates were still low by comparison to most American cities. His office had recently issued a press release debunking the idea that immigrants and refugees were any more prone to crime than native-born citizens, and yet the association persisted.

"Image is everything," Kempf said. "You can pay so much attention to race that it perpetuates itself, to a certain extent."

His phone kept buzzing as we spoke. Something had happened the previous evening in the parking lot of a nearby Walmart, something that would go on to become national news that week. Amber Hensley, a woman from the Fargo suburb of Mapleton, got into an argument with three young women of Somali heritage because she felt they had parked their car too close to hers. One of the Somali women began recording the incident on her phone; on the video, which quickly stirred a viral uproar, you can see the woman with permed blond hair lean in menacingly and threaten: "We're going to kill every one of you fucking Muslims . . . why are you in our country anyway?" The next day, Hensley took to Facebook to apologize for not acting like a Christian, but she still lost her job at a local accounting firm.

As Fargo's cultural liaison officer, Kempf helped to facilitate a meeting between the women involved in the confrontation at the headquarters of the Fargo Police Department. And what happened there was truly unexpected, as I learned firsthand from the Somali women, when I had the chance to meet them in person that evening at an Italian restaurant in West Fargo.

"She started crying as soon as she saw us, and we cried too," one of the women, Sarah Hassan, related. They learned that Hensley was still grieving the death of her father in Iraq, and that she'd made a rash association with their hijabs. Hensley apologized profusely for what she'd said, and the refugees from Somalia forgave her, explaining that they'd fled Al-Shabaab militants themselves. They went to Hensley's employer to ask that she get her job back and had even made plans to celebrate their birthdays together in September.

I wanted to understand why these young women were so keen on reconciliation. One of them, Rowda, put it simply: "We are neighbors, we should be united."

With us at the table that evening was a Somali American community leader, Hukun Dabar, who shared his own sense of what precipitated such outbursts. "They fear the unknown," Hukun said, as he described what he had come to feel about many of the Americans he had met in the Midwest. Social interaction was much more cautious and restricted than what he knew back home. "This is a civilized country," Hukun said with a wry smile. "You don't know your neighbors." And when others preferred to keep to themselves, newcomers too were reluctant to reach out.

"You knock on the door to say hello. The next day they might call the police and say, *He keeps knocking. I don't know what he wants.*"

In the face of such suspicions, what these Somali American women did seem all the more generous and courageous—their making amends with a stranger in the wake of a violent outburst. Paul Krabbenhoft and I talked about it the next morning. He was a Lutheran himself and the son of Lutheran missionaries. He and his wife often volunteered with Lutheran Social Services, working alongside Bhutanese and Nepali immigrants in a community gardening project called Growing Together. As Paul saw it, people in the area were slowly getting used to these new immigrants. "Everybody's evolving. We're all God's people."

I brought up Matthew 22:39: *Thou shalt love thy neighbor as thyself.* How did he think about this teaching? "When I was young, I would have thought of that word 'neighbor' more literally," Paul replied. "Now I think of it as whomever I'm engaging with, whomever I'm talking to, like we are, right now. If there's respect, if you can have a dialogue. It shows that you can be kind in that relationship."

Paul found it tragic that a newcomer to Fargo might worry about conversing with a stranger. "For the majority of people in this town," he insisted, "if he took the risk to say *Hello*, I think they'd say it back." As a runner, he made it a point to greet everyone he passed. And it wasn't until very recently that he and his wife began to lock their front door when they left the house. "I came from the country, and I don't have those fears," he said. "We grew up trusting people, that people are good, giving them the benefit of the doubt until we're wronged."

Hukun Dabar also knew the importance of such trust. He had settled there as a teenager in 2014, finally rejoining his mother in Fargo after a decade of refugee itineraries that had scattered his Somalian family into far-flung countries. He began to take classes at the Moorhead campus of Minnesota State University and started a nonprofit organization, the Afro American Development Association, to assist refugees resettled in Fargo and Moorhead with language and employment training. In 2017, the city recognized Dabar with a Fargo Human Relations Award for his community work. Only in his early twenties and a newcomer still to the United States, he had quickly become a prominent advocate for refugee rights and welfare in the region.

"Immigrant families are trying their best, they are integrating well, they want to learn the American culture," Hukun told me. But he had also seen how challenging divisions of race and culture could make the most basic circumstances of social interaction. In Somalia, he said, neighbors would reach out to one another for charcoal, for a little cooking oil. They might even show up unexpectedly at your door in the middle of the night, and even then, you might sit to eat together. "Here it's very difficult," he said. "Being a Black person, a person of color, it's automatically a red flag. You go to your neighbor's door, it's like you're disturbing them. They look at you from a small window; they don't know who you are. *Who is this person? What do they want?* You have that fear."

"You're a community activist, a social activist," I said to Hukun. "What do you think it would take to change these things?"

"Right now, there is fear on both sides," he acknowledged. The problem was bigger than what any individual person might want or refuse to do. These dynamics would change only if institutions brought people together in unlikely ways: partnerships between churches and mosques, for example, to organize interfaith dialogues, joint potlucks, "know your neighbor" campaigns in the cities and towns where migrants had come to settle. He told me that he had volunteered at events of this kind organized by the Islamic Society of Fargo-Moorhead, billed as chances to "Meet Your Muslim Neighbor."

The Somali American community leader was signaling the importance of what the sociologist Eric Klinenberg calls "social infrastructure," the everyday places that make it likely for people to meet and engage with others they may not know very well, or even at all. "Building places where all kinds of people can gather," Klinenberg writes, "is the best way to repair the fractured societies we live in today."[26] In Fargo, as in so many other places around the country, we can see how porches, sidewalks, and other neighborhood public spaces had long served this essential function. When people retreat into isolated homes, other occasions for encounter must be devised and supported, settings less stark and imposing than a barred door.

"Nobody knows each other right now, that's the problem," Hukun reflected. But this could also change, he argued, with more opportunities for people to interact with strangers as potential neighbors, rather than as potential threats. "You reach out. You become friends. You go to the lake together. You eat food together. You become like family."

Hukun said these things with conviction when we first met in 2017. Over the next few years, he remained active in civic matters in the Fargo-Moorhead area, while the population of the region continued to grow more diverse. In 2022, Hukun ran for the office of mayor in Fargo, campaigning on a platform that highlighted affordable housing and ways to address the problem of homelessness. In an introductory campaign video, he said that his attention to these matters was inspired by his grandmother, who had taught him the importance of loving one's neighbors. The video introduction closed on this theme as well: "I'm Hukun Dabar. I'm a life-long hard worker. I'm a change-maker. I'm your neighbor."[27]

Incumbent mayor Tim Mahoney was ultimately re-elected that year, and Hukun placed fourth, with the support of 18 percent of the voters.[28] But he had knocked on the doors of thousands of city residents while campaigning, sometimes a few hundred of these doors each day, and Hukun was ebullient about the experience when we spoke the week before the election. "It's all about telling your story," he recounted. Older white men were more difficult to connect with, and there were those who had set their dogs loose or told him to get out. But most of the people he encountered were warm and en-couraging when they met.

"Is Fargo ready for a Black mayor?" I asked him candidly.

"We're gonna make them ready for a Black mayor," Hukun said with a smile. "Give it ten years, and you're gonna see a Black governor in North Dakota."

His enthusiasm was infectious. I too wanted to believe that this was possible.

THREE
PLACE AND BELONGING

DENTON, TEXAS

The county courthouse is the symbolic heart of Denton, a bustling town laid out in the dry brushlands of north Texas. The Romanesque Revival structure sits at the center of the town square, surrounded by the commercial buildings of what has been an important market hub and center for higher education in the region since the late nineteenth century.

It was at the courthouse square that Denton's Juneteenth Parade began in 2022, leading through the southern reaches of the town to Fred Moore Park on its southeastern outskirts. The route would have been long and tiring to take on foot in the blistering summer heat of Texas, and most participants made the journey by car and truck, or on flatbed trailers hitched to a motor vehicle. Among them was a maroon SUV sporting a sign for the parade's grand marshal that year, ninety-six-year-old John W. Bettie.

At the park, where the parade ended, his family members escorted Bettie by wheelchair to a covered pavilion, where the organizer of the event, Donald Norman-Cox—a Denton public historian and author of a recent book called

Juneteenth 101: Popular Myths and Forgotten Facts—introduced the elderly man to the small crowd gathered there on bleachers and camp chairs.[1] The identical T-shirts sported by Bettie and all the members of his family proudly declared that they had come back from Liberia for this event. "Good afternoon to everybody here," the grand marshal said, but he couldn't say very much more before he began to sob. One of his daughters gently took the microphone from Bettie to explain why they'd left Texas and had moved so far away.

"Daddy, welcome home," she said, adding in a wish for Father's Day. Her voice too was quavering with emotion. "My dad's grandmother took a journey from here to Liberia with her entire family, seeking freedom because she felt that she wasn't free," she explained. "She and her husband owned a business, and they lost everything. When they got driven out, she thought that she couldn't take that anymore. And then she took a journey from here to Liberia."

These words were a reminder of the forced exile a century ago in Denton that made this a moment of homecoming for those like the Bettie family. The Black community of Denton at that time was anchored not on the outskirts of the town but instead at its very heart, in a prosperous enclave known as Quakertown. Like many other Black townships at the outset of the twentieth century, Quakertown had thrived, with a school, many churches, and businesses like the café owned by Bettie's grandmother. But white civic leaders in Denton led a campaign to appropriate the Black township's land, raze its buildings, and place a public park for white families there instead. Many Black families left Denton altogether, for other towns and states or farther afield. Those who remained gathered once again in the early 1920s on a tract of land southeast of the town, an area that remains the nucleus of Denton's Black population to this day.

The Denton park that hosted this Juneteenth celebration was named after Frederick Douglas Moore, longtime principal of the school for African American children that was also established in this distant area when the original Black community school in Quakertown burned down mysteriously—many suspected arson—in the 1910s.[2] The parade that June day in 2022 had to travel far from the center of Denton because the Black community had been flung out of the heart of the town a century earlier. Even so, due to many years of collective struggle by those who had since made and maintained a community in Denton, people like the Bettie family still had a place to which they could return.

"I want to say that the love of liberty brought us back to Texas," Bettie's daughter said at the Juneteenth celebration, gesturing toward the motto of Liberia—"The love of liberty brought us here"—emblazoned on the caps that she and her father were wearing. "We hope that this will not be our only journey home," she added. "Even when daddy is gone, we will still come back home to Texas because Texas will always be home for us."

Texas has long been a difficult home for people of color. This paragraph was written on a summer day in 2023. It was a day marked by the announcement from the governor of Texas that the state would build floating walls along the Rio Grande to keep away migrants, only one of countless longstanding efforts to downplay the fact that Texan prosperity has always depended on the presence and labor of its non-white residents, back to and beyond the centuries of enslavement registered by Juneteenth itself.[3] But these histories of forging a homeland founded on denial and exclusion have also been accompanied by acts of homemaking in a very different spirit.

"Despite the brutal reality of racial apartheid, of domination, one's homeplace was the one site where one could freely confront the issue of humanization, where one could resist," cultural critic bell hooks notes. "This task of making homeplace was not simply a matter of black women providing service; it was about the construction of a safe place where black people could affirm one another and by so doing heal many of the wounds inflicted by racist domination."[4]

This idea of home as a space of cultural resistance remains a crucial counterpoint to the consolidation of fortress homes and residential landscapes in the United States. Like so many other American places, Denton has had its share of violent displacements, as the shameful fate of its Quakertown attests. At the same time, generations of Dentonites—especially Black women civic leaders and other Black, white, and progressive allies—have fought for a vision of home and belonging in a far more generous and inclusive sense.

Over many decades, Black residents and organizers in Denton have responded to the hardships of institutionalized racism with practices of mutual aid and collective caretaking. From the creation and destruction of Quakertown to the antiracist organizing pursued by Black and white women together in Denton in the 1960s to more recent Black Lives Matter protests, contemporary efforts to combat racism are built on the legacies of these historical struggles, and on the more inclusive vision of home and community these activists have summoned.

These struggles have much to teach us about the work of making and sustaining livable places, which may always need walls of some kind to hold and secure them, but also invite an appreciation of those within and beyond who made their shelter possible. Those cast into exile by divisive and exclusionary visions of home often have no choice but to pursue a wider and more collective imagination of domestic care and belonging. At a moment when this imagination is more crucial than ever, there is much at stake in recovering the history of such efforts.

———————

Juneteenth marks the emancipation of enslaved Americans, celebrated first in Texas and now across the country. Freedman Town, the first Black settlement in Denton, was founded in the early 1870s, not long after the town had been established as the seat of Denton County in north Texas. In the following years, formerly enslaved people purchased plots of land to settle with their families in various parts of Denton, including the tract north of the courthouse that became known as Quakertown, or just Quaker.[5] As Randy Hunt, founder of the Historic Denton nonprofit, suggested to me, the very name implied "this is a safe haven, come."

The history of Quakertown reflects what anthropologist Karla Slocum has described as "the pull of a Black space" in her book *Black Towns, Black Futures*, "a space that is inclusive, economically vibrant, and socially engaged — that is, committed to Black community."[6] What drew settlers to Quakertown, in particular, was the Frederick Douglass School, which was established here in 1878 as the first free school for Black children in the county. "The community school seeks as its primary purpose to improve the quality of human living, both individual and group," school principal Fred Moore declared, and indeed, commitments to collective well-being were reflected not only through the work of such educational institutions but also in the efforts of

Quakertown's churches and fraternal organizations.[7] When someone in the community died, for example, the Grand United Order of Odd Fellows would shoulder not only the cost of burying them but also caring for their family for two years.[8]

Denton's central square was a white public space, organized for the needs and values of the town's white citizens. Meanwhile, a few blocks northeast of the square, Quakertown's Black residents lived in a social world of their own. In the early decades of the twentieth century, the area was a thriving neighborhood of more than sixty middle-class and working-class Black families, most of whom owned their houses, reflecting both the wealth and self-sufficiency of the community. Photographs from the time reveal well-kept homes and gardens framed by picket fences, children in fine clothes playing with wagons and tricycles. The settlement boasted its own grocery and drugstore, restaurants and barber shops, numerous churches and fraternal lodges, a medical office and mortuary.[9] As Alma Clark—widow of Reverend Willie Clark, who grew up in Quakertown—put it, "it was a city within a city."[10]

This very distinction, however, between one city and another in its midst, calls attention to the systems of racial segregation that prevailed for decades in the American South. So distinctive were these customs that Americans had come to take for granted, historian C. Vann Woodward noted, that foreign diplomats often discounted stories of these practices as simply propaganda, until they were shocked to confront their reality in person when posted to the United States. Separate railway compartments and hospital wards, telephone booths and public toilets, drinking fountains and swimming pools, even school textbooks and courtroom Bibles set aside for use by whites or Blacks alone—these measures insisted that "subordinates had to be totally segregated and needlessly humiliated by a thousand daily reminders of their subordination."[11]

The very word "segregation" was a medical term referring to the physical separation of sick individuals from a healthy population, until it began to assume a racial connotation in the 1890s. "As long as our colored people continue irregular habits, and herd together in immorality and dissipation," a 1905 Virginia pamphlet on tuberculosis warned, their homes will be hotbeds of infection, fresh from which they will enter into intimate relations with our white people, drinking from public cups, spitting around kitchens and public places, as nurses fondling and kissing children, as cooks waiters and barbers handling food, tableware and clothing, inevitably spreading infection.

And it was the pursuit of this racially charged vision of public health, medical historian JoAnne Brown has argued, that best explains some of Jim Crow's most troubling excesses, measures that intertwined racial anxiety with fears of disease.[12]

Black Quakertown occupied some of the lowest land in Denton, on the banks of the flood-prone Pecan Creek. On the hilly land just to the north was the College of Industrial Arts, a women's college that opened in 1903. As the college expanded, bidding to draw young white women from towns around Texas, the Black settlement on its periphery became a source of anxiety and embarrassment to whites. The college screened the D. W. Griffith film *Birth of a Nation* in 1917, bringing to Denton its incendiary portrayal of violent Black men. While concern over such "menace" grew, leading Dentonites also argued that the city lacked a public park. "We owe it to our boys and girls to furnish them with a place for innocent recreation and diversion," Emma Lipscomb of the city's Women's Clubs urged at a Rotary Club meeting in the spring of 1921.[13] A plan gradually took shape among Denton's white elite: the idea of moving Quakertown out of the city altogether, and laying down a public park in its place.

On April 4th of that year, a lengthy editorial on the plan by Denton Chamber of Commerce Secretary H. F. Browder took up nearly half the front page of the *Denton Record-Chronicle*. "The city should have charge of this district and see that it is allowed to become a beauty spot instead of a nucleus of disease and a menace to the health of the whole town," Browder wrote. He attributed the higher death rate of Denton's Blacks to their lack of personal responsibility—"they are not able to keep their premises in sanitary condition"—rather than to the failure of the city to provide for sewers and drainage. Moving them out of Quakertown, the white public official wrote, was better for the health of Blacks and whites alike. The land could become a spot "where the public can find a breathing place," rather than "a place where we are ashamed to allow [visitors] to pass thru."[14]

The next day, the citizens of Denton voted in favor of a $75,000 bond measure to purchase Quakertown's land, remove and resettle its Black residents, raze the neighborhood, and build a park in its place. The KKK, meanwhile, was also making deeper inroads into Denton, going so far as to declare, in a boisterous address before a crowd of hundreds on the courthouse square in 1922, "Be a white man or get out of a white man's country!"[15] In the months that followed, many Black families left Denton altogether. Those who agreed to sell their land had their houses moved to a new area called Solomon Hill, on the southeastern edge of the town. Others who refused to sell and vacate the land found their places condemned by the city. By 1923, the Black people of Quakertown had been cleared out completely.

———

"The ordering of White life seems to require and demand the disordering of Black life," Jovan Scott Lewis writes in a book-length meditation on the afterlife of the white race riot and massacre perpetrated in Tulsa, Oklahoma, in 1921.[16] Such disordering takes many forms. There are physical and social acts of eviction, of the kind that Quakertown residents experienced in the very same years just a couple hundred miles to the south of Tulsa. There are also narrative modes of displacement, such as the way that the destruction of Quakertown was justified in retrospect, as the rightful clearing of "a settlement of dilapidated shacks through which ran a dirty stream," according to the *Denton Record-Chronicle* in 1939.[17] The memory of the prosperous Black district was so thoroughly erased from the official public record of the town that when a utility crew digging in the park that replaced Quakertown discovered some of its remnants in 1989, an officer of the Denton County Historical Commission went so far as to plead publicly for more information about their provenance: "I want to know where the people lived, what they did."[18]

Traces of Quakertown remained in Denton, however, along with many descendants of its exiles, still living on the southeastern outskirts of the town, past flour mills and two sets of railway tracks, over a mile from their original location near the courthouse square. Many residents had lived for years in the houses that were wheeled there in the 1920s. Alma Clark was one of them, and she spoke proudly with an oral historian in 2006 about the four decades she spent in that well-built house before it was finally torn down the previous year: its large covered porches, the ten- to twelve-foot ceilings throughout, and the three children she had raised there with her husband.

I met Ms. Clark for the first time at the American Legion Senior Center in Southeast Denton one afternoon in 2017, when she was eighty-nine years old. She scoffed at the official rationale given for Quakertown's removal. "We went into the homes of white folk and cooked their food and cleaned their houses. We took care of their children. We were good enough for that," she told me with a tart smile.

However much labor the Black women and men of Denton contributed to the well-being of the town's white residents, they lived themselves in a space of public neglect.[19] Solomon Hill had been a cow pasture, and those displaced here from Quakertown had to make do for years with outhouses and without utilities or running water.[20] Until the late 1960s, dirt streets were the norm in Southeast Denton: "sometimes we were in mud up to our ankles because if it rained those streets weren't paved," one resident recalled.[21] Conditions there were a revelation to the occasional white visitor, such as Euline Brock, wife of a professor at North Texas State College, who recalled seeing, as late as the 1960s, a "row of one-room shanties or two-room shanties" with outdoor privies and a single outdoor faucet among them to share.[22]

In 1964, the year that brought the passage of the Civil Rights Act, Brock and other liberal white women in Denton began to hold regular meetings with a small group of Black women in the town, creating what came to be known as the Denton Women's Interracial Fellowship. They began simply with an effort to talk with one another, following up with organized discussions about racial and social issues and public campaigns that eventually drew dozens of active women participants from the town.[23] As Euline Brock—who would go on to become a Denton City Council member and eventually mayor of the town in the 2000s—recollected, "we felt that the first thing that was needed was a forum for Black women and white women to get together as equals and just get to be friends and get to know each other as human beings rather than as a Black person or a white person."[24]

Racial integration had finally begun in Denton's public schools in the early 1960s, and women in the fellowship aimed in part to support their children. The organization ensured that its membership remained Black and white in equal measure at any given time and alternated its meetings regularly between Black and white homes. These domestic visits were themselves influential, as white women in the group had to confront the many stereotypes they held. "When we visited their homes, we noticed how well-kept they were," Dorothy Adkins recalled with respect to her Black colleagues in the group:

I always came back to feeling, *How on earth do they do it all?* I just couldn't imagine. For so many of the women at the time, the only job that was available to them was keeping someone else's house; and to know that they had gone off to somebody else's house, probably a different house every day for a whole week, and then go into their own home and see that it's spotless too, really impressed me.[25]

Women in the organization led a successful campaign to pave Southeast Denton's streets and equip them with streetlights. They organized voting drives to register new Black voters. They took to visiting local restaurants in Black and white pairs to support their desegregation and would attach notes to the bills they paid, stating, "As your customer I welcome being served by any qualified person, regardless of race, color, or creed."[26] In the same spirit, they distributed cards that encouraged Denton city residents to sign a "Good Neighbor Pledge" that affirmed the right of every person to rent, buy, or build a home anywhere they wished: "I will welcome persons into my neighborhood without regard to race, religion, or national origin; and I will work with them to build, to improve, and to maintain a community which is good for all," the cards declared.[27]

The efforts of the Women's Interracial Fellowship sparked various forms of controversy by making visible the harsh realities of racial segregation. Early interracial social gatherings for children in one white neighborhood "caused quite a furor," one member recalled, with white neighbors going so far as to throw rocks at the gathering.[28] One white leader of the organization stirred outrage by documenting the dilapidated houses that some members of her congregation had rented out to Black families in Southeast Denton, placing a poster in the vestibule of her church each Sunday morning with photographic evidence and the caption: "These are the Houses Owned by Elders in Our Church."[29] The landlords eventually agreed to clear debris from these lots and repair the rental properties. But despite the open housing campaign led by the women's organization, social and economic forces conspired to keep people mostly where they were, and the heart of Denton's Black community remained on its southeastern periphery.

In *All Our Kin: Strategies for Survival in a Black Community*, her classic 1974 study of Black kinship in a midwestern city, anthropologist Carol Stack described how Black "families cooperated to produce an adaptive strategy to cope with poverty and racism," relying on "extensive networks of kin and friends supporting, reinforcing each other."[30] In the same years in Southeast Denton, Black families had to do much the same, as they had in previous decades in Quakertown. Women relied on one another to help with their children, as they juggled work and other responsibilities. Families added rooms to their homes to house Black students who had been admitted to local universities but denied a place in university dormitories; "we all opened our homes," recalled Billie Mohair, one member of the fellowship.[31] Those with cars would drive these students to the universities each day so they could attend classes and study.[32]

"We had to help each other to survive," Alma Clark recollected to me, adding a striking analogy. "It's like making cornbread. You need meal, you need flour, you need baking powder, you need eggs. You need to put all those ingredients together to make that cornbread. You can't do anything if you keep them separate."

———

Although the Women's Interracial Fellowship wound down its activities in the 1970s, its legacy remains widely visible in Denton today. A vivid mural depicting Alma Clark and several other Black women activists with the organization spans both sides of the railway underpass leading into Southeast Denton.[33] An art installation commemorating their work for racial justice now adorns a small park close to the courthouse square.[34] These monuments are part of a larger public acknowledgment of the town's troubled racial history. The Denton County African American Museum also has a place now in downtown Denton, hosted within a restored home that was moved out of Quakertown in the 1920s. The park itself that replaced the Black township was renamed Quakertown Park, and it now includes much interpretive signage marking the lives of those displaced a century ago.

In 2020, Denton elected its first Black mayor—Gerard Hudspeth. I had the chance to meet him for coffee one morning a couple of years later. He was candid

Women's Interracial Fellowship leaders Alma Clark and Betty Kimble pictured on a mural in Southeast Denton.

about the challenges of serving a mostly conservative population as a minority in public office—like the white colleague of his, for example, who'd gestured toward the empty chair beside him at a public event with the startlingly casual words, "Come on, segregation's over." Hudspeth talked about managing social change in a slow and pragmatic manner, with the conviction that "absolutes don't exist." For while a Republican himself, he too had to wrestle with being wrongfully detained while driving, with being confused at times for other Black leaders in town, with the anxiety of fiddling with doorknobs while hanging campaign brochures in the evening twilight. As late as the 1980s when he was in high school, Hudspeth told me, he had seen a KKK rally take place—peaked hoods and all—at the Denton public park that replaced Quakertown.

For many decades, the most prominent symbol that consecrated Denton as white public space was the Confederate monument looming over the southern edge of the courthouse square. Placed here by a local chapter of the United Daughters of the Confederacy in 1918, the structure featured a granite archway supporting an impassive soldier made of stone — a young white man facing south, rifle in hand, and a knife and water canteen strapped to his waist. The archway columns described the war's Southern martyrs as "a song heard far in the future . . . their examples reach a hand through all the years to meet and kindle generous purpose and mold it into acts as pure as theirs." Below these words were a disused pair of drinking fountains built into the structure and etched with the years of the Civil War, 1861 and 1865.[35]

Denton's leading white women took the creation of the monument as a matter of civic duty in the early twentieth century, holding plays, dinners, and benefits to finance its construction, even baling paper and selling sandwiches.[36] For Denton's Black residents, the Confederate monument was something else altogether: "a giant *Keep off the grass* sign," as former city council member Deb Armintor described it to me, a way of asserting the heart of the town as white residential property. As Katina Stone-Butler, a Black singer and activist put it, there were "spiritual barriers" that persisted around the courthouse square.

Stone-Butler had come to Denton from Memphis nearly thirty years prior to study music at the University of North Texas. Our conversation yielded deep insights into the history of the square as a "stronghold of white supremacist ideals" and an abiding symbol of an oppressive legacy. "Our Black ancestors and elders passed down a legacy of survival, teaching us to navigate around these oppressive structures," Stone-Butler told me, describing the square as a manifestation of a "spiritual redlining" that "used architecture and invisible lines as a form of terror and gatekeeping to instill fear. This fear is so ingrained that younger generations of Black locals often avoid the square," she added. "This adaptive response to trauma has been continuously passed down and reshaped through generations."

Denton's Confederate monument was finally taken down in June 2020, in response to the Black Lives Matter protests that summer led by Stone-Butler and many others, but most especially thanks to many years of dedicated campaigning by civil rights activist Willie Hudspeth, Gerard Hudspeth's father. For twenty-one years, Willie Hudspeth had kept up a weekly public vigil at the monument on Sunday afternoons. He also testified countless times to the Denton County Commissioners Court, the political body responsible for the courthouse square. He did not typically argue for removal of the monument on these occasions, as though its racist legacy could simply be erased with such a gesture. Instead, Willie Hudspeth maintained that the two water fountains at its base ought be restored to service once again, so that anyone might drink from them regardless of race.

Willie Hudspeth's forefathers had survived the horrors of slavery in west Texas. He grew up in Fort Worth, and first came to Denton as a university student in 1971, after serving in the Air Force for several years in Vietnam. He was wearing an old camouflage jacket when we met for the first time in Denton in late 2017. "Turn them back on, that's what I'm asking," he explained, as we talked about the monument and its fountains over lunch at a nearby rotisserie. "Turn them on now so I can drink from them. You didn't let my ancestors drink, but let me. It'll be a proud day when we can all stand in line and drink from those fountains."

Willie Hudspeth's journey had taken him through a local chapter of the Black Panthers, the unexpected racial solidarity of his service overseas, and the sad truth of persistent segregation once he came back to Texas. He had taught at a local high school in Denton for many years and led a local chapter of the National Association for the Advancement of Colored People. As we talked, I could hear the past come alive in his voice, which took on a hard and menacing tone as he recounted what it was like to grow up with "Whites Only" facilities in the Jim Crow South, the things that white strangers were willing to say, even to a young child. "Get out of my way, n—! You need to drink from that water over there, boy!"

Hudspeth spoke about his crusade to restore water to the fountains on the Confederate monument as a search for closure, in the face of wounds that had lingered for decades. "I can visualize it," he told me. "I can see myself doing it, with my six granddaughters in front of me. They'll drink. I'll drink. And then it'll be over. That freedom . . . now we can drink."

He was imagining, I could see, a kind of homecoming in the city, the possibility that Denton might yet become a place for the sustenance of Black life. As it happened, the taking down of the Confederate monument on the courthouse square a few years later did not unfold in such a spirit of collective caretaking and acknowledgment, happening instead under cover of darkness, with no word of warning to Hudspeth and the many others who had waited so long for the moment. But Hudspeth accepted the monument's removal as a good and necessary thing. And a few months later, when Katina Stone-Butler and other producers of the *Black History for White People* podcast interviewed him about his long struggle, he spoke again about the need for a collective healing. "We all need to get together and work on some things together," he said.[37]

The podcasters reminded Hudspeth of the city's plans to name June 9th—the day the Confederate monument was removed from the courthouse square—as Willie Hudspeth Day henceforth. "How would you like to see that day celebrated or commemorated moving forward?"

"One of the things that I've learned in this whole process is that we keep separating ourselves from each other," Hudspeth told Stone-Butler and the other podcasters, reflecting on the long shadow of segregation. "Get with another race and do something. If it's just going to the park, letting the kids play, and sitting there doing nothing. . . . Get with somebody of a different race and just chill with them—that's how I want the day remembered." Against the backdrop of a radically segregated history with persistent and thorny legacies, something as simple as sharing space with racial others could stand out as a political act.

———

For bell hooks, homeplace was in Kentucky, as she writes in *Belonging: A Culture of Place*. It was in the rural green hills where she grew up, "a life where the demarcations of race, class, and gender did not matter."[38] But it was also in the Kentucky town of Berea where she settled for the final decades of her life, making a home among others equally committed to building an antiracist community. "Living in a community where many citizens work to end domination in all forms, including racial domination, a central aspect of our local culture is a willingness to be of service," hooks writes:

> Those of us who work to undo negative hierarchies of power understand the humanizing nature of service, understand that in the act of caregiving and caretaking we make ourselves vulnerable. And in that place of shared vulnerability there is the possibility of recognition, respect, and mutual partnership.[39]

There is a profound truth to what hooks says about the vulnerability that comes with openness and care. It is also true that so often—in Denton, Texas, as in many other places—such exposure is distributed unequally. Many residents of Denton struggle with the basic problem of affording a place to live, as is the case in so many other American cities. But local laws and codes are structured to pass this burden elsewhere, beyond the vicinity of the city's wealthier and predominantly white neighborhoods. Active regulations restrict the construction of duplexes in downtown neighborhoods built for single-family homes, limit the creation of additional dwelling units as a more affordable alternative for renters, even deny the right to sleep in their own cars to those with no other place to stay, former city council member Deb Armintor told me. Such rules are like "walls that follow you wherever you go."

Under such circumstances, the historically Black area of Southeast Denton has once again emerged as a place to meet the needs for dwelling otherwise unmet in the city. Most of the affordable housing built in recent years by Habitat for Humanity is located in this southeastern area of Denton. More recently, the Southeast Denton Neighborhood Association has raised concerns that a large-scale real estate project to build an upscale apartment complex in the area could propel its gentrification and the displacement of residents of color. "Will Southeast Denton see the same fate as Quakertown?" one report on the matter in the *Denton-Record Chronicle* asked.[40] "I don't understand why everything in Denton, Texas, got to come over to us in Southeast Denton," one resident stated pointedly at a public meeting about the project in November 2022. "Does anybody else have land somewhere?"[41]

It remains to be seen how these developments will go, and what they will imply for the larger trajectory of desegregation in the city. But it is clear that Black community leaders who have wrestled with such matters for decades will continue to do so in a characteristic spirit of mutual caretaking. I think, for example, of Betty Kimble, longtime resident of Southeast Denton and one of the founding members of the Women's Interracial Fellowship. Even into her early nineties, Kimble served as an advisor for a local organization providing home rehabilitation services to low-income Denton seniors. And such service was folded into the very rhythm of her daily life, as I learned myself when I visited Denton for Juneteenth in 2022.

Ms. Kimble and I had first met five years earlier at the American Legion Senior Center in Southeast Denton, which she was still directing in her eighties. I learned, over the course of a few conversations, how she had paid her way through college by doing custodial work at the University of North Texas and how she'd gone on to lead an assembly-line team at Texas Instruments for more than twenty years. She told me about the interracial organizing that she and other women had done together in Denton and what it was like to grow up there under Jim Crow. She recounted taking narrow steps up to a theater balcony to watch Westerns with other Black children, how someone or other would always have something for them to eat at the back door of nearby restaurants. "We knew what we could do and what we couldn't," she told me. "We enjoyed what we could do."[42]

It was a real privilege to meet Ms. Kimble once again in 2022, and to pick up the thread of our conversations. She invited me to attend a Juneteenth service at her church—Mt. Pilgrim Christian Methodist Episcopal Church— that Sunday morning, where Reverend Keaton Fuller spoke of the essential company of God in times of chaos, and invited me to stand together with all the fathers in the congregation being celebrated that day for Father's Day. Later that afternoon, Ms. Kimble asked me to join her and a grandson at home for Sunday supper.

There were many things to commemorate her life of public service in that small bungalow on Lakey Street, just a few hundred feet from Fred Moore Park. I savored what she had cooked for us to eat together, and I cleaned my plate again and again. As we sat around a table beside the kitchen, Ms. Kimble recalled all the Black students she and her husband would pack into their car each day when driving to the University of North Texas campus, during the many years when Black students were forbidden from those dormitories; the way that her and other Black families worked together to ensure their children would make it through school; the boxes of food that her church had been handing out more recently during each week of the coronavirus pandemic; the free vegetables from a local community garden that Ms. Kimble would keep on her driveway each week so that others could stop by to pick them up.

"I ask God to let me help someone every day, and I do," she said to me, with all the warmth and dignity held in the words she spoke. "See, I fed you," Ms. Kimble added with a knowing look, and indeed it was true. She had opened her own home to me. She taught that such care for others was still possible and necessary, despite the fraught character of our domestic boundaries.

PART II

LIFE ON THE ROAD

FOUR

IT'S A BRICK

A few years ago, my family had an opportunity to move to Los Angeles for a few months. My wife had a fellowship at the J. Paul Getty Museum. I had the chance to pursue my own research sabbatical in a different environment. We rented out our rowhouse in Baltimore and found local schools in LA for our kids. We were lucky to get a spot for our daughter Uma at a friendly nursery school a few blocks down the road from where we would live, a pink stucco apartment complex on Sunset Boulevard. It was quite appealing—the idea of walking Uma to school each morning—something we hadn't done back home.

The name "Sunset Boulevard" conjures all the mystique and romance of movieland Los Angeles. Just a few miles to the east of where we stayed was the Sunset Strip, with the celebrity clubs, hotels, and bars that bring flocks of gawkers from all over the world. Where we lived, though, was more like a winding artery for westside traffic. Here, Sunset was a surprisingly narrow two-lane road. When there wasn't much traffic, vehicles would hurtle down the asphalt at 50 miles an hour. This doesn't sound that fast, unless you think of it from the perspective of someone walking, say, down the sidewalk beside the road. Walking or running however fast, those vehicles were doing something altogether different: clipping through the same space at more than seventy blistering feet each second.

Each morning, we took turns helping Uma, just four years old at the time, get dressed for the day. We'd pack a sandwich and some snacks into her Hello Kitty lunchbox, help her get her shoes and jacket on, and slip out the side gate of the complex onto Sunset. We mostly had the sidewalk to ourselves at that hour each morning, while the road itself was hopelessly snarled in traffic. All these automobiles, pickup trucks, buses, and utility vehicles made for a fearsome din as they inched down Sunset, thousands of individual engines thrumming and rattling side by side in unison. The first time Uma and I walked down the street to her nursery school, she was terrified. Both her hands were clamped tightly over her ears all the way.

We had landed in Brentwood, one of the most exclusive neighborhoods in Los Angeles — so exclusive, in fact, that many of the smaller roads spurned sidewalks altogether, asking maids, caretakers, and occasional walkers to take to the asphalt instead. We would often see bright red signs planted on the edges of these meticulously groomed and landscaped properties: "Drive as if your children live here." But the children themselves were hardly visible on these streets, ensconced within their homes or backyards, or else inside the bulky vehicles that took them from place to place. Never had I seen so many big SUVs as we did there: Range Rover, Cadillac Escalade, Chevy Suburban, Porsche Cayenne, Mercedes GLC, GMC Acadia, each following another like a parade of gleaming tanks down the road.

Walking Uma to school each morning meant weaving our way between these lumbering giants parked out front, leading her through the sweeping driveway to the nursery school door. On foot our child was dwarfed by their wheels and grilles. Now and then a door would swing open and another child would come into view within that vehicle, too small to clamber down from the vehicle's height without help. I couldn't help but think about the profound mismatch of scale. Such massive conveyances, such tiny cargo — why?

It's not just our homes that are styled now like defensive fortresses. Over the last decade, imposing vehicles like SUVs and trucks have come to dominate the American car market, far outpacing smaller sedans in sales. These are automobiles designed with aggressive profiles and built as defensive steel cocoons, often marketed as ways to survive an uncertain and even hostile world.[1] Pedestrian deaths on American roadways, meanwhile, have soared by more than 50 percent over the last decade. Someone in an armored cockpit, someone else on their own two feet: this too is a polarized and difficult encounter. The automotive metropolis of Los Angeles provides a stark exposition of these challenges of life on American streets.

One morning in Brentwood I walked past a brand-new white Cadillac Escalade, the dealer placard still fixed to the back. I stopped for a brief chat with the driver, another nursery school dad like me. I was curious about what, to him, appealed in the vehicle. They had three kids, he told me, "and a nanny too, of course." Somewhere in the back was his golf bag, his son's T-ball gear, other stuff they carted around with the weekend in mind. He admitted they were getting about 12 miles per gallon, but this didn't seem to bother him too much.

Why an Escalade? "My wife wanted to go with this one, for safety," he told me. "It's perceived to be safe. You know, more mass."

More mass. The phrase kept playing on my mind as I walked back home—so light on the tongue, and yet so ominous. Whose safety was secured by all this mass hurtling down American roads, and at whose expense?

———————

The vehicles that make up the personal automobile fleet in the United States are the biggest, heaviest, and most powerful in the world.[2] Automakers learned to manufacture much lighter vehicles in the wake of the oil crisis of the 1970s; with the acute need for fuel efficiency in mind, the average weight of an American automobile dropped by over 20 percent between 1975 and 1981. But then the weight of these vehicles began to climb once again, and remains on the rise, standing now at the highest point on record, according to the US Environmental Protection Agency: 4,303 pounds per vehicle. The average "footprint" of American automobiles—the space they take up on the ground, the area defined by the points where their tires touch the road—also has risen steadily, having increased by 6 percent between 2008 and 2022.[3]

These developments mark the ascendence of sport utility vehicles and pickup trucks in the American automobile marketplace beginning in the 1980s.[4] Ford F-Series trucks have been the most popular vehicles on American roads for decades. But such utility pickups increasingly keep company with passenger vehicles built and styled like heavy-duty trucks. Passenger sedans now account for just about one-fifth of annual automobile sales, a market share that has been eroding steeply: when I lived with my family on Sunset Boulevard in Los Angeles in 2017, sedans still comprised a third of the American auto market.[5] In a telling sign of this shift, auto plants around the country have been retooling their assembly lines from passenger sedan to SUV manufacture, from GM's historic factory in Lordstown, Ohio,[6] to Ford's Chicago Assembly Plant and Fiat Chrysler's Belvidere Assembly Plant in Illinois,[7] to manufacturing plants operated by Mercedes-Benz,[8] Mazda, and Toyota in Alabama.[9]

Ideas of greater personal safety and security have propelled the steady rise of the SUV.[10] And it is true, in one important sense, that the occupants of a "light truck"—as SUVs, pickups, and vans are known—are less likely to die in a crash than the occupants of a passenger car. This margin of protection on the inside, though, comes at the price of greater danger to those on the outside of these vehicles. Their higher center of gravity makes them more difficult to handle, more of a challenge to steer clear of potential accidents. When a light truck collides with a passenger car, those in the car are several times more likely to die than those in the truck or SUV, according to the National Highway Traffic Safety Administration (NHTSA).[11] The pressure to go big in the face of such odds is so powerful, one economist has suggested, that something like an "arms race" is taking place on American roads.[12]

Then there are those others who share these spaces with motorists: pedestrians, cyclists, and children on scooters, skateboards, roller skates.[13] In 2022, more than 7,500 pedestrians were likely killed in crashes with motor vehicles in the United States, a fatality rate that increased by 77 percent between 2010 and 2021.[14] Studies have shown that pedestrians are two to three times more likely to die when struck by a light truck than by a passenger car.[15] This has to do with the greater rigidity of vehicles like SUVs and pickups, and with the geometry of their front ends: high hoods and grilles are much more likely to strike a bystander in the torso than in the lower extremities. Armored against the outside world, these vehicles are more lethal to those outside. Small children are especially vulnerable to such hazards, for drivers of such vehicles must contend with a much larger blind zone around them.[16]

The features that shield and cocoon those within the hard shell of an SUV also add mass that must be carried from place to place. Fuel economy, therefore, is an intrinsic casualty of their design. The overall mile per gallon rate of the American personal automobile fleet has been climbing year by year, but lags significantly behind the European Union and Japan, where fleets of smaller and lighter vehicles require 30 to 40 percent less fuel to travel a given distance.[17] As a class, light trucks like pickups and SUVs are exempt from the "gas guzzler" tax that Congress levied in 1978 to discourage the production of inefficient vehicles. Transportation is responsible for more greenhouse gas emissions than any other sector of the American economy.[18] Greater emissions and more serious effects on climate change are another consequence, therefore, of the American love of big, strong vehicles. And yet their popularity is only growing.

The Escalade in the nursery school driveway that day, like so many others gliding through the streets of Brentwood, came from Casa de Cadillac, a historic dealership in the nearby San Fernando Valley—not far from where I grew up and went to school in the 1980s. One Tuesday morning, I took the 405 freeway into the Valley to take a closer look at these machines.

Built in 1949, the dealership is an icon of modernist roadside architecture in Los Angeles. The building meets Ventura Boulevard as a wall of glass panels—the Casa de Cadillac logo set down in a neon cursive that bends the letters over to the right, as if they were being carried along at speed and trying gamely to keep up. Mid-century roadside buildings like this one—like the vehicles they carried—promised a physical embodiment of speed, of matter in fluid motion.[19] Think of how Cadillacs and other luxury cars of the 1950s mimed the form of spaceships and jet planes, with sweeping tail fins and lights laid out like rocket nozzles in chrome. These features and their aspirations sit uneasily with the more rigid conveyances sought out now.

Gleaming in all that light from the wall of windows at Casa de Cadillac was a long black Escalade, parked in one corner of the showroom. Richard, a sales consultant, walked me around the car and opened up the back, showing me how to fold down all the seats with the touch of a button. My first thought, looking into that cavernous bay, was that our Honda Fit might just roll right into the belly of this car, park in that space behind the front seats. More mass: this particular model weighed in at nearly 5,800 pounds.

"What are people looking for in a car this big?" I asked Richard, taking in the extraordinary volume of the hulking vehicle.

"It's all about that Caddy feel," he said with a smile, pointing out the emblem on the grille. He let me try out a "Platinum" model parked in the lot outside, priced at nearly $90,000. Without the footboards that rolled out smoothly when the doors unlocked, I noted, it would have been tough to clamber up into the cabin.

As we pulled out onto Ventura, I found myself looking nervously all around, eyes darting from the windshield to the various mirrors, trying to get a feel for that expansive armature of metal and glass moving along with us down the road. It was a surprisingly hot day in early March, temperature in the high 80s. "Feel how cool that seat is?" Richard asked me, pointing out the air conditioning system that chilled the leather under my pants and back. I couldn't help but wonder about all the heat that this three-ton behemoth exuded, the window sticker promising 15 mpg in the city.

"What about fuel economy?" I asked Richard. It was a March morning in 2017; President Trump had addressed an audience of hundreds of auto executives and workers in a former automotive plant near Detroit that week, announcing a halt to the more stringent fuel economy standards imposed by the Obama administration. "The assault on the American auto industry is over," Trump had declared.[20] In Los Angeles, meanwhile, the salesman chuckled at my question. "People who drive a car like this aren't really thinking about mileage."

What were they thinking about then? "Safety, for one thing," Richard said. "You're higher up. You can see everything around you. You're not the one trying to see behind some other SUV. Someone hits you, and you think, "Oh, what was that?" he suggested, looking lightly over his shoulder as if to brush away the landing of an insect or something else just as inconsequential. He spoke as if the vehicle was armor for the body of the driver, truly a *tank*, as he put it, impervious to incidental contact with others.

This sense of safety that he talked about, while we drove, was assertive as well as defensive. "When you see an Escalade coming, with that V8 engine and all that power, you get out of the way," Richard explained. I could feel it when I stepped on the gas pedal, the sense of an enormous and arbitrary force at my disposal, something I could muster up if I chose to do so, the question of whether it was necessary left solely up to me. "Get out of my way!":

driving an Escalade was like shouting this down the road, Richard said with a laugh. The pleasure was caught up with a threat of aggression.

We walked back into the dealership to find a middle-aged couple, coffee cups in hand, looking at the black Escalade on the showroom floor. They wanted to know whether this version came equipped with a feature they'd read about, a refrigerator between the two front seats. Sensing my own ambivalence, meanwhile, the salesman turned his attention to them, telling me that I might be better suited for a Range Rover.

———————

I followed Richard's cue the next afternoon, deciding to walk down from Brentwood to the Range Rover dealership on Santa Monica Boulevard. Here, as always, this meant walking at times down blocks without sidewalks, skirting around parked vehicles and sharing the asphalt with passing cars. Going on foot allowed me to take in these vehicles more carefully than if I'd been behind the wheel of a car myself. I stopped to look at the sticker plastered to the back of a green Chevy Tahoe: "KEEP CALM AND BACK THE FUCK OFF."

A salesman named Mikhail met me at the Range Rover dealership and took me out onto Santa Monica in a Land Rover Discovery. We could see the roofs of other cars lined up ahead, almost as if we were peering over obstacles between us and the open road. Mikhail had just come back from a company-sponsored off-road expedition in Arizona, where they'd learned to motor down rock slopes as steep as forty-five degrees.

Almost no one would do this with their own Range Rover, he admitted to me, but the idea was there in the way he talked about driving through Los Angeles: the city as an urban wilderness, an unpredictable space of hazards and exposures, one that demanded preparation and defense.[21] It was there even in the geometry of this imposing vehicle: the high flat snout of its face, a hard vertical plane that reached above my abdomen when I stood beside it, with a promise to push through space with the implacable force of a battering ram.

Another dealer on nearby Olympic Boulevard put it this way, talking about the shape of the GMC he had to offer: "it's a brick." I found the analogy arresting. We'd come so far from the idea of the automobile as a sleek embodiment of speed. The parallel with a walled enclosure went even further, the dealer implied, because of the space set out by the rectangular frame of an SUV. "Get kicked out of your house?" he asked, opening the rear hatch of a Yukon and gesturing to all the room inside. "You can just sleep in here."

The automobile has long been imagined as a kind of mobile dwelling to live in and inhabit, "a simulation of the domestic environment," as the sociologist John Urry has noted, "a home-from-home moving flexibly and riskily through strange and dangerous environments."[22] Such spaces can be true and essential resources under conditions of rampant housing insecurity, as is the case in contemporary Los Angeles. But it isn't simply their availability that is at stake in these observations from an automotive dealer in the city. There's also the psychology of the American car buyer manifest in these evolving designs. What was the attraction of a brick-like vehicle, one that approximated not just the security but even the shape of a house?

This question took me a few weeks later to the CARLAB, a small consulting firm based in Orange County. I plied a world of concrete rivers to get there from West Los Angeles, the 10 to the 110 to the 105 to the 605 to the 405 to the 22, the sky a hazy white and the mountains a vague presence on the horizon. The founder of the firm, Eric Noble, taught in the transportation design program at the ArtCenter College of Design. At the CARLAB, they interpreted consumer behavior for manufacturers based on the values and circumstances of current and potential buyers, gleaned through extensive research. "I tend to want in my car what I want for myself in the future," Noble explained, describing how they made sense of consumer desire.

We looked at some designs for the "crossovers" that have opened a new space in recent years, between passenger sedans and conventional SUVs built on top of a pickup chassis. Later, over lunch at a nearby taqueria, the designer spoke of pendulum swings in automotive design, as the form of vehicles adapted to broader social currents. Cars in the 1960s were "long, low, wide, and open" like the mood of those years, embodied in vehicles like the Corvair, with a roof that almost floated on wispy pillars and giant sheets of glass. Now, Noble mused, "it's pretty clear that the entire West is suffering a broad case of insecurity."

Why are brick-shaped SUVs so popular in the United States? "What is the appeal of a brick-like structure in general?" he asked by way of reply. "It's the same thing. It's considered more substantial. That's just what Americans have learned to want."

Automotive designers think of the shape of a car in human terms: wider wheel wells as "hips," for example, curving beyond the sides of a narrow body. You could think of the harder and more angular profile of an SUV as a masculine form, Noble suggested, one that might convey "his big strong arms enfolding me."

Such comfort and safety, however, necessarily added weight to a car. Airbags were heavy, as were thick panels of safety glass and reinforced pillars to protect a cabin from rollovers. Passengers in a luxury vehicle were insulated from noise with dense pads of asphalt, and the countless electric motors of a high-end vehicle were built from weighty coils of copper wire. All this meant that a vehicle would carry more mass, more force and potential danger to others in a collision, the automotive researcher acknowledged. But what they encountered time and again in interviews and focus group discussions was something like a kill-or-be-killed pragmatism, when it came to the possibility of contact between two vehicles on the road. "If there are two cars in an accident," people would tell them, "I want my kids in the bigger car."

––––––

The rise of the SUV is now a global phenomenon, its prominence in international automotive markets representing the second-largest cause of increasing carbon emissions over the last decade, more impactful than shipping, aviation, and heavy industry.[23] The conversion of automotive fleets from gas-powered to electric vehicles is often conceived as a panacea for their carbon footprint, especially in the United States. The nation, it would seem, is prepared at last to confront the effect of American lifestyle on the world beyond. The years of the pandemic have also stoked interest in "complete streets" hospitable to pedestrians, cyclists, consumers, and drivers alike.[24] But what will these streets look and feel like if the dominance of oversized vehicles continues, especially for those who aren't barricaded within such vehicles themselves? An electrified SUV remains an SUV: a mobile machine with the same magnitude and force.

Automobile manufacturers insist that sensor technologies are capable of addressing roadway hazards, for both the occupants of their vehicles and people outside. Take, for example, Cadillac's promotional brochure for the 2021 Escalade line, which outlined a package of safety features—augmented reality navigation, automatic emergency braking, "front pedestrian braking," a side blind zone alert, even a "safety alert seat" that would vibrate in warning—to identify and react to potential problems.[25] But, as journalist Andrew Hawkins noted on a 2021 episode of *The War on Cars* podcast about the Escalade, "if you weren't up so high, if it wasn't so wide, you wouldn't need all these features. . . . They wouldn't even need half the cameras that they had, or half of the radar or ultrasonic sensors if the vehicle was just smaller."[26]

The War on Cars is a quirky and insightful production. In late 2021, the show released ads for a mock pickup called the Chevy Inundator, built with a steep front grille so absurdly high that the windshield was reduced to a narrow horizontal band. "Here's to the men who do the manly things," a narrator intoned in a gravelly deadpan.[27] Two months later, I caught up with one of the founders of the podcast, writer and activist Sarah Goodyear, for a long conversation. She talked about her faith in younger people, their awareness of the dangers of climate change and the consumer treadmill, and her fascination with the steady rise of motor-assisted e-bikes all around the United States—in urban, suburban, and rural zones. But she also expressed serious concerns about where American roadway culture seemed to be headed—the possible effects, for example, of relying too much on the vehicle's sensors and other autonomous systems.

"Humans are too fallible," too unpredictable as pedestrians and casual users of the road, Goodyear told me. "My biggest fear is that we're going to go to a hardened streetscape that is predictable enough for sensor-enabled cars." She could see a proliferation of barriers that would tightly govern where and how people could move through streets, yielding "urban environments where streets are more like freeways, so that people don't encounter these vehicles that can't understand them." In the name of addressing the problem of unreliable and distracted drivers, these technologies could land us in a more "dystopian future, where the kind of free movement we're used to will be increasingly constricted." Goodyear invited me to imagine a binary logic of future roadways: zeroes and ones, cars on roads and people elsewhere, "less and less of the gray areas, the soft edges," the spaces to sustain any non-automotive use of streetscapes.

How did she make sense of the stunning rise of the SUV in recent years? "I could just say *capitalism*," Goodyear joked:

But after thirty to forty years of systematic disinvestment in the public realm, increasing precarity in terms of healthcare, a general deterioration of public life — all these things incite a survivalist mentality, the sense we all have that ruin is around the corner for any one of us at any moment, that society is not going to save me, that I have to save myself, I have to save my family.

These needs could be read from the very structure of vehicles like the SUV, their aggressive grilles, for example, acknowledging that their occupants have little else in their hands to control, that these vehicles at least would embody the idea of "doing something to take control of your environment, when you feel inherently out of control all the time."

Such impulses have had a special salience, of course, in the recent years of the pandemic, which gave us many new automotive rituals enacted through distant commingling: curbside haircuts and photography sessions, drive-in movies and church services, drive-by graduations and birthdays, and so on.[28] The fall of 2020 saw automakers making bold new promises to prospective car buyers, offering up vehicles that would filter pathogens and other dangerous particulates from the sheltered air of automotive cabins.[29] Goodyear herself had remarked on these developments in a *War on Cars* episode released that May of 2020. "I see people starting to use cars as PPE [personal protective equipment], as the ultimate form of protection against the virus," she observed. "It really worries me that once we start getting back to more economic activity and more people going back to work and shopping, that there are going to be people running around, wearing their cars instead of wearing masks."[30]

The activist chuckled when I brought up this episode a couple of years later, when we spoke in the winter of 2022. "I was absolutely on the money with that prediction." She told me how things were going in her eminently walkable Brooklyn neighborhood, all the new license plates on the road, the kids being dropped off at school instead of walking, people trying to drive into Manhattan instead of taking the subway. "Traffic in New York is so much worse than it used to be," Goodyear noted, with public transit usage yet to recover to pre-pandemic levels.[31]

At the same time, she observed, the problem was social as much as infrastructural. "Now people have cars, and they see the world around them as hostile" in a way that they didn't before, Goodyear suggested. "Protection against the virus is becoming a more generalized protection against the other vagaries of urban life. The more that people wall themselves off from other human beings, the more threatening those other human beings seem."

———————

In the fall of 2021, a few months before Goodyear and I talked, I had a small accident on a busy road not far from our house in Baltimore. I was driving home that morning from an outing at a nearby nature reserve. What I remember most vividly is the feeling of a wall of green metal, suddenly coming at me. I swerved and braked instinctively but was hit anyway, just in front of where I sat behind the steering wheel. The front corner of our compact Honda Fit was mangled. The other vehicle, a Subaru Forester SUV, was a little scratched and dented.

The other driver, it turned out, was a sixteen-year-old who had gotten her driver's license just a few months before. She was upset by the collision—she had veered into my lane, hadn't noticed me at all. Later, I learned that Subaru was actually marketing the Forester as a safe option for parents who were nervous about handing their keys to distracted teen children.[32] I worry now about my own teenage child who'll be driving soon. We love our compact car and how agile and maneuverable it is on narrow city streets. But would it endanger our son to put him behind the wheel of something so small and clearly vulnerable? What does care look like when the potential for violent impact is so endemic to a society like ours?

The market is already answering such questions for us. Auto manufacturer Honda recently revamped its compact Fit hatchback line for global markets everywhere *but* the United States, where the sale of its smallest and most affordable vehicle was discontinued in 2020, due to slumping demand.[33] Small cars continue to disappear from the American automotive market, even as gas prices rise. It's nearly inevitable, I'm beginning to realize. When we replace the compact car we have now, it may well have to be an SUV.

American automobility has long been founded on the dream of an escape capsule, a safely sealed cocoon. "The only way for Americans to be *together* in the postwar city," historian Andrea Vesentini writes, "was to be kept safely *apart*, each inside a private interior."[34] For most of its history, the automobile itself could be imagined as that insular bubble, modeled on the suburban interiors it traveled between. But now, as the automobile itself grows in interior depth and volume, the logic of seclusion also deepens. And all of us will have to wrestle with what this implies for the character of shared and public space.

A friend of mine, whom I'll call Sahana, also lives in Los Angeles. A few years ago, her husband came home with a grand surprise: the keys to a brand-new Nissan Infiniti SUV. She'd been hauling their three kids around LA in a decade-old Odyssey minivan. Pieces had literally begun to drop from the aging vehicle. She and the children had to pull off the freeway once when something started smoking under the hood. Her husband looked carefully for a hybrid SUV with decent mileage. My friend was relieved. "I'm just glad I'm in a car that's safe for my kids."

I tagged along with Sahana and the kids on a day of errands one summer Friday, a few years ago. She had warned the children that her anthropologist friend was trying to understand what it was like to travel in a bigger car. Her youngest child, who was five then, wasted no time in teasing me about this. "Look at how big our car is!" he exclaimed, as we stepped into their garage in Studio City. We were headed first to a nearby swim school for his weekly lesson. As we pulled into the small lot at the school, it struck me that each of the seven vehicles parked there was an SUV, but Sahana wasn't surprised. "I don't know anyone who doesn't have one."

Later I hung out with the kids in another parking lot, windows down, while my friend ducked into a grocery store to pick up a couple of things. From the front, I could barely see her daughter, the oldest of the children, who had made the third row of high-backed seats into something like a room of her own. She gave me a detailed inventory of all that she had to herself: four cupholders, two windows, two vents, a second seat to fold down into a table, and spots she'd marked out below her feet for each of her two shoes. The child was fastidious with her room at home, and here too, she said, "I like to keep it neat."

The row between us was shared by the two boys. "Write down everything I have," the youngest one instructed me, pointing out the cubby holes tucked into his door and car seat, the folding seat that he could also claim as a table beside him, and the packet of wipes kept below it. "I have my own section of books," he added, showing me the basket of picture books below his dangling feet. "Did you write down my dragon?"

Behind the wheel, Sahana was engulfed by the gleaming black mass of the Infiniti. "It's not that I feel grand or anything, driving an SUV," she said that day as we headed down Ventura. "It's just efficient for the life we have now." On school days they might be in the car together for as much as two hours. "The kids would just fight all the time in a regular car," Sahana observed. "Here, my daughter has her own space in the back. The boys each have a place for their own activities."

Here was a crucial lesson to absorb. The safety promised by the shell and shape of the car was one thing, but on a day-to-day basis, it was the space inside that mattered most. And this was a space that worked well because this too could be divided, as it was at home—because this too, for so much of each day, had to be a place in which to wait and dwell.

Growing up in Los Angeles, spending countless hours with my sister and brother on those freeways and roads, I knew about the importance of this kind of space. The first car we had in LA was a maroon Oldsmobile Cutlass sedan. When we were very young kids, before my brother came along, I would always claim the right side of the back seat, my sister would always have the left. I can still clearly picture the two brown lines of vinyl beading that ran down the center of that wide bench seat. These borders were an essential feature of our American childhood, not to be crossed or infringed upon in any way, lines we came to police so zealously on our own.

Then and now, in a city like LA, traffic can snarl for the nuttiest reasons. On the day that I spent driving around with Sahana and her children, a Cessna, of all things, had made an emergency landing on the 405, closing off that essential artery. As we crawled south along Sepulveda Boulevard instead, her older boy, a dreamy child, piped up cheerfully about the car he wanted when he grew up: a yellow Camaro with black stripes.

"I want it to look like a bumblebee," he said as we inched and idled our way down the road, one gleaming shell among thousands of others, windows sealed against the noxious air, each as if a world of its own, each enveloping many more worlds within. Everything was set up to give each of us that sense of a place apart.

FIVE

ROLLING COAL

MIDWEST AND BEYOND

With video clips, so much depends on what you see, where the stream picks up. This one on the Reddit forum r/PublicFreakout in the summer of 2020 begins on an intersection in Marquette, Michigan, just a couple of blocks from Lake Superior.[1] There are young people with signs, kneeling on the asphalt. A GMC truck pulls up, engine rattling, rearview mirrors caked with mud. People get up, brandishing messages:

"I SHOULDN'T BE WORRIED ABOUT A SIMPLE TRAFFIC STOP"

"WHERE THERE IS OPPRESSION THERE WILL BE RESISTANCE"

"STOP KILLING!"

"#BLM"

The truck keeps inching forward, looming over the human bodies on the road. A young woman holds out her palm as if to say "Stop." She does this hesitatingly, as if she knows that the truck may not stop, finally bringing her hand to rest on the hood of the vehicle. Behind the wheel is a white man in a baseball cap. "We got the license, let him through, nobody needs to get hurt," someone calls out.

A drum begins to beat as the protestors gather on both sides of the truck, slapping the metal body with their hands. The diesel engine lets out a low and guttural thrum. As it bolts ahead, the truck releases thick black gobbets of smoke, engulfing the crowd. "Oh my fucking god. Holy shit. That's unbeliev-able," someone cries out.

Most of them are wearing masks in these early months of the pandemic—this small, multiracial gathering on the streets of a very white northern town. Maybe this helps a bit, with all that smoke. The black plume hangs overhead, dissipating slowly. People are waving their cardboard signs to try and clear the air. The truck meanwhile is long gone, already somewhere else.

Later, a debate about the incident erupts on Facebook.[2] Young women at the rally report that they'd been kneeling on the road for a moment of silence, that the truck had circled around to face off against them, that the young man behind the wheel had laughed and flipped them off. There are people who vouch for them, on the forum. But many aren't buying it, insisting in-stead that the protestors were the aggressors, that they'd broken the law by blocking the road, that they had asked for trouble. "People illegally blocking public rights of way should be treated no different than a speed bump," one resident declared.

Protestors for social justice have been struck by vehicles around the coun-try, even run over in sporadic acts of terror. Take a look at Facebook groups like Do Not Block Roads When Protesting and you'll find heartless memes like "All Lives Splatter," stick figures tumbling over the high hoods of vehicles like that truck in Marquette.[3] This threat was no doubt in the air that day, actual-ized here in coal rather than collision.

Diesel trucks "roll coal" when retrofitted to spew black clouds of smoke. Coal rolling is a notorious and uniquely American phenomenon of recent years.[4] Many states have banned the gesture as an environmental nuisance, a flamboyant indulgence in burnt hydrocarbons at a time of mounting concern for the climate crisis. But the practice also carries a strongly racial politics: white men (mostly) playing with the blackness spilling from their oversized trucks, sometimes even putting their faces to exhaust pipes as blackface gags.[5]

Throughout the country in the spring and summer of 2020, coal rolling was a widespread feature of local responses to the Black Lives Matter protests that galvanized the country.[6] From Oregon and Montana in the Northwest to Tennessee and North Carolina in the Southeast, people chanting "I can't breathe" were met with gusts of choking smoke. The tactic is a window into a prosaic practice of vehicular aggression in the United States. In a moment of deep concern about carbon emissions and grossly unequal exposure to pollutants, here was a culture celebrating exhaust, even its imposition on bodies already struggling to breathe.

In 2017, I began to explore the menacing aesthetics of this diesel culture, spending time at truck shows and races in Iowa, Tennessee, Colorado, and elsewhere. I came to see that excessive exhaust can be a sign of celebration in such spaces, a mark of freedom instead of pollution, a way of claiming the American road as a space for the pleasure of drivers alone.

One third of the transportation fleet in the United States runs on diesel fuel, according to the Environmental Protection Agency.[7] These are primarily heavy-duty vehicles for freight and commercial trucking and transport, but they also include passenger cars and trucks. Diesel engines are one of the most significant sources of air pollution in the United States; the nitrogen oxides they produce contribute to ground-level ozone and acid rain, and the particulate matter or "soot" they release has been linked to many health problems like asthma, respiratory illness, and heart and lung disease, a pollution exposure burden borne especially by communities of color and socioeconomically disadvantaged populations.[8] In 2012, diesel exhaust was classified as "carcinogenic to humans" by the World Health Organization.[9]

Automaker Volkswagen was plunged into a scandal—widely known as "Dieselgate"—in 2015, when investigators discovered that the company had quietly installed software devices on millions of its diesel cars so that they could bypass emissions testing standards.[10] But the coal rolling by diesel trucks in the United States, which leapt into public view around the same time, was something else altogether: a celebration of the visual spectacle and sensory kick of thick, black clouds of billowing exhaust. "Pollution porn for dudes with pickup trucks" is how the online magazine *Vocativ* described the phenomenon in the summer of 2014.[11]

The "coal" that issues from a diesel truck is a byproduct of excess fuel, partly combusted carbons released in the form of soot and smoke. With an exhaust stack kit and a modified fuel delivery and emission control system, any diesel vehicle can be retrofitted to flood the engine with extra fuel and make this happen, as diesel enthusiasts know. Take country singer Granger Smith's 2020 song "Diesel," for example — something like an anthem for these possibilities. The video features Smith atop a lifted pickup truck on massive wheels, hefting a "Don't Tread on Me" flag as he leads a belching caravan of heavy-duty pickups down a narrow country road.[12] Orange flames and dark smoke are everywhere as Smith keeps coming back to an aggressive chorus:

> *Yeah, we love smoking that diesel*
> *It screams out freedom like a big bald eagle*
> *Like a rooster on a June bug beetle*
> *Country boys are left foot lethal*

The video recalls what the cultural critic Cara Daggett has named "petro-masculinity," an imagination of burning fuel as "a practice of white masculinity, and of American sovereignty, such that the explosive power of combustion could be crudely equated with virility."[13]

I got a sense of this myself a few years ago at a diesel drag race event in Crossville, Tennessee, called the Rocky Top Diesel Shootout. Hood ornaments, paint jobs, and merchandise logos featuring skulls, knives, jagged teeth, and automatic rifles all gestured to the outlaw and militia culture of the truck scene, the hint of violence in revved-up machines. As a brown man, I was nervous about being there on my own. But the people around me — so many of whom were grizzled white men — seemed much less interested in me than in the trucks, each of which was lining up for a chance to go whining down the track in a trail of dark vapor.

Among the market tents and tables selling mechanical gear and other merchandise, a brand called Diesel Life stood out for the scale of its operation. They had set up shop in a trailer rig doubling as a mobile storefront, with their death-dealing logo — a menacing skull perched atop a pair of fuel pumps arranged like crossbones — laid out on the side in massive proportions. Inside were T-shirts that declared "Smoking is not only permitted, it's encouraged" and the hashtag #DieselLivesMatter, framing an old diesel pump against a spooky twilit landscape.

These designs were interesting for their ambiguity. I was drawn to one with a skeletal hand in a tattered work glove, drowning a leering skull in a lake of yellow fuel. "Diesel Life," the brand said again, but associating this life with death seemed inescapable. You could easily imagine a critic of fossil fuels embracing the shirt as much as a diesel enthusiast.

I talked with Ashley Feldkamp, who had founded the Diesel Life brand with her boyfriend a few years prior and had come to Crossville to sell merchandise and represent the company. "There's something very unusual and honest about your designs," I suggested to her. "It's as though they're saying, *It is dangerous, it is deadly, but still, this is your life.*"

"We go to more than a hundred truck and diesel shows a year," Feldkamp told me. "I walk around, talk to people, ask myself, *What would this person wear? What are they thinking? How are they feeling?*" The aesthetics of the brand, as she saw it, had to be faithful to the character of a unique culture, that of "the diesel family," as she named it. "Truck drivers are a different breed, they *are* rough," she said. "The image we want to portray is that it's a life that you live. The truck drivers, they believe that — this is their life, this is their livelihood."

I couldn't help but recall the skull-and-fuel-pumps of the Diesel Life logo, the way this image seemed to condense and amplify the many other skulls plastered onto the T-shirts, stickers, and truck bodies all around us. Cartoonist Nate Powell has addressed the prevalence of such "death's head" imagery in an incisive visual essay published in the magazine *Popula* in 2019.[14] The appeal of such ominous forms in white, male American circles, he argues, attests to the popularization of a military style teetering on the edge of lawlessness, calling up the vigilante anti-heroism of Marvel's *The Punisher*, the assertion of a power beyond the very divide between good and evil. "All of this — skulls, trucks, flags, guns — form the edges of a commodified, weaponized identity," Powell writes, emblems of a popular culture founded on the "romance of dark power," a picture of ordinary life steeped in a casual violence.[15]

This sense of a complicity with dark power was in the air that morning at the dragway in Crossville. It was in the thick clouds of billowing black smoke that would drift and hang over the packed bleacher stands with every pair of souped-up pickups that lined up to race. It was in the way that the men in these stands kept a casual patter going over the rattling scream of the doctored engines, indifferent to breathing in that smoky pall.

On the far side of the track was a billboard for a local gun shop, the promise of "1000's of Guns!" for sale just down the road. On the near side of the track was a young man in a black T-shirt, taking pictures of the passing trucks. On the back of his shirt was a diesel pickup leaving behind a big black cloud of its own. "Money may not buy happiness," the shirt declared, "but it'll buy a diesel, and I've never seen a sad person rollin' coal."

The joy of rolling coal likely has as much to do with where a diesel truck is headed as with the smoke it leaves behind. The freedom these vehicles declare is that of the open road, the speed and distance promised by a powerful engine, the vision of a clean break from whatever might be lingering in the rearview. But leaving things behind is never such a simple matter. Take the big rigs conjured up as fantasy by every pair of angle-cut smokestacks mounted to the bed of a diesel pickup. Here's long-distance truck driver and country singer Tony Justice on that experience in "Highway Junkie," a 2016 track with a wicked and infectious bass line —

> *Hundred cups of coffee, five hundred cigarettes*
> *a thousand miles of highway, and I ain't forgot her yet*
> *but I'll keep on movin', keep on movin' down the line*
> *Ain't nothin' in my mirror, just a cloud of dust and smoke*
> *what do you expect when some old trucker's heart gets broke?*
> *Yeah, truckers' hearts get broke . . .*

Sporting a Stetson hat and a denim shirt, Justice kicked off a set on the main stage of the 2017 Truckers Jamboree in Walcott, Iowa, with this track, playing for a crowd of all ages gathered on hay bales and folding chairs. The massive sign looming 139 feet overhead on a post behind the stage explained where we were: Iowa 80, which bills itself as the "World's Largest Truckstop." About a thousand trucks and four thousand cars pull in each day at this exit along Interstate 80, a few miles west of the Mississippi River and the Illinois border. For decades, the truck stop has sponsored an annual Truckers Jamboree, drawing thousands of truckers, truck enthusiasts, and curious onlookers to its sprawling grounds along the interstate.

Tony Justice has a devoted following as a singer and songwriter, a career he kindled while also trucking goods out of Tennessee to Texas, Illinois, and Florida for the Home Shopping Network and UPS. He'd just released his fourth studio album — *Stars, Stripes, and White Lines* — in 2017, available at truck stops along the interstate and chronicling a life spent mostly on the road. Between songs at the jamboree, Justice shared some of his own tales of the road, drawing appreciative chuckles from even the most stone-faced men in the crowd.

"I grew up in east Kentucky," he told me the next morning when we sat down for a chat at the Redeye Radio booth. "It was mean, tougher than pine knots." His father was a trucker too, with three coal haulers of his own parked in front of their house. Justice and his brothers would have to scrub the coal dust off those trucks every weekend before they could play. This kind of experience gave him perspective on the lightness of commercial country music today, he told me, the "make-believe little world" that the industry typically conjured up as an escape from hardship. "Reality always has a way of coming back and slapping you in the face," he mused.

Many of his songs are driven by a wry sense of fairness on the open road. I think of these lines, for example, from "Elvis Was a Truck Driver, Too," the last track of *Stars, Stripes, and White Lines*: "Well we laughed when we passed that ragtop red Corvette / I bet he ain't got the diesel smoke out of the leather yet." Tony laughed off the lines as just a good rhyme when I brought it up, pointing out that a big rig's smokestacks would reach a good dozen feet above any such car. But he also recalled what it was like when one of his father's coal haulers would take off down the road with a full load of coal, 130,000 pounds at a time.

"The black smoke would just roll, it'd be following down the road like a jet, like a jet stream," he recalled. "Diesel engines, they've got to breathe to do what they need to do. Let that engine breathe a bit, give it some fuel, there's gonna be some exhaust."

The public is quick to judge big rigs, maybe their drivers too, for being heavy, noisy, and intimidating. No one likes being on the tail end of a diesel semi picking up speed down the highway or rumbling up a steep hill. But people also forget so easily, Tony pointed out, that wherever they were in America, nearly everything they own and love was brought to them by one truck or another. And those who drive these vehicles are struggling day by day with the limits laid down on what they can do—like the 2017 federal mandates for electronic logging devices (ELDs) to monitor and regulate the hours when drivers can operate their vehicles, meant as a precaution and safety measure but making it all the more difficult to meet a tight schedule or to pull over and take a quick nap when needed.

"Drivers," Tony said, "we feel like we're being squashed with regulations. I'm all for the environment, but there's got to be a happy medium."

Such frustration was palpable at the Truckers Jamboree. There were the stickers plastered onto some of these trucks: "Fuck MPG" or "Certified Dirty Idle," mocking the "Certified Clean Idle" tags that many states and lo-

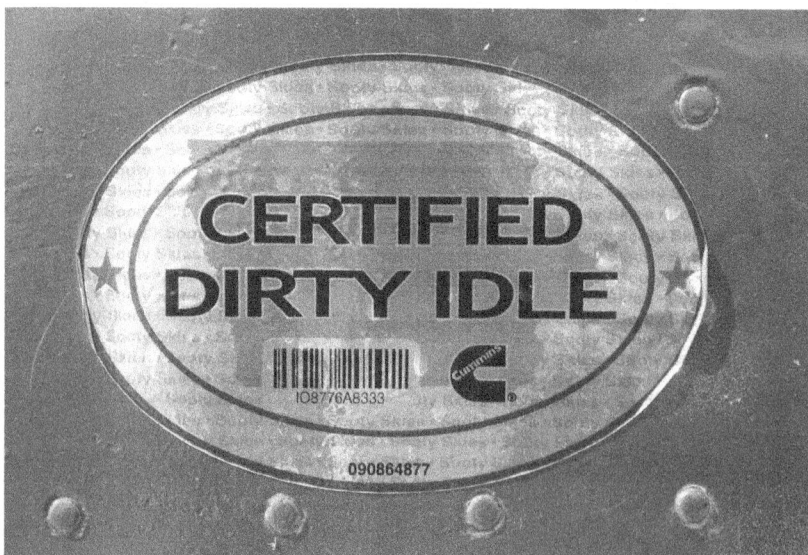

calities now require. Or the magnets for sale in the Iowa 80 gift shop, which declared a proud defiance with slogans like "I like truck fumes" or "Nobody governs my truck." Older truckers at the jamboree scoffed at the latter idea. Big rigs today are set up with so many sensors, monitors, cameras, speed-limiting governors, and fuel-regulating devices, they told me, you just couldn't figure out anymore what was actually going on when your truck broke down by the side of the road. All you could do was call a tech and wait.

There are structural reasons why the freedom of a life behind the wheel on the open road has become an illusory dream, sociologist Steve Viscelli argues in a book-length ethnographic study of American trucking called *The Big Rig*. As Viscelli shows, the evisceration of the rights and protections of American truck drivers ironically began with the deregulation of the industry in the 1980s, which "transformed trucking from an industry with some of the best-paid workers and one of the strongest unions in American history into one in which unions play almost no role, and workers live for weeks at a time out of the machine they operate, often earn less than minimum wage, and work hours equivalent to two full-time jobs, sometimes more."[16]

Most big rig drivers work now as contractors rather than employees, preferred by carriers because of the cheap and flexible labor they represent and the willingness of such drivers to bear the costs of truck ownership and maintenance themselves. The industry actively promotes such arrangements by idealizing drivers who own or lease their own trucks as entrepreneurs and "owner-operators," Viscelli notes, even as working conditions leave these drivers entirely at the mercy of big shipping companies.[17] Drivers are left to do what they can with the few elements in their control, like the fuel economy of their road habits, which can determine their chances of actually earning a livable income. It's little wonder that, under such conditions, the idea of an extravagant wastage of fuel becomes a symbol of freedom and the substance of fantasy.[18]

Hence the magnetic attraction of what was on display at the Super Truck Beauty Contest that year during the Truckers Jamboree in Walcott, Iowa. Tricked-out big rigs came alive each night—their gleaming grilles and faces towering over avid passersby, banks of LEDs pulsing in flashes of red, blue, orange, and green, shimmering in the glitter scattered under their wheels.

Engines thrummed and rattled from all sides. One truck sent out tongues of propane flame from its ten-foot stacks. The smell of diesel fumes and cigarette smoke was heavy in the air.

There was something menacing and almost infernal in the aspect of these giant machines. And indeed, one of the trucks that seemed to have the most visceral and enthusiastic appeal had rings of wicked spikes on each of its rims and piping that glowed in green-like bones, facing the world with a small army of leering metal skulls mounted on corner after corner. "LAWLESS," said the back of the matte black cab. Every now and then, someone would step on the pedal within the cab, and dark gobbets of smoke would come spilling from the stacks as the engine began to roar, slowly dissipating into a July sky smoldering in red with a late sunset.

————————

Rolling coal is controversial even among diesel enthusiasts. Online forums dedicated to Powerstroke, Cummins, and Duramax diesels reflect ambivalence about the practice. There are those who ask for tips on how to modify their engines, and sometimes crow about what they've managed to do to others on the roadways once they have. But many others on these forums will meet such boasts with dismissal or condemnation, blaming those who roll coal deliberately onto others for ruining the hobby and forcing the EPA and state agencies to bear down on diesels everywhere. Indeed, while rolling coal remains largely legal throughout most of the United States, six states — Colorado, Connecticut, Maine, Maryland, New Jersey, and Utah — have passed laws prohibiting the practice over the last decade.[19]

Colorado was one of the first states to do this, in 2017.[20] Section 42-4-314 of the Colorado Revised Statutes now reads as follows:

(6)(a) *Nuisance exhibition of motor vehicle exhaust—prohibition.* A person shall not engage in a nuisance exhibition of motor vehicle exhaust, which is the knowing release of soot, smoke, or other particulate emissions from a motor vehicle with a gross vehicle weight rating of fourteen thousand pounds or less into the air and onto roadways, other motor vehicles, bicyclists, or pedestrians, in a manner that obstructs or obscures another person's view of the roadway, other users of the roadway, or a traffic control device or otherwise creates a hazard to a driver, bicyclist, or pedestrian.[21]

I spent some time in Colorado a few weeks after this prohibition was passed in 2017, tracking reactions to the new law. I had the chance to speak about the measure with a patrol officer in the city of Fort Collins, where coal rolling had been reported as a regular problem.

"We get a few reports each weekend night," the officer with the Fort Collins Police Department told me. Kids in high school or just past that age would come into the city each weekend from the surrounding country, cruising College Avenue in modified trucks. The officer was a diesel enthusiast himself, and when he wasn't charged with pulling them over, he struck up conversations with these kids about what they'd put under the hood of their trucks. "Yeah, we smoked 'em out," they'd tell him slyly, recalling an encounter with some "pansy Prius driver."

Going home after duty one afternoon, the officer recounted, he had pulled up at an intersection behind a small Smartcar and a diesel Dodge with a raised chassis. He watched as a guy leaned out the passenger window of the Dodge and called down to the driver of the Smartcar with a bit of a sneer. "What's it wanna be when it grows up?" the Dodge driver said, his truck engulfing the car in a black cloud as it sped off. Like many, the officer interpreted coal rolling as a matter of masculinity and defiance, thumbing a nose at a state that threatened to go after their trucks and guns. "This is America. You're not gonna tell me what to do with my truck."

The day before the officer and I met, I attended the Five-R Trucks and Trailers Truck Fest at the Bandimere Speedway near Denver. An ominous picture on the flyer promised plenty of black smoke, which came in loud and regular bursts from the racetrack throughout the day. I assumed that people at the event would be angry about the new law, but most replied with an earnest and law-abiding tone when I asked them about coal rolling.

"We're not assholes," a welder with two Tea Party stickers on the back of his 2005 Dodge told me. "People don't understand that about us. Come after my guns, and I will do what I can to hang on to 'em. But we need laws. You have to keep people safe. This is a civilization. If everyone just did whatever they wanted, there'd be chaos."

It took me a long time to find someone willing to admit that they'd actually rolled coal deliberately onto someone else. The founder of a local truck club called over a friend, whom I'll call Michael, a guy in his twenties who delivered pool tables for a living. He smiled slightly when I asked whether he'd ever smoked anyone on purpose. "Only if they're tailgating me, or if they cut me off," he said. "If they keep their distance, it's okay. Some of these drivers, even people on bicycles, they don't always follow the rules they're supposed to follow."

Michael had a black F-350, a pair of exhaust stacks mounted to the flatbed. "It was my dream truck," he told me. He couldn't race it because it leaked too much fluid, and they wouldn't allow it onto the track. But he'd put in a lot of work on the truck, which he used each day to haul tables from place to place. He'd trained as a diesel mechanic and insisted that diesels were cleaner than gasoline cars. The smoke was just soot, he said; it would fall to the ground.

Michael wasn't ashamed to admit that he smoked a driver every now and then. And the new law wouldn't change how he drove or what he did. As he saw it, what mattered was the aggressiveness of others, not his own. "It's a way of saying, *Hey, give me some space*."[22]

It isn't an easy thing to do — communicating with others on automotive roadways. Lights and signals, paint and styling, flags and stickers: there's little more to rely on when every other driver around you is sealed off in their own private compartment, navigating the strange nature of roads as public spaces. There's always the risk of being misunderstood, even provoking an unintended confrontation. "Within the private cocoon of glass and metal," British sociologist John Urry notes, "intense emotions are released in forms that would otherwise be socially unacceptable."[23] Most everyone has seen this happen, maybe had such feelings themselves.

"Let me ask you something," I suggested to Michael in our conversation that day. "Say you had your window down, they had their window down. Couldn't you just shout at them and say something like, *Hey asshole, why'd you cut me off?*"

Michael laughed and shook his head. "Then you'd get into things like road rage. Who knows if they're carrying a gun. It's just not something I'd want to do." Better, it seemed, to make your point and speed off quickly before they managed to react.

What Michael said took me back to one of the trucks I saw hurtling down the speedway earlier that day in Colorado, not one flag but three fluttering from its bed: an American flag, a Confederate flag, then yet another Confederate flag with an assault rifle planted at its center. "COME AND TAKE IT," the words at the bottom of the third flag screamed, knowing full well that at that speed, such a response was simply impossible.

These gestures made with diesel trucks: they seemed no different from the impasses into which communication had fallen in so many other spheres of American public life. In this arena, as with so many others, dialogue was not the point.

———————

Trucks are vehicles of identity in the United States. What people say with these vehicles—and with their exhaust—reveals much about how they see themselves and others. "The pickup truck is deeply ingrained in our national life and culture," American historian James C. Cobb observes in an essay describing how trucks have emerged as "lifestyle statements" for many Americans keen on conveying personal relationships with the rural and rustic, even as the cost of making these automotive statements continues to climb. "For a sizable contingent of Americans," Cobb writes, "the pickup truck has emerged as a means of establishing their ties to a distinctly blue-collar identity in the course of flaunting their bourgeois prosperity."[24]

Rolling coal is always an assertion of both identity and power, a way to express who truly belongs on the American road, and who or what ought not to be there. Plumes of black diesel smoke were gleefully cast as "Prius repellent" when the phenomenon first surfaced in the 2010s, as if the hybrid Toyota and its ilk were vermin to keep away. Targets of the gesture often include others who might seem out of place on a roadway dominated by cars and trucks, like pedestrians and cyclists—as evidenced most disturbingly, perhaps, by the six cyclists struck and injured on a Texas country road in September 2021 by a teenage driver in a Ford Super Duty pickup who was trying to harass them with diesel smoke.[25] It should not surprise us that when people occupy roads and sidewalks to share messages of other kinds, trucks and smoke surface once again as ways to push them off or crowd them out.

One of the most popular coal rolling videos on YouTube is billed as a "Rolling Coal on Protesters Compilation (BlackLivesMatter, Trump Haters, Tree Huggers)."[26] "In this video we showcase some of the best videos of protestors getting coal rolled on them," the producers of the compilation—a YouTube account called Show Me Diesels—explain. With more than 5.5 million views since it was first posted in 2017, the video has met with plenty of caustic commentary, but also many rounds of chortling adulation. "I currently don't have a Diesel, but I'd gladly spend the 70 grand to have this much fun," reads one of the most liked remarks on the lengthy comment thread accompanying the video.

The eight videos pulled together as a five-minute compilation are pretty poor in production quality: shaky and blurry recordings made on cell phones from the inside of truck cabs, showing off what smoke can do to sidewalk demonstrators as the trucks speed past. You can't really tell what these people on the street are protesting against, unless you pause the playback and squint at the screen. One person is carrying a "Stop the Hate" sign. Another alleges that "GOD H8S F-GS." There's a group with a banner insisting that circumcision is cruel to boys. Other activists have signs that say "Honk for Bernie." The driver who smokes that last crowd crows the slogan back at them gleefully as he races by in his truck, leaving a thick black trail that engulfs the demonstrators and slowly dissipates into the bright blue sky.

"Tastes like America, right? Whoow! Make America great, baby! Yeehoow!"

On close examination, most of the protestors visible in these videos appear to be white, their causes quite varied. And yet, for many viewers of the compilation, it seems to be the Black Lives Matter movement that stands for the identity of these various activists. Some of the most-liked comments on the video joke that "Black smoke matters," or quip, to great effect, "Does rolling coal on BLM count as black on black violence?" Why are the protestors lining the streets for various reasons tagged so readily as campaigners for Black lives, as if BLM had become a code word for any advocate with a sign by the side of the road? "We need these guys now!" someone commented in June 2020, as demonstrations for George Floyd convulsed the country.

As we now know, many people with diesel trucks felt this call in the spring and summer of 2020, reacting to Black Lives Matter protests in numerous places around the country with precisely this gesture. There was the truck that smoked out a rally organized by high school kids in the Oregon town of Milton-Freewater in June of that year. And the truck that barreled through an intersection crowded with people in Pasadena, California, trailing a cloud of black exhaust.[27] And the young guy in bronzed sunglasses who smoked a rally in central Tennessee and then posted a clip to Facebook to "spark conversation."[28] And the large diesel trucks that doused hundreds of protestors who had gathered on a rainy Saturday in Kalispell, Montana.[29] And the trucks that came through like clockwork—one every ten minutes—to slow down and smoke out a crowd gathered in front of the county courthouse in Logan, Utah.[30] What were these gestures about?

Racism, Ruth Wilson Gilmore writes, brings "group-differentiated vulnerability to premature death."[31] The politics of race is at stake in the harassment of social justice protestors with diesel smoke, but so too another kind of social difference: between those who navigate American streetscapes in increasingly armored enclosures and those who occupy and traverse these spaces on foot. It's almost as if this difference is becoming something like a racial divide in the United States, between those on the inside and those on the outside of an automobile's walls. For isn't it the case that so much of the pleasure in these incidents has to do with the privilege of flying away, escaping exposure, leaving others behind, avoiding the suffering of those less fast, less mobile? One coal roller put it starkly that June of 2020, crowing about the rally he'd just smoked in northern Idaho: "If they want to support the black lives matter, we'll make 'em black."[32] What would it take to address the sense of impunity reflected in such statements?

On May 30, 2020, hundreds of demonstrators gathered on the corner of Greenwood and Wall Street in the city of Bend, in central Oregon, to protest police violence and the murder of George Floyd in Minneapolis. Reports described the protestors as peaceful and largely masked, in that early moment of the pandemic.[33] But here again, a diesel truck appeared on the scene to attempt a disruption with black exhaust. One demonstrator later told a police investigator that the driver seemed to be aiming the smoke at the protestors, stating that "it felt gritty and painful," and that he had observed "families with kids grabbing their kids and running away from the harmful smoke."[34] Multiple witnesses described seeing the truck come around again and again alongside the protestors, subjecting them to the exhaust each time.

"I did give a little soot and I'm not ashamed to admit it," the twenty-year-old driver of the Dodge Ram pickup, Dylan Freville, admitted publicly on Instagram. "If I'm going to drive downtown through a protest and be shit on for my political beliefs and my skin color, you best bet y'all are getting a little coal." Law enforcement saw the circumstance otherwise and charged Freville with harassing the demonstrators. "Perhaps no right in our country is more fundamental than the right of peaceful assembly," Deschutes County District Attorney John Hummel noted in a public statement. "Those who disagree with messages being shared by those who assemble have the right to share their opposition, but they have no right to resort to violence. To the rolling coal practitioners in our community, I say: use your words, not your smoke."[35]

Freville implied to the police officer investigating the incident that he was compelled to resort to this usage of smoke, that he acted out of fear of the protestors, their shouting of political slogans, that "he started to become scared at how upset they were getting." This claim was belied, however, by what witnesses of his actions reported: that the truck kept circling back to the intersection where the protestors had gathered, returning as many as ten times to douse them with diesel smoke. "I know how much [the black smoke] hurts, it's been done to me," Freville told the investigator. And yet he came back again and again to impose this pain on the demonstrators, as if he was dramatizing their vulnerability to him, his invulnerability to them.

With these findings in hand, Freville was charged with harassment later that summer. But then, in a spirit of restorative justice, the coal roller was invited to take part in a mediated public dialogue with a leading Black activist from the region, Luke Richter of the Central Oregon Peacekeepers. The session was organized by the district attorney's office and facilitated by a well-known clinical psychologist and mediator.[36] Participants were asked to take a "decency pledge," promising to offer respect and listen attentively to others.

There are no public records of Freville's reaction to the hour-long dialogue and exchange, which exonerated him from any further responsibility for his harassment of the protestors. But what the Peacekeepers organizer Luke Richter later said to a news reporter applies to the violent contradictions of American road culture as much as anything else. "If people just aren't willing to stand with each other and just talk about the differences," Richter mused, "then we're not going to get anywhere."[37]

The activist's vision brought personal commitments and structural conditions alike into focus. Take just the environment of the American roadway. What would the shared space of our streets have to look and feel like to make such progress possible?

SIX

WALKING BAREFOOT

FLORIDA PANHANDLE

The 2017 Truckers Jamboree took me to a lackluster motel just off I-80 in Iowa for a few nights. One morning, I went on a run past gas stations and convenience stores, a truck supply company and a Vietnamese evangelical church. On foot, I felt out of place. The grassy shoulders of the roads were littered with crumpled cans of Busch beer, takeout containers and straws, and jagged bits of rubber tire tread and plastic tubing. I passed a raccoon splayed out woefully on the asphalt and made it as far as an overpass farther east down the interstate. Someone had sprayed two words of advice onto the low concrete wall of the overpass bridge, framing the essential lesson of the vehicles speeding constantly underneath: "THINK QUICK."

You could really feel it here, the challenge of simply keeping up with the pace of things. And this is what roadways like the American interstate have long been teaching us—the idea that, as Earl Swift has put it, "its pilgrims, windshields and chrome flashing in the sunshine, were moving with a speed and purpose that made our own seem puny."[1] Roads built for automotive speed seem to embody the idea of a future coming along so quickly that it's already here before you know it, a destination plotted and fixed before you've even had the chance to think about where you mean to go in the first place. But it's never been just this. Our roads have always carried many different ideas of a possible future, other visions that matter even now.

Interstate 80 cuts across the continent along routes marked out previously by Route 30 and by the Lincoln Highway, dedicated in 1913 as the first modern roadway to span the United States. The Lincoln Highway was envisioned as a "transcontinental boulevard" by Henry B. Joy, president of the Packard Motor Car Company and head of the Lincoln Highway Association. In the early 1920s, the association chose a 1.3-mile stretch between the Indiana towns of Schererville and Dyer to construct what they called the "Ideal Section" of the highway to come, built as an "object lesson" in roadway design and described by Joy as "an instrument to be used in educating all the people." One report billed it as "the show road of the world."[2]

The Ideal Section was developed as the first lighted highway in the United States. The model road was laid down with a ten-inch slab of concrete forty feet wide, allowing for two lanes of traffic in both directions. But what stands out most about these designs, looking back from a century later, is all the space they reserved for purposes other than driving—such as walking. The Ideal Section included a gravel footpath for pedestrians five feet wide, winding its way alongside the concrete road. Telegraph and telephone wires and poles were placed out of sight, advertising signs were prohibited altogether, and the entire stretch was landscaped extensively with native plants. The footpath "curves through the trees on the south side of the road so that the pedestrian, though only a few feet from the concrete, has constantly in view a delightful vista of timber and shrubbery," the Lincoln Highway Association noted proudly in 1935.[3]

Early photographs of the Ideal Section and its graceful walking trail— wending through those trees and shrubs, set off from the paved ribbon of concrete by a bank of vegetation—allow us to imagine what our highway system may have become if walkers and other non-automotive travelers had remained a priority to transportation designers. Early plans for the Ideal Section even included a campground with space set aside for those who wanted to break their journeys beside the road. But now, a century later, this same stretch stands as a profound lesson in what American roads have since become. The farmlands have long given way to strip malls, I saw after finding my way there along I-80 from Iowa in 2017, and the forest that remains is a thicket of gleaming signs for the dozens of businesses strung along the way.

Vast parking lots flank both sides of the Ideal Section—Route 30—today. There were many gas stations, as you might expect for this southeastern fringe of greater Chicago. More startling was the sheer number of drive-thrus packed into this short stretch: six fast-food franchises, one drive-thru car wash, five drive-thru banks, two drive-thru coffee houses, two drive-thru dessert places, a pair of drive-thru postal boxes, even a drive-thru dry cleaner and a drive-thru pharmacy, all nestled into the chain of strip malls along those 1.3 miles, trumpeting their convenience to passing vehicles. You could hardly imagine a better object lesson in modern American roadside culture: the idea that being outside means being inside your own private automobile.

"That's progress, you can't stop it," Bonnie Ludwig, an eighty-five-year-old volunteer at the Dyer Historical Society told me. "When it comes, it comes." She counted up the many buildings in the heart of Dyer—hotel, creamery, hardware store, drugstore, beauty shop, tavern, and so on—that had been razed when the road was widened in 1997. Her first job as a teenager in the 1940s was at a drive-in restaurant along the Ideal Section. "We used to try to name each of the cars that went by—that's how few of them there were," she recalled. Now, over the course of one hour late the next morning, I counted 2,184 cars and trucks passing by a spot along Route 30 not far from where that restaurant used to be. A handful of motorcycles drove by during that hour, but I did not see a single pedestrian making their way down the road.

Apart from scattered and discontinuous concrete sidewalks, no traces of the Ideal Section's famed pedestrian pathway remain. To walk along this highway now is to pick your way mostly through parking lots and grassy roadside shoulders, navigating a landscape built for cars. I got a vivid sense of this one evening that July, when I stepped into a crosswalk from a sidewalk curb. The traffic signal told me I had plenty of time, but I must have stopped a moment too long to stare at the Walgreens drive-thru pharmacy sign towering overhead. "Get out of the street, you asshole!" someone in a white minivan shouted out as he passed.

I couldn't help but gape as he sped off, making his way to the Wendy's drive-thru down the block. What would it take to renew the idea that pedestrians and others belonged on these streets too — that walking, cycling, even loitering along this road was just as rightful a thing to do with this public space as to race through it as quickly as possible?

"One day everyone will be able to walk down the middle of the road, free from all the violence this society has built," the American poet and environmental activist Mark Baumer foretold on January 21, 2017.[4] He was walking west that day along an isolated stretch of US 90 in the Florida Panhandle, still near the beginning of a barefoot walk across the country to raise awareness of the climate crisis. Tragically, he was struck and killed by a speeding vehicle the very next day.

The story of Mark Baumer's pedestrian odyssey across the United States is at turns surreal, humorous, poignant, and heartbreaking. There is so much to learn from the heartfelt musings that the activist shared during that ill-fated journey, and the radical revisioning of roadway space that he and other advocates for more inclusive streetscapes have propelled.

———————

"The United States is a driving culture," transportation planner Angie Schmitt notes in her recent book on pedestrian safety, *Right of Way*, a culture in which "police, juries, the media, and even traffic safety officials are all susceptible to what pedestrian advocates call windshield bias."[5] Pedestrian deaths have increased by an alarming degree in the United States, climbing about 50 percent over the last decade. This circumstance ought to be understood as a systemic crisis, even an epidemic, according to Schmitt, a symptom of roads designed for automotive speed rather than public safety, a consequence of more recent developments like the boom in SUVs and trucks and the surge of driver distractions.

When walking, older people, poor people, and people of color are impacted more by roadway hazards, suffering disproportionately from injury and death. And yet these incidents are blamed all too often on irresponsible walkers, as Schmitt notes, reflecting "the relatively low status of those being killed."[6] The hard shell of an automobile seems to insulate its occupants both from the risks of the world beyond and from responsibility for it.

"Something weird happens when you're in a car," environmental activist Mark Baumer observed in 2016. "Your mentality changes. You're blocked off from the world, and you're going like, *Only I matter. Only where I'm going matters.*"[7]

Baumer shared these thoughts with a reporter from *Vice* in early December that year, as he walked barefoot down the shoulder of Interstate 70 in southwestern Pennsylvania. He'd set off on foot from Rhode Island, intending to spur American concern for climate change with a shoeless trek from the East Coast all the way to California. "In many ways, there's nothing more frightening to the American way of life than a man walking barefoot down the side of the road while eating a bag of kale," Baumer, a vegan, mused in one of his daily blog entries.[8]

An award-winning poet with an MFA from Brown University, Baumer had taken a leave from his job at a library to pursue the trek. He had walked across the country once already, in 2010, that time with shoes on his feet. *I Am a Road*, his self-published book recounting that journey, reads like a surrealist portrait of an America quietly coming undone, or like the memoir of an interstellar traveler dropped down to earth to report on the unlivable rules of an alien land. Here's one moment in Texas, rife with both deadpan humor and dark perspective:

> I began walking. People were quietly sipping on coffee inside their automobiles while they slowly moved towards a place their bodies didn't want to go. Some of the automobiles were dressed like things that won't be real after the world ends. Every day it was the road's job to make sure a large number of Americans ate greasy food. I stopped at a store. It only sold cans. Someone wearing cutoff jean shorts rode his bike down the bread can aisle. Something with white hair and a dark mustache was inspecting a can of hot dogs. I covered my face with a red, white, and blue piece of cloth and began walking on the highway again. The highway was still full of automobiles. A large recreational vehicle was pulling a smaller recreational vehicle, which was pulling a sports utility vehicle. Two men yelled at me because they thought I liked being yelled at. Both men were wearing the same colored shirt. There was probably a law in this town requiring people who yelled to wear the same colored shirt when they yelled.[9]

When he set off once again on foot in 2016, Baumer chronicled the walk on Instagram, YouTube, and a daily personal blog that more and more readers began to follow. He had aimed to raise funds to support a Rhode Island activist group, the FANG Collective, that organized against the dominance of fossil fuels in American life. Perhaps not surprisingly, his blog became a running meditation on the perilousness of American road culture, what this automotive space looked and felt like from the standpoint of someone navigating it on foot for hours on end, day after day. "The road seemed to have a lot of trucks on it." he mused on a December day that happened to be his thirty-third birthday. "I tried asking them why they were on the road I wanted to use but like every pedestrian walking in an area dominated by motor vehicles I was ignored."[10]

Baumer had taken a bus from Cincinnati to Jacksonville that month to start the cross-country trek all over again, winter conditions in the Midwest too much to manage barefoot. Making his way west once again across northern Florida, he spent his nights in a bivouac sack behind churches and bus stops. The reports he made along the way revealed countless moments of zany exuberance and communion with the natural and manmade landscapes he traversed. But they also carried a desperate awareness of the explosive yet somehow intangible violence built into the ordinary course of American life. "Your comforts are killing people," Baumer mused as he stepped along a road from Monticello to Tallahassee beside a stream of rocketing cars. "Change the way you live, so other people can live as well."[11]

As someone walking through spaces designed for cars alone, Baumer had to remain acutely aware of the absurd quantum of mass and force careening down American roadways. The web address he created to blog about his journey was notgoingtomakeit.com. "Oh wow, someone's driving a house at me, I hope that house don't run me over," he joked on the blog one day, gaping at the wide barn hitched to a pickup speeding in his direction. Cars were like "death machines," he ranted one rainy afternoon as he walked along a roadside in Pennsylvania: "Don't say, *you're in the road, you're gonna get killed.* No, you're in an automobile, you're gonna kill someone. I'm not gonna die because I was walking on the road. I'm gonna die because someone in an automobile couldn't control their automobile."

This prophecy came to pass less than two months later in January 2017, when a Buick Encore SUV struck and killed Baumer as he walked along the shoulder of US 90 through the Florida Panhandle. He was traveling from Mossy Head to Crestview, on the 101st day of his journey, wearing a high-visibility safety vest and walking against the flow of traffic, as safety conventions dictate. The driver had veered carelessly onto the shoulder from the road, Baumer's father later wrote, unable to control "her 5,000-pound lethal weapon."[12]

Mark Baumer's tragic demise was national news. "Many Americans have been searching for ways to incorporate political activism into their everyday lives, to get out of the echo chambers that keep them among only like-minded people," Anna Heyward wrote for the *New Yorker*. "Baumer was an eccentric model for both, someone for whom activism was both a life style and a form of self-expression."[13]

In the years that followed, Mark Baumer's father started a newsletter in his memory, called "Mark Still Walking." And indeed, the ideas that motivated Baumer's barefoot journey remain essential today, as we grapple with the question of what American roadways may yet become.[14] "I need people to understand this earth does not only have to create systems of death and wealth," he wrote the day before his death in Florida.[15] What would it mean to realize his vision of a truly livable road, hospitable to living beings of many kinds?

Questions of road safety in the United States have long centered on the well-being of those inside cars and other motor vehicles, rather than those outside these automobiles. Vehicle safety tests focus almost exclusively on the hazards posed by accidents to the occupants of a motor vehicle, neglecting to measure what such vehicles in motion can do to pedestrians, cyclists, and other roadway users. Hence the paradox encountered all too often now in the American automotive marketplace: dangerously oversized vehicles emblazoned with five-star safety ratings, shielding their occupants from most every harm while simultaneously contributing to the steep rise in pedestrian fatalities of recent years.[16]

Federal regulatory agencies seem to have caught onto this problem at last, with the National Highway Traffic Safety Administration expected to issue new safety standards meant to assess the dangers that speeding vehicles may pose to pedestrians and other "vulnerable road users," as those who use the roadways without steel shells of their own are known.[17] These walkers and other road users themselves, however, must keep vigilant about these dangers, and their advocates have struggled for years to bring focus and redress to their concerns.

So much of what Mark Baumer documented during his barefoot journey across the United States was his vulnerability, as a walker, to the harshness of the road. With few sidewalks to rely on as he walked, he kept to the shoulders of the road, or the painted white lines, softer on the feet, that divided them from automotive lanes. The soles of his feet registered the difficulty of this passage, and he marked each day with an Instagram post that recorded their condition, as his feet grew ever more scarred and encrusted with roadway grease and grime. Chemical salts meant to clear northern roadways of snow were designed for rubber tires, not bare feet, and his revised southern itinerary through Florida occasioned a new series of foot selfies from small towns west of Tallahassee along US 90: Gretna, Chattahoochee, Sneads, Grand Ridge, Marianna, Cottondale, Bonifay, Westville, Defuniak Springs, and, lastly, Mossy Head.

US 90 extends from the Atlantic shoreline of Jacksonville to the town of Van Horn in west Texas, where the road gives way to Interstate 10. Mark was walking west along the eastbound shoulder of the road when he was struck and killed in January 2017, a few miles east of the town of Crestview. For some months, I'd been reading about his story and corresponding intermittently with his father in Maine. In early 2018, I had the chance to go to this part of the Florida Panhandle to try to get a sense of the final days of Baumer's journey.

In this area, US 90 is lonely country, a two-lane road laid down through sandy flats, flanked by a railway line and scrubby stands of pine. Eglin Air Force Base occupies most of the land south of the highway there, much of it set aside as a testing range for new airborne weapons. There were many vultures circling high above the road I took to Crestview—the roadway strewn, mile after mile, with heaps of red flesh and matted fur. I sped past a yellow sign I'd never seen before, urging caution for some mysterious mammal in silhouette that might cross. I couldn't help but laugh to myself, thinking back to some of Mark's deadpan musings in Pennsylvania: "Someone should educate people how not to kill raccoons and maybe someone else can educate raccoons how to not get killed but educating humans should be the priority."[18]

This portion of US 90 has been designated part of the Lawton Chiles Trail, marking the 1,000-mile trek that state legislator "Walkin' Lawton" took in 1970 across the Panhandle and down to the Florida Keys, propelling his successful run for the US Senate and eventual governorship of Florida.[19] "It zooms by fast," Chiles reported glibly on about the traffic on his walk along US 90 from Crestview to Mossy Head fifty years ago, describing how his hat would get blown off his head by every livestock hauler passing by.[20]

Lawton Chiles had walked along the side of the pavement back then, and even now, there is nothing like a path or walkway for pedestrians along this stretch of the nominal "trail" that commemorates his historic journey on foot. Florida, in fact, of all the states in the country, according to the National Complete Streets Coalition, has the highest statewide Pedestrian Danger Index, the highest risk of fatality for walkers.[21] In 2016, the year that Baumer began walking west from Jacksonville, 667 pedestrians were killed in motor vehicle crashes on Florida's roadways.[22]

The Florida Highway Patrol office in Pensacola gave me a copy of the homicide report recording the circumstances of Baumer's death. The driver of the vehicle was a fifty-one-year-old woman on her way home from a stop at a pharmacy in Crestview, where she'd picked up medications for pain, anxiety, and attention deficit disorder. It was not known whether she had driven under the influence of these medications or any other drugs, for she declined to submit to a voluntary drug test. The driver declared under oath that she had seen Baumer walking along the shoulder and intended to move aside to avoid him. Technical analysis by the Highway Patrol, however, showed that she had veered from the eastbound lane *into* the shoulder when she had hit Baumer and that he was struck three feet beyond the line that marked the limit of her lane.

Mark Baumer sustained multiple immediate injuries to his body. He was a formidable young man, standing 6' 3", but as with all SUVs the front end of the Buick Encore had a steep face and high vertical profile. This, as we know, is one reason why collisions with SUVs are much deadlier for pedestrians: a sedan with a lower profile is more likely to strike and injure the lower limbs and extremities of the body, while a vehicle with the high and aggressive styling of a typical SUV is built to hit the torso on impact.²⁵ *Like being hit by a wall,* I kept thinking to myself, sitting with the homicide report at the patrol office in Pensacola.

Baumer was thrown over a hundred feet by the collision and was pronounced dead at 1:22 pm on the grassy shoulder where his body came to rest, still clad in a reflective safety vest. Fragments of his eyeglasses, phone, and backpack fell to the ground at various places. The driver also veered into the grassy shoulder, finally coming to a stop 291 feet beyond the point of collision; she'd been driving over 65 miles per hour when she noticed the young man walking. Her windshield shattered on impact, but the airbags deployed within the cabin. Both the driver and the little girl in the front seat beside her were unscathed.

The homicide report included a VIN number for the vehicle involved, and it wasn't hard to track down its history. The vehicle was a white 2015 Buick Encore, brought into the country from South Korea that February, sold once by the Lee Buick GMC dealership in Crestview in 2015 and then once again to someone else the following year. In April 2017, shortly after the collision, the SUV was declared a total loss and issued a salvage title. That May, a report from Carfax showed, the vehicle was exported from Savannah to the port of Klaipeda in Lithuania.

The Crestview Lee Buick dealership is on S. Ferdon Boulevard, a few miles south of US 90. The salesman I met at the dealership was sympathetic to Mark's story, when I recounted it. He was a cyclist himself and told me that he had lived unhoused on the streets for a few months during a rough patch in his twenties. He had seen firsthand how isolated and indifferent one could become as the driver of an automobile. "It's like you're in your own little world," the salesman said as we took an Encore on a test drive around the town together. "You're not thinking of the guy ahead of you, or whether the person behind you has had a bad day."

As we drove and talked, the frame of the small SUV curved around us like a hard shell. "People that are drawn to these kinds of cars," the salesman observed, "they like the feeling of being enclosed." Back at the dealership, he passed me a promotional booklet for the Encore promising exactly this. "A sense of well-being envelops you," the booklet foretold.

The promotional materials for the SUV broached the subject of safety and protection, but only from the point of view of those within the vehicle. What beyond its boundaries would trigger these safety systems, if necessary? The illustrations in the booklet presented only other automobiles in motion, as if the road was a space for motor vehicles and nothing else.

Roads in the United States haven't always been imagined as purely automotive spaces. Before industrialization, urban geographer David Prytherch notes, "American streets were public ways for foot and horse-drawn transportation, but also open spaces for public gathering and markets."[24] This social function of the streetscape was eroded by the heady surge of motorized vehicles over many years, with streets redefined as arteries for traffic and redesigned as "physical infrastructure limited to vehicular flow."[25] But now, as a century of such design has yielded ample evidence of its destructive and unlivable nature, Prytherch notes, efforts to "reconceive streets as public places for social interaction and conviviality" are on the rise.[26] Urban and transportation planners have once again begun to conceive streets and roadways as spaces "to support social relations beyond just circulation, whether public gathering or social intercourse or political protest or commerce."[27]

Mark Baumer admitted that his own experience on the American road was often quite lonely. Highways afforded few occasions to say or feel much of significance in the company of strangers. One day in north Florida, he reported passing the first walker he'd seen in ten days along US 90, a man in a white shirt who simply said "yep" as they crossed paths.[28] And the sight of a lonely house on acres of lawn, Baumer also noted that day, "made me think of the refugees fleeing unstable countries due to war or the rising oceans," a sense of kinship likely inspired by his own experience on foot and out of place in bunkered landscapes.

At the same time, however, his very presence changed these transit corridors into spaces of social interaction and exchange in many different ways. "I still get sad whenever I touch a piece of earth that automobiles don't want humans to touch," Baumer reflected.[29] Often, as he passed through such spaces, people would stop to offer food or a pair of shoes or slow their vehicles to throw him a bag of stuff through an open window. As a curious observer, Baumer also communed with the countless anonymous things that litter the edges of any highway, his video logs lending a bit of life to an abandoned spoon or a shredded length of rubber. His journey was charged by such connections, the chance to nurture a more expansive sense of solidarity, the realization of communion in atomized space.

Like so many others in the weeks and months after Baumer's death, I too found myself caught up by this spirit of connection. I came to Florida on the first anniversary of his death, hoping to find the place of the accident and honor the walker's passing in some manner. Jim Baumer told me about a cairn of rocks that he had raised to commemorate the site of his son's death. I was worried that he might find it odd that a stranger would want to come here to mark this anniversary. But in this too, like their son, Baumer's parents were kind and understanding.[30] Jim Baumer told me about the many others who had joined them in remembrance. "I think it speaks volumes to the kind of person that Mark had become and demonstrates the resilience of his life and legacy, as it ripples outward," he wrote me.

That January of 2018, I got myself a room at a truck stop motel two miles east along US 90. I found the heap of rocks that Jim Baumer had described, clustered in a spot along the grassy shoulder. I could feel the loneliness of this place where Mark Baumer came to rest. There was a sand mine across the railway tracks that ran alongside the highway, but otherwise there were just pines and roadway, cars and trucks speeding past that shoulder at breakneck speed.

The rocks had come apart, and I gathered them up once again, arranging some flowers and fruit around them. Baumer was a vegan, passionate about fruit. I figured he would appreciate the bananas and grapes, oranges and plums. "We have a custom in India of marking a death anniversary with offerings of the person's favorite foods," I told his parents.

Two mornings later, I walked from the motel back to that spot one last time to pay my respects. I'd been compulsively watching his roadside videos, and as I made my way carefully down the highway shoulder, Baumer's voice kept echoing in my head. I could imagine his delight at some of the relics strewn in the grass: the blue paisley bandanna, the lottery ticket for a $200 million cash prize, the Shopkins Happy Places box—"The Lil' Shoppies have found their Happy Place at Sparkle Hill High School!"—and the packet for Big Mama pickled sausage. I could see him yukking it up with that empty tin of

Grizzly snuff, "Never go mudding with a full spit cup." Some of this could have been here when Baumer walked the road.

At first I stuck to the grassy slope, looking mostly at the debris. Then it struck me, as I kept thinking about Baumer, that I should try myself to walk the shoulder barefoot. It was a cold morning, in the low forties. The concrete was hard and smooth, surprisingly free of any litter, and at first it wasn't bad, this walking. Within minutes, though, my feet began to prickle with little jabs of pain from the stones embedded on the roadway. Motor vehicles kept roaring by, so many so big, one raised truck with huge tires swinging into the opposite lane ahead of me to hurtle past an SUV. I could feel every one of them pass beyond me: a looming whine in my ears, the tremors in the concrete as the vehicle closed in, the rippling air as it swooped by. I kept making plans to leap off the shoulder if one veered my way, not knowing if I'd have the time.

I was going west, as Baumer had been doing. And I kept walking once I reached his cairn, wanting to make it a little further along, at least to the next intersection, to carry his journey onward in some small way. When I stopped to take a break, I could see that the soles of my feet had already taken on a black sheen, little bits of anonymous matter pressed into the skin. I was shaken by the feeling of exposure. I couldn't help but think about Baumer's courage, his openness to whatever might happen on roads like this one.

"Part of me wanted to curl up and wait for my brain to melt but instead I began walking in the rain," Baumer reported on the final morning of his barefoot trek.[31] Trump had just been inaugurated as president of the United States, and his proud indifference to human suffering and natural disaster vexed Baumer deeply. "I am out here in america. Please bring me your hatred and pain," the walker and activist declared. And then he set off on foot once again.

———

Efforts to make American roadways more habitable for pedestrians, cyclists, and others have gained momentum in recent years. Over 1,600 places in the United States—states, counties, cities, and other localities—have passed "complete streets" policies promoting the development of infrastructure that prioritizes the needs of vulnerable and diverse road users, through amenities like sidewalks, crosswalks, bike lanes, public transit shelters, and other spaces demarcated for non-automotive uses.[32] The coronavirus pandemic led many American cities to establish "Slow Street" zones for outdoor exercise and socializing, roadway experiments that have endured in many cases beyond the "stay at home" era.[33]

Inspired by successful efforts across Europe, dozens of American cities have now made a "Vision Zero" pledge to eliminate traffic fatalities and severe injuries altogether, including the city of Providence in Rhode Island, where Mark Baumer began his barefoot journey in 2016.[34] "The only way to assure that others are safe is to promote a sane infrastructure policy," a writer for the *Transport Providence* blog wrote in a reflection on Baumer's fatal accident in 2017.[35] A few years later, thanks to the efforts of safe streets advocates and committed local leaders, the Providence City Council adopted a "Green and Complete Streets" ordinance that acknowledged that city streets and sidewalks are shared by "motorists and non-motorists, residents in wheelchairs and parents pushing strollers, kids biking and walking to school, and people who can't afford or don't want motor vehicles."[36]

Advocates have pushed for many such measures in Florida too, which remains one of the most dangerous states in the country for pedestrians. Florida law considers it safe, for example, for children to walk along any road with fewer than six vehicles passing each minute, or to cross any road at a stop sign or stoplight as long as there are fewer than 4,000 vehicles passing each hour, as retired school transport director Rob Doss noted in an editorial for the *Gainesville Sun* in 2021:

> Can you imagine your child or your grandchild — or yourself — in either of those two scenarios, looking over your shoulder every 10 seconds to avoid being hit by a car as you walk along the road, or finding yourself in an unwinnable and potentially tragic race to cross the road at an intersection while dodging vehicles at a rate of more than one every second?[37]

For many years, Doss has been advocating for a revision of Florida's Hazardous Walking Conditions statute, which he hopes will encourage the construction of more sidewalks and other pedestrian infrastructure. When we spoke in 2022, he said this is the central question: "What does it take to make a safe pathway for children to get to school?"

In recent years in Florida, the safety of US 90 has also emerged as a specific concern. Mark Baumer was only one of many pedestrians killed along this highway in Florida in 2017, on a road that has been identified as one of the most dangerous in the United States.[38] A new master plan process led by the Emerald Coast Regional Council aims to create multimodal corridors along several stretches of US 90 in northwest Florida, suitable for those seeking to travel along the highway by foot, bicycle, skateboard, and other non-automotive means.[39] Pensacola has already begun such work along a portion of the highway that passes through the city; inspired by a wrenching hit-and-run that took the lives of an infant and woman crossing the street there in 2018, the project has widened sidewalks and regulated pedestrian road crossings to designated crosswalks, while narrowing lanes and reducing speed limits for automobiles.[40]

"People are crying out for slowing down the cars outside their doors," environmental activist Christian Wagley of Pensacola told me. More than two decades ago, Wagley committed himself to navigating the city by bike and by foot. Simply for doing this, he noted, he's been mistaken for someone unhoused more than a dozen times, even run off the road now and then. But he has also been organizing to make the city's streets more hospitable to cyclists and walkers. As the executive director of Bike Pensacola, Wagley has led monthly "Slow Rides" through the city for more than seven years, typically drawing around 250 cyclists each month.[41] The events take people into neighborhoods that they are otherwise unlikely to see.

The issues are complicated, Wagley acknowledged: "cities are cool again," and people are moving back into central districts; but often, when they do, "they're bringing their suburban expectations with them." He described monster vehicles that don't fit into garages or parking spaces and "epic battles over sidewalks" as people claim those spaces as their own. At the same time, however, progressive visions for urban development continue to take hold in the designs that planners are putting forward. The Florida Department of Transportation, Wagley noted, has even begun to describe inhabited places in ecological terms, working holistically to make sense of the kinds of movement and activity appropriate for different contexts of social life.[42]

On roads as in neighborhoods, so much comes down to the kind of company people are willing to seek out and accommodate. Wagley knew of Mark Baumer's journey. In fact, a similar experience more than two decades ago —

when Wagley biked one summer from Pensacola to his hometown in Annapolis, Maryland—shaped his own mission as an advocate. "On a bicycle, it's very easy to pull up and talk to people," he recounted. "I looked vulnerable. People would feed me, slip me money, *You look like you could use a little help*, they'd say." Those thousand miles by bicycle taught him that roads could also be fully social and sensory spaces. "Walking and biking, you use your senses fully. Wrapped up in an automobile, you don't do that."

As Wagley saw it, roadways could become spaces for such experience once again, but the changes needed would only come incrementally. "It's really hard to move around and rearrange the infrastructure that's in place. It's a giant ship you're trying to turn around. It's going to work ultimately, I know it will, calming the traffic, reclaiming space for people, but it's slow. It's going to take decades to make these changes."

The activist was speaking of specific streets and traffic patterns in Pensacola, but his words led me to think of the path the country seemed to be traveling along in broader terms. For here too was a fork in the road: between the isolation and indifference that our automotive culture seemed to push ever further, or a more honest acknowledgment of the many others we shared our lives with, whether on the road or anywhere else.

PART III
THE
VULNERABLE BODY

SEVEN
WHITE BODY ARMOR

SHELBYVILLE, TENNESSEE

Shelbyville is a town of 24,000 in central Tennessee. Like many places in America, the population there is changing. Somali refugees and Latino immigrants who settled there in recent years were the focus of a 2009 PBS documentary, *Welcome to Shelbyville*. Walk down North Main Street today and you'll see Thai and Japanese restaurants, taquerias and Latin American supermarkets, signs that say "Hablamos español."

Like most everything else, these businesses were shuttered on the morning of Saturday, October 28, 2017. Police sedans had cordoned off many of the roads heading into the town. A pervasive thrum was in the air, from the helicopters circling overhead. Armored vehicles were planted on the streets that surrounded the town square, dozens of riflemen and officers in riot gear massing on the roofs of low buildings.

"How are you feeling?" I asked the Nepali woman behind the counter of a gas station the previous night.

She replied with a single word and a tight-lipped smile. "Scared."

117

Scheduled that Saturday morning was a white nationalist political rally, meant to show that "White Lives Matter." The rally was expected to be the largest such event after the "Unite the Right" rally in Charlottesville, where clashes between demonstrators and counter-protestors had left dozens injured and one young woman dead. The Shelbyville rally was organized by a Southern separatist group called the League of the South, working together with a larger umbrella of white nationalist groups that called themselves the Nationalist Front.[1]

On their minds were the resettled refugees and other new minorities of Shelbyville and the region, what organizers called "the demographic transformation of Middle Tennessee."[2] It also mattered that this was Bedford County, birthplace of Nathan Bedford Forrest, Confederate general and first grand wizard of the Ku Klux Klan.

Conditions were potentially explosive. "Many business owners have boarded up their windows, and people who live in the area have been advised to stay away," a local news reporter said on television that morning. "It's the uncertainty of it all that's prompting these precautions."

This was advice that I had plainly flaunted in coming here. My skin was conspicuously brown, and there was no question that I fit the racial demographic of what these activists would rail against. My wife was upset that I'd even thought of going, especially after what had happened in Charlottesville. Still, it kept gnawing at me. The lines seemed too sharply drawn: American Nazis and their radical leftist critics, each cast as outliers in American society as a whole. Could I find some other vantage point on what drove this politics?

As an anthropologist, I had the intuition this was possible. I knew that essential insights could come from putting yourself where you don't quite belong, putting your own body on the line. But I'd also be the first to admit that I'm not exactly imposing in bulk or stature. Thinking about what I could do to protect myself, my mind flitted nervously between wild ideas. Could I get myself some makeup to lighten my complexion? Or a Kevlar bodysuit of some kind?

Vulnerability comes down to the body, that fragile vessel of flesh and bone in which we pass through the world and weather its countless storms. The body is home to our most visceral feelings of anxiety and unease. "Insecurity is often dealt with through borders, fences, and protective barriers, and the body is the last frontier," sociologist Barbara Sutton notes, on the parallels between architectures of protection at individual and collective levels. "Enclosing the body in this way, while maintaining a sense of autonomy, is consistent with other individualistic strategies prevalent in late capitalist societies, such as gated communities."[3] Think, for example, of phrases like this tagline for Body Fortress whey protein: "Your body, your fortress."

It isn't surprising that in an age of heightened anxiety concerning the American body and its vulnerability, an upstart clothing brand from Baltimore called Under Armour swiftly rocketed to national preeminence, boosted by the motto "Protect this house."[4] Nor is it an accident that several of the top news stories on WKRN-TV that October morning in Tennessee — the white nationalist rally, a home invasion arrest, a series of attacks on daters who met online, and a plan by the Drug Enforcement Agency to avert prescription drug abuse — all had to do with bodies at risk in one way or another. "The body as a fortress" may be one of Western civilization's most abiding notions of what it means to live in good health, as Susan Sontag observed, but this is indeed "an image of the body that features catastrophe."[5]

It was a cold and blustery day when I set out on foot that morning, down North Main Street from the Econo Lodge Inn. In the end, no makeup or body armor, just a beanie cap and black jacket to ward off the cold. Well, there was also the T-shirt I had on under the jacket, one I'd picked up at a gun show a few months back, that I felt I had to wear. The image on the black shirt was striking: a warrior before the ruins of an ancient temple, wearing the tactical vest and combat gear of a modern soldier, as well as the helmet and chainmail of a medieval Christian knight. Around the illustration were words from Ephesians 6:10–17:

> *Finally be strong in the Lord and in the strength of his power*
> *Put on the whole Armour of God*
> *Fasten the belt of Truth and take the shield of Faith*
> *Put on the breastplate of Righteousness*
> *Take the helmet of Salvation and the sword of the Spirit*

It had to matter, I told myself, that I would enter this space with good faith, that I belonged here as much as these white nationalists did. And ultimately, what I gained that day was a glimpse of the peculiar *ordinariness* of American white nationalism, its grounding in masculine feelings of bodily insecurity and everyday strategies of self-protection.

––––––––––––

The League of the South was founded in Alabama in 1994. Designated as a hate group by the Southern Poverty Law Center, the organization has publicly defended the South's secession from the United States, homophobic and antisemitic violence, and the Confederate battle flag as a symbol of Southern white heritage.[6] Founder and longtime leader Michael Hill, a historian by training, describes such positions as a matter of existential peril in an essay called "In Defense of Our Blood."[7] The essay celebrates European settlers who had "carved a rough civilization out of a howling wilderness," making no mention of the enslaved Black labor on which these settlers relied. Southern whites were "bound up in a long community of blood," Hill argues, long devoted to "defending our native soil of Dixie," yet threatened anew by a "modern American regime" bent on "bringing in a new, more compliant population from the Third World to overwhelm and replace us."

The racial replacement of whites by others has become a galvanizing idea in American white nationalism and conservative spheres more generally, inspiring chants like "You will not replace us" and "Jews will not replace us" at the August 2017 rally in Charlottesville.[8] With the violence and chaos of that demonstration, official plans for the event two months later in Shelbyville were far more restrictive. I decided to try to attend in person only after reading about these extensive security precautions. And as I walked that morning to the site of the rally, I saw that there could have been as many law enforcement officials as there were demonstrators at the event: the local police and the county sheriff's office, the Tennessee Bureau of Investigations and the federal Department of Homeland Security, canine units and officers on horseback, counter-sniper teams on the rooftops of surrounding buildings.

"Which side are you on?" an officer asked as I approached the site. I was surprised that the question came up at all, given the color of my skin. But the answer was consequential. Long lines of metal barricades and a hundred feet of empty roadway divided the white nationalists from the counter-protestors who were also gathering that morning, held to a distinct area across the wide expanse of Lane Parkway. The way the barricades were set up and foot traffic routed, it could take more than half an hour to walk from one side to the other.

I followed a handful of men and women with press passes into the security clearance area for the white nationalists. Like me, there were a few others on this side who weren't white. A Japanese film crew was documenting the rally, and a Black woman from Shelbyville was walking around quietly, making a point through the simple fact of her presence. "I really would like to meet them," she told me, "but I know it would mess with their heads."

She warned me to be careful. "You don't have anyone to watch your back."

The security protocol was arduous and time-consuming. Signs declared that "All persons entering the demonstration area will be subject to search for weapons and dangerous items and will be scanned by metal detectors," including a long list of potential hazards — everything from clubs, torches, and masks to drink bottles and fanny packs — subject to confiscation. Everyone was forced to mill around the checkpoint, waiting to submit to a pat down and other bodily indignities in the name of safety, so much so that it helped break the ice between a brown ethnographer and the white nationalists in his midst. Here was something we could complain about together, as if this was a painfully slow line at an airport terminal.

I struck up a conversation with the bearded man ahead of me in line, who worked at a uniform factory in northern Alabama. He was wearing a red MAGA cap and had an American flag draped around his shoulders, because flagpoles had been banned from the event. He admitted to me that he felt stupid with that flag hanging over his back.

"What would look cool is a SWAT vest and a gun," he said, eyeing the officers nearby. "Yeah, I'd love me a SWAT vest and a gun."

The League of the South and other groups like the Traditionalist Worker Party and the National Socialist Movement came down to the checkpoint in quasi-military formation, with helmeted young men in rows marching behind plastic shields as a ruddy-faced man with a thick white beard led them in a chant: "Closed borders! White nation! Now we start the deportation!" When they halted, I could see that some of them had swastikas and the letters KKK tattooed on their arms. Although they were forced to relinquish pocketknives and many other items — I even had to give up my ballpoint pen — they were allowed to keep their shields, their signs emblazoned with enigmatic slogans like "STOP SOUTHERN CULTURAL GENOCIDE."

Close behind me was an elderly man, somewhat frail-looking, carrying a portable breathing machine and wrapping himself in a Confederate flag as if a shawl to ward off the biting cold. Although male, like most participants in the rally, his appearance brought into focus the undercurrent of vulnerability that ran alongside this spectacle of belligerent masculinity, giving it an ironic twist. He'd come up to Shelbyville from Tuscaloosa.

"We want to secede from the union, be our own nation," he explained somewhat plaintively. "I'll never see it in my lifetime . . ."

"White power can be understood as an especially extreme and violent manifestation of larger social forces that wed masculinity with militancy," Kathleen Belew writes in a study of the history of contemporary white supremacy and white nationalism in the United States, *Bring the War Home*.[9] Women have rarely been as prominent as men in movement events, and yet they remain ever present as a symbolic and organizing ideal. "White power women were both symbols of and actors in a common struggle," Belew notes, "to protect white women's chastity and racial reproduction and, with it, the future of whiteness itself."[10]

All of this came through in an exchange I had at the security area with a middle-aged man wearing a Confederate bandanna and a medic backpack, as the security detail slowly did their work. A pipe fitter by trade and a volunteer fireman, he belonged to the medical team for one of the white nationalist groups. He told me that he'd served in the same way at the Charlottesville rally, tending to white demonstrators who'd been hit with pepper gel by protestors. He wasn't from Shelbyville but had friends who lived in the town.

"Does it feel dangerous to you, being here?" I asked.

"I ain't sayin' I'm not scared," he replied. "I'm not fearless. But I work 250 feet off the ground, hangin' pipe, it don't bother me."

"I'm here to understand where we are as a country," I told him. "I know there are people here who want the South to secede again. What would they do with people who aren't white?"

"I ain't sayin' they'd do anything with such people," he said. "It is frustrating when you bust your ass your whole damn life, you pay your damn taxes, then your benefits get cut down with all these people getting this and that.

This was a nice town. When they let all the immigrants in, the refugees, shit started happening worse, burglary, stealin' shit, everything."

There was someone else on his mind as well—his teenage daughter. "She's sixteen," he told me. "Yeah, I want her with a white man. That's just the way I was raised."

It wasn't that she would suffer if she married a Black guy, an Iranian, or an Indian, he acknowledged. "It's the kids, the children, they'd catch hell at school, all their lives."

I was surprised that he brought this up, and a little unnerved that he mentioned Iranians as well as Indians like me. He had to have noticed whom he was talking with. "I was born here," I volunteered after a slight pause. "My parents came here. It wasn't my choice. Now I've got kids who were born here. Would people be bothered by the idea that we're citizens?"

"Not me, it don't," he said. But what he added next made that reply far more ambiguous. "You can ask twenty people here, you're gonna get twenty different answers."

Bodies are tangible in their presence. But the desire for safety and protection can lend the body a porous and even phantasmatic quality. Armor anticipates threats and dangers of countless kinds, lurking in the shadows of the world beyond. "Armor surrounds, protects, and insulates a fragile, sensate body," anthropologist Kenneth MacLeish observes in an ethnographic study of the American military and the experience of its soldiers. "Both the rhetoric and the material logic of armor is that of an impenetrable surface, a hermetic seal between inside and out," as MacLeish writes, but the lived reality of such protection is only partial and far more complicated than this ideal would suggest. As soldiers know all too well, imagination of the armored body always carries the threat of failure, even annihilation.[11]

Finally clear of that security checkpoint in Shelbyville, the white nationalists walked down to the place designated for their demonstration, chanting "blood and soil" while a bagpipe played a seventeenth-century Scottish marching tune. I tagged along near Matthew Heimbach, the young founder of the neo-Nazi Traditionalist Worker Party.[12] He was infamous for the "White Students Union" nighttime patrols he had organized at Towson University in

Maryland and for a disturbing incident caught on camera at a Trump campaign rally in Louisville in 2016, when he and other men shoved and assailed a young Black female protestor with words—"Get out! Get out!"—echoed by the presidential candidate himself onstage.[13]

As he walked, Heimbach talked with a camera crew about his hopes of balkanizing the United States into smaller, racially exclusive ethno-states. "If you're a progressive that wants multiculturalism," he said to the reporters, "you have the right to your own nation-state; it's a pretty big area. But as whites, we have the right to opt out. We can have our own nation, we can build our own communities, built for us and by us. That's our vision."

It was well past noon by the time the demonstrators could finally gather at their rally location, past yet another security checkpoint. A much larger crowd of counter-protestors had already massed across the road, hurling insults at the white nationalists for being late to their own event. The counter-protestors seemed to be equipped with better loudspeakers, and their soundtrack—songs like "La Bamba" and "Hit the Road Jack" and the "I Have a Dream" speech by Martin Luther King Jr.—overpowered what the white nationalists had to say.

Where I stood, a young man wearing a black MAGA cap took the microphone to cheer the wall prototypes being raised along the border near San Diego. "You like those examples they gave us? Yeah! I like the one with the spikes on top!" He goaded the counter-protestors across the road, shouting "Hey, you all like the wall? 'Cause it's goin' up, the wall is goin' up, and it's gonna get higher, and higher, and higher!" His shout broke into something like a guttural scream as it continued. The chanting, meanwhile, continued from the other side of the road. "No hate, no fear, immigrants are welcome here!"

This is mostly how it went on the frontlines of the demonstration that day in Shelbyville, verbal slingshots cast back and forth across a desolate expanse of asphalt. "Come on, let's see that Nazi salute," came the taunts from across the road. "Why are you pounding your shields like that, Nazis? You look mighty insecure. Why did you have to bring World War II combat helmets, Nazis? That's sad. You must be afraid. Man, the KKK are apparently K-K-Kowards . . ."

The young American fascists in antique black helmets and combat boots were carrying clear plastic shields, which were now spattered with stains. On social media, they avowed that they carried the shields to protect themselves from the bags of paint and other noxious fluids that protestors might hurl at them. And this is indeed how we typically think about shields, as ways of defending ourselves from outside threats, attacks on the body from beyond its bounds. If there is reason to fear, it lies out there, elsewhere.

In an intriguing study of the psychic life of Nazism, however, the German historian Klaus Theweleit suggests something different and more complicated. For the Nazis, Theweleit argues, aggression was indeed interlaced with fear. But this had as much to do with perils on the inside as on the outside. German military culture in the early twentieth century called for the development of a hard masculine shell, capable of protecting soldiers from the pervasive dangers of femininity: soft, fluid, threatening always to swamp and overwhelm, whether from without in the form of lawless populations and disorganized masses, or from within, in the shape of tempting pleasures and seductive desires. The body's defenses were both physical and imagined, meant to ensure that "each and every feeling is tightly locked in steel armor."[14]

This image of a highly regulated self was a kind of a fantasy, Theweleit acknowledges, far from the degree of self-control mustered up by actual men. But this gap itself was crucial, helping to make sense of the incessant and obsessive drilling of fascist society. For the nation too could be imagined as a living body, liable to bleed from the injury of omnipresent threats, relying like individual citizens on the safety of its walls. For the manly German soldier, Theweleit observes, "the army, high culture, race, nation, Germany—all of these appear to function as a second, tightly armored body enveloping his own body armor."[15]

Like the National Socialist German Workers' Party led by Adolf Hitler in the 1920s, the contemporary American Traditionalist Worker Party has outlined a twenty-five-point manifesto for its ambitions. "The nation is like a living and breathing organism," the manifesto declares, "comprised of its families, communities, and comrades — our hearts beating as one." And this imagination of a collective body might explain why certain dangers — incursion by other races and "hostile foreign influences," the temptations of homosexuality and other forms of "antisocial behavior," even "dangerous foods that weaken and poison the bodies of our people" — are taken so seriously. The vitality of this white society would depend on the firmness of its boundaries, the "bright white line" encircling and protecting its most vulnerable lives.

These were ideas that looked to be written onto the bodies of the uniformed cadres at the rally's frontlines, radiating from their carefully groomed appearance, their impassive faces, the straight lines they formed with their black boots and shields. Styled as foot soldiers, many startlingly young in age, these men were a deliberately provocative spectacle of fascist unity.

They were also, however, a minority among those who joined the white nationalist demonstration in Shelbyville. That left me curious about the others on the periphery of all the commotion. What was on their minds? How did these ideas speak to them?

Experience of the body is influenced by ideas about its nature, what it might need and what would secure its well-being. These ideas can pull us in profoundly different directions, with deep consequences for our lives with others. As sociologist Barbara Sutton writes,

> [T]he fortress body reproduces the logic of separation and suspicion. It may protect individuals from a concrete attack, but armor also embodies a particular way of being in the world that may be detrimental to basic relationships among people. It is hard to imagine a sense of openness to the world, to the connections that are essential to our lives, if we relate to each other in armor.[16]

I was standing on the edge of the white nationalist demonstration, trying to follow what was happening from a slight distance, when I fell into conversation with a tall white man in a black Carhartt jacket. He didn't want to divulge who he was, and nor, frankly, did I, but it turned out that he was raised in Brooklyn, not far from the Bronx borough where I was born. In his late forties, with a neatly trimmed salt-and-pepper beard, he had gone to the rally in Charlottesville earlier that year and had come to Shelbyville for this event.

"I have an affinity for this side," he admitted. "I don't agree with everybody on this side, but there are some very important points that need to be made."

I introduced myself as a writer, and we wound up getting into a long and animated discussion, one that pulled in a few others also standing around on the edge of the rally, even as the loudspeakers kept broadcasting strident chants and shouts back and forth across the road.

"What do you think of this idea of an ethno-state?" I asked the man, getting the sense that he was open to a conversation. I thought to be frank. "What would you do with people like me?"

"What's your heritage?" he asked.

"My family is from India," I said. "I was born and raised in this country, but my parents immigrated here."

"Aren't you guys Aryans?" Both of us laughed uneasily.

He asked when my family had come to the United States, adding that he had ancestors who came here during the Revolutionary War era, and that Southerners also had Scotch Irish forebears who had been here for centuries. "Our ancestors built this country for their posterity. We feel this is our inheritance, that it's a specific culture that made it what it is."

"Let me tell you why I'm here," I told him. "In the 1970s, there was a shortage of doctors in the United States. The government put out a call, and a whole bunch of them came from India. My dad's a cardiologist. Over the years, he's probably taken care of tens of thousands of patients, saved a lot of lives. Does that give us a place here, or not?"

"Yeah, that's a part of our history," he replied. "We can accept that. We can absorb a certain amount of other cultures." The way he spoke, he seemed indeed to be thinking of a national organism, its ability to tolerate some degree of foreign bodies in its midst.

A young man with wire-rimmed eyeglasses was also listening in. "You're familiar with the concept of brain drain?" he interjected. "When you take the best and the brightest from other places, you inflate the higher echelons of the country, and you expand its base. All of a sudden, more and more people can't compete."

Wearing an olive-green jacket and hoodie, he was twenty-three years old. He'd come out for the rally from Florida, and I gathered that he was in a construction trade. He talked about getting pushed out of his field by immigrant workers from the Caribbean. "They're stealing from us," he said. "In a decade or two, my children won't be able to start out as apprentices."

The young man wasn't wearing any sign of an insignia or affiliation. I had no idea who he'd come there with or how closely he identified with any of the groups that had organized the rally. "To be honest with you, as an absolute best-case scenario," he told me, "I would like to live in an ethno-state. But I realize that's unreasonable. I realize we have responsibilities."

"If a lot of this began with European expansion," I responded, "isn't that where you'd want the ethno-state? Why North America? Why not Europe instead?"

"I can't go back. I'm not European. I'm a mutt. I'm German, Irish, English."

"I can't go back either!" I exclaimed.

"I know, I know you can't send people back. Logically, I accept that. But stop bringing them over here until we can figure out what to do. We need to pause and really think about what we're going to do with people who don't share our cultural values."

I objected to this idea of an impasse. "Working on this book," I said to him, "I've been talking to people all over the country. I'm not always bowled over by what they say, but I find I can connect with folks who are different from me. I believe that's possible."

"I really can't relate on the same level with people who haven't had my up-bringing, who come from similar families as me, my own people," he replied. "It's harder for me to relate at the soul"—he thumped his chest twice for emphasis, with his fist—"with people who are from a different culture than me, as opposed to people who grew up the same way I did."

The gesture was earnest and unexpected, and I found myself moved to greater candor, both disarmed and slightly alarmed by what he had done with chest and fist.

"I'll tell you something," I said. "Being an immigrant, for us, the soul, so to speak, is always torn. You grow up in one place, you're surrounded by those things, but then your heritage comes from somewhere else. I think our souls are a little more divided, if that makes any sense."

"As somebody from a minority group," he replied, "I don't expect you to understand what I'm saying. You probably mostly grew up around other Indians."

"I grew up in America," I interjected. "Most of my friends growing up were white, most of my colleagues are white. I've always had to talk to people of many different kinds. I find my life is bound up with people of many different kinds. What worries me is the idea that we'd do better if we hive off with our own kind. I wonder whether that wouldn't be a whole lot worse than now. Ultimately, we don't just share a country, we share a planet."

All this I meant as an expression of a common fate. But he heard it as a justification for caution, as if I had signaled a reason for alarm. "I understand," he said, "that Europeans are the dominant power on this planet right now, but power ebbs and flows, societies grow and fall, for every civilization from the Mesopotamian all the way up to this one. And that's definitely a threat that you have to worry about, that another group will come over and wreck your shit."

I realized how differently we imagined what it meant to live side by side with others. I saw differences as natural and necessary. He took them as signs of a looming dispossession.

The chanting, meanwhile, had grown in volume. The police pulled up at the curb to take away a young white man whose hands they'd zip-tied behind his back. We later learned that he was a counter-protestor who had come into the white nationalist area. A scuffle ensued, and he was escorted away by the officers, eventually charged with disorderly conduct.

"I can't understand why they have the opinions they have, and I was hoping to shed some light on this for myself," the young man later explained to a reporter, describing how he was put into a headlock by one of the demonstrators. "I didn't have any success."

With whatever luck, meanwhile, I found myself among people willing to speak more candidly about what brought them there. And what struck me most about these conversations was their familiarity. There was nothing unfathomably strange about any of the conversations I had that day in Shelbyville. The concerns these men expressed echoed what I'd often heard from many others around the country. They talked about the security of body and soul, their own well-being and that of their kin, what they thought it would take to care truly for them.

What they said was so banal. And this, if anything, made it more frightening.

"There's no living with the other," the man in the Carhartt jacket told me. What seemed to have gone missing here was the faith that one could live alongside others unlike oneself, sharing a collective life with them rather than living at the other's expense.

"You gotta put your own air mask on first," he said. "You gotta take care of yourself before you can take care of someone else. You can't help people if you cut your own throat."

———————

In recent years, as it happens, the white nationalist movement in the United States has dealt with many self-inflicted wounds: severe bouts of infighting and organizational dysfunction have taken a heavy toll, with many of the leaders of the 2017 rallies in Charlottesville and Shelbyville facing deep legal troubles and criminal convictions, and with the organizations facing dwindling membership. The League of the South, for example, now "struggles to exist" according to the Southern Poverty Law Center.[17] In another important sense, however, these last years have seen less a collapse of white nationalist politics in the United States than its consolidation as a mainstream position, manifest in a pervasive imagination of rightful self-defense.

Conservative media outlets often traffic in the idea of a white America being flooded and "replaced" by racial others. Echoes abound of the "Fourteen Words"—"We must secure the existence of our people and a future for white children"—that have long stood as the credo for white nationalism in the United States.[18] Critics have found echoes in the rhetoric of influential media personalities, such as Tucker Carlson, who argued, in an infamous 2020 diatribe against Somali American Congresswoman Ilhan Omar and Asian American Senator Tammy Duckworth, that "We have every right to fight to preserve our nation and our heritage and our culture."[19] This is a politics, however toxic, pitched to shield vulnerable bodies from existential threat, one in which protection and aggression are bound up tightly together. Its widespread appeal has to be understood.

I think, for example, of an older man I spoke with at the 2017 rally in Shelbyville, a thick white mustache on his face and a Confederate States of America buckle cinching up his blue jeans. He confided his suspicion that all the rally participants, both nationalist demonstrators and counter-protestors alike, had been paid to conjure up a spectacle. He kept poking fun at what the neo-Nazi foot soldiers were wearing. "A lot of them seem really odd, like that feller with the big holes in his ears, or the feller with the Nazi scarf and the funny beard. It's just odd, not what I'd call regular people."

"I wonder where the hell they're all from," he mulled aloud, as we watched with a shared feeling of curiosity. But it also looked like this mood of estrangement had tainted his imagination of the country itself. "They keep bringin' so many people in, I don't know where they all come from," he'd said earlier to me and to the man from Brooklyn. "I cain't find an American that owns a convenience store or a motel no more."

The older gentleman was ambivalent about the rally and its racial politics, both intrigued and repelled at the same time. He looked to be caught on the edge, asking himself whether to join in. I came away with the sense that there were many others who felt the same way.

Chanting among the demonstrators—"White lives matter! White lives matter!"—reached a crescendo as we spoke. Someone tapped me on the shoulder, a counter-terrorism consultant I had met earlier. He told me to turn around: "You don't want your back to this."

The young men in uniform were banging their shields in unison, preparing to march away from the demonstration site. One of them taunted us with a "Love over Hate" flyer ripped from a telephone pole—"You lost a sign, buddies"—as they stomped past. They kept going, and I followed them out of the pen built to contain them for the day. I remained unscathed.

A white journalist later told me that despite the close quarters where we were all hemmed in together, the color of my skin had guarded me from any potential violence: "In a strange way, you were the safest one inside that pen." Again, it was a matter of optics, of preserving the impression that this was a peaceful event meant only to affirm a certain way of life. He'd wound up in a scuffle with some of the demonstrators, meanwhile, and had a small cut on the side of his nose. "They used their shield as a weapon," he explained, pointing to the cut on his face—a means of protection, once again, deployed as an instrument of aggression.

I walked back along North Main Street toward my hotel, stopping into a place called El Mexico for a bite to eat. I could see, when I sat down at a booth, that my hands were trembling with the strain of having passed the day on an even keel, coils of tension finally easing into a state of normalcy. I texted home to say I was okay.

The Latino man who seated me at the restaurant was born in the United States and had lived in Shelbyville for nearly fifteen years. He told me something curious, almost funny, about the people streaming into the place now that the rally was over. "They go to the rally and come sit down here to eat. We don't know what side they were on."

Indeed, having seen what I'd seen, it seemed entirely plausible that someone could spend the day rallying on behalf of a white nation, then stop in for a quick burrito. That feeling stayed with me as I walked down the road back to my hotel, trailing all the big black pickup trucks rolling out of town. Who could say what side they were on, those walled within those massive vehicles with dark tinted windows. All of it, as I walked, took on an ominous tinge: that feeling of an armored reality, and the mystery of all that might be obscured within.

EIGHT

SKIN OF THE COUNTRY

AUGUSTA, GEORGIA

In April of 2018, President Trump issued a memorandum to the secretary of defense, declaring a national security crisis on the southern border of the country.[1] Within days, hundreds of National Guard troops were deployed by the governors of Texas and Arizona to assist with border security measures. Many were alarmed by the spectacle of military intervention. But one former immigration judge and attorney for what used to be known as the Immigration and Naturalization Service (INS), Andrew R. Arthur, argued that this was indeed a matter of national defense. "The border is about more than illegal aliens," he said to the *Daily Signal*. "The border is like the skin of the country. If something penetrates that skin, it gets inside."[2]

The comparison may be unusual, but it shouldn't surprise. Modern nations are often imagined as individual organisms. In the discourse of immunology itself, meanwhile, as the medical anthropologist Emily Martin has observed, bodies have often been described as "imperiled nations continuously at war to quell alien invaders. These nations have sharply defined borders in space, which are constantly besieged and threatened."[3]

If we tend to think of bodies and their boundaries in this manner, it would seem to follow that a national border must also secure something akin to biological integrity. Indeed, as one border wall advocate suggested on a Reddit forum later in 2018, "picture the US as a person with an insanely strong immune system, but open sores all over its skin." For many, thinking of the border as a defensive layer of skin is a habit, almost unconscious. "Our Southern Border has long been an 'Open Wound,'" Trump himself has said.[4]

The logic of such ideas can be easier to grasp in images than in words. Take, for example, this cartoon penned by Rick McKee. A low wall runs across the drawing, a boundary around the United States. We are looking at America from the outside, from beyond its southern border, a saguaro cactus implies. There are two dark-haired men in baseball caps and sneakers, clambering over the wall. They frown at the small creatures who've approached them with hopeful smiles. Microbes, you might guess from how they look, and one of them, in fact, has a hobo's bindle stick in hand, the cloth bundle at the tip labeled with the word "disease." "Mind if we tag along?" these friendly-faced invaders ask.

One of the country's most prominent conservative cartoonists, McKee is

Rick McKee/*The Augusta Chronicle.*

syndicated in hundreds of newspapers across the United States. This cartoon, published in August 2014, was quickly picked up in many news features, blog commentaries, and social media posts warning against the dangers of unlawful immigration; even now, the image remains in circulation. The image framed an April 2020 editorial by conservative commentator Michael Shannon on how best to handle what he described alternatively as "China Flu" and "Kung Flu." Calling for new pandemic-era measures to restrict immigration and curtail the rights of illegal migrants, the writer insisted that "being the ER for Latin America is a luxury we can no longer afford."[5]

There is nothing unusual about such sentiments. "Suspicion against migrants as carriers of disease is probably the most pervasive and powerful myth related to migration and health throughout history," noted members of a Lancet Commission on Migration and Health in 2018, warning against "the prejudice and unfounded fear" that can be stoked through the misuse of public health data. "Although historical examples exist of the introduction of disease into new settings through human mobility (eg, the spread of infection from European colonial settlers)," the commission observed in its broad global survey, "the risk of transmission from migrating populations to host populations is generally low."[6]

And yet, when the coronavirus pandemic reached the United States about a year later, arguments about immigrants from such countries and the diseases they might bring surfaced once again to devastating effect. In the spring of 2020, countries around the world closed their borders to stem the spread of the virus. Here in the United States, the Trump administration called on a hitherto little-known provision of the 1944 Public Health Service Act—infamous now as Title 42—to mandate the immediate expulsion of asylum seekers and other migrants seeking refuge in the United States, on the grounds that they could spread communicable disease.[7] Although public health experts rejected the measure as "scientifically baseless and politically motivated," Title 42 has been used to expel millions of migrants from the United States, and the policy remained in use until 2023.[8]

How best to explain this impulse to isolate and seal off? How did the threat of infection gain such a powerful hold on American ideas of security? To what extent is disease even the problem conveyed by such measures, rather than the sense of palpable and embodied uncertainty that any encounter with

foreign lives increasingly seems to carry? I reached out to conservative cartoonist Rick McKee with these questions in mind, and through our many exchanges, began to see how deeply contemporary debates about immigration
and disease were tied to the racial histories of public health.

When we first met in the summer of 2018, Rick McKee was the editorial cartoonist of the *Augusta Chronicle* in Georgia. I arranged to meet him at the
newspaper office one afternoon that summer. He was friendly in correspondence. "Call me Rick," he insisted right away. He also wanted to make sure—
mostly in jest, I think—that I wasn't Sacha Baron Cohen in disguise.

A year back, Cohen had pranked a conservative radio host in Augusta for
his Showtime series *Who Is America?* pretending to be a Reed College professor named Nira Cain. What his production team had maintained about Cain—
that he was a liberal academic seeking out dialogues in Trump country for a
show called *Bridging the Divide*—felt eerily similar to what I was trying to do
myself. It gave me pause and made me wonder whether this book project of
mine also amounted to an elaborate bluff, whether there was any real value
to these exchanges. McKee, in any case, was gracious enough to hear me out.

The *Chronicle*'s offices on Broad Street looked empty and understaffed, a
symptom of the ongoing crisis in American print journalism. McKee met me
in the paper's vaulted lobby, the walls commemorating the historic triumph
by Tiger Woods at the Augusta Masters in 1997 and the terror attack on the
Twin Towers in 2001. He was much less rumpled than I expected a cartoonist might look, with a clean-shaven face and a checked button-down shirt
tucked into his khakis. He took me to a shuttered office suite upstairs where
we could talk, flipping on a light switch and inviting me to take a seat beside
an unused desk.

McKee had grown up in Chattahoochee, a small town on the Florida-
Georgia state line. He'd worked at the *Atlanta Journal-Constitution* for a
few years after college, before joining the *Chronicle* in 1990. "Editorial cartoons are typically a negative art," he observed. "We're usually attacking
something, some concept, somebody." The challenge lay in crafting a cogent
punchline that people could figure out quickly on their own. "Visually, you
have to get it in such a way that everybody can look at it, understand it, make

sense of it," all this, he explained, in eight to ten seconds of glancing at that image, at most.

We took some time to look together at his first retrospective collection of cartoons, called *Painting with a Broad Brush*.[9] "I'm usually trying to come up with the image that's going to make the most impact on that particular topic, that particular day, trying to get at the nub of the truth," McKee explained. Behind every cartoon was some news story, some reported incident that sparked the drawing he would make. In the case of the microbial border crossers he had sketched in 2014, which I pulled up for us to talk about, McKee had been following stories about unaccompanied minors from Central America apprehended that year on the southern border, and the question of whether they were a possible vector of illness.[10]

"This was when kids were pouring over the border in the tens of thousands," McKee recalled. "Because we didn't know their shot records, their vaccinations, and they had no papers, we had no idea what was coming with this wave of humanity. That's when I came up with the concept of the disease tagging along, like a little runaway. He's got his little runaway stick with his belongings," he said, pointing out the microbe he'd drawn with a bindle stick. "They're also like unaccompanied minors. They're little runaways along with the other kids."

I was startled when McKee said this, so much so that I fumbled for words in response. This aspect hadn't even struck me until he pointed it out—the idea that these germs could stand in for migrant children, that these kids could be imagined as literal embodiments of disease. Didn't this verge on racism, I asked him.

McKee acknowledged that the racist rhetoric prevalent in American public discourse was a serious problem. "This stuff that's out there, the virulent racism, it's just stomach-churning, disheartening, the way it's being given voice. I don't want to play into those fears."

I was glad that he said this. But I still wanted to understand how a drawing like this one could be interpreted in any other way. I brought up the conversations I'd been having with others, the ways that many conservative people I had met thought about the country and the question of how to secure its well-being. "There are people who think of the country as a body. And then it wouldn't be so unreasonable to think of the border as the skin of the body.

When I look at an image like this, that's what comes to mind for me. Are we talking about the infiltration of foreign elements into an organism?"

McKee said he wasn't thinking in those terms when he drew the cartoon, but he was willing to talk out the idea. "Let me get my brain around that, as an analogy. The logical extension of that idea would be that the people coming here illegally were like invaders, or outside elements breaking the skin. That personalizes it for a lot of people. I don't know, maybe that's where they are, subconsciously."

"Of course, you're not the only one to call attention to this danger of disease," I pointed out. "Even Trump said it at one point."

"I think there's just a fear of the unknown," McKee responded. "People are afraid of things they don't know, they don't understand. I don't have a paralyzing fear of disease. But when you have an unsecured border and people are just coming in, you don't know. You just don't know. You have no idea what could be going on."

An image can bring such uncertainty into sharp focus, lending substance and meaning to what may otherwise remain a vague sense of unease. So much turns on the feelings that readers themselves carry. As Rick McKee's border disease cartoon began to circulate in 2014, there were those who found it to speak precisely to their own concerns. "This is honestly one of my biggest fears in the coming months," one contributor to the Reddit forum r/conservative wrote. Others, meanwhile, pilloried the drawing as racist and misguided.

"That one got hit pretty hard," McKee admitted to me. There were readers who found the cartoon "reminiscent of the 1800s, when we criticized the Irish or the Chinese, that they were diseased." I was struck by the cartoonist's mention of this historical parallel. Do images such as these address a familiar and recurrent problem, or do they speak instead to a habit or pattern of response? Could they have more to say, in other words, about the ideas that motivate American critics of immigration than about the objects of their criticism?

On April 13, 1840, the Augusta *Daily Chronicle & Sentinel*—as the *Augusta Chronicle* was known at the time—published an extract of unusual length from the *Charleston Courier*. The subject was a crucial one: a possible breakthrough in the understanding of yellow fever and its etiology. Year after year, coastal Charleston had seen devastating outbreaks of the lethal disease. One local physician now claimed to have unraveled why the disease "kept pace with West India commerce and followed in its wake," how it had reached these shores from the Cuban ports of Havana and Matanzas.

The doctor's hypothesis was a curious one, having to do with rotting tropical fruit and the poisonous vapors they might exude in an unhealthy local atmosphere. However strange this idea might seem to us now, it was highly significant at the time. For yellow fever was known then as "the disease of strangers in warm climates," or, more simply still, Stranger's Fever. And whether the disease was attributed to human immigrants from elsewhere or to imported fruit gone bad, the question of its transmission was crucial. As the newspaper's editors put it, "our chief danger is from abroad."

For more than two centuries, popular imagination in the United States has associated immigration with disease — so much so, argues historian Alan M. Kraut, that public health and immigration anxiety are bound together like a double helix in American history, reappearing time and again in familiar patterns. Take, for example, the infamous 1883 cartoon of cholera as a Grim Reaper in Indian garb, a shipborne stowaway seeking to slip undetected into the country, repelled at last by a wall of disinfectants on the shores of New York. The cartoon's caption anticipates today's concerns with eerie precision: "The Kind of 'Assisted Emigrant' We Can Not Afford to Admit."[11]

Newcomers to the United States, Kraut explains, have long been met with "nativists' suspicions and accusations that they are accompanied across sea and land by silent travelers — germs and genes of an inferior sort — well capable of polluting the sturdy American population mainstream."[12] Such ideas are especially potent when the origin and transmission of a disease are misunderstood.

In 1900, a team led by US Army pathologist Walter Reed established that yellow fever was communicated by the *Aedes aegypti* mosquito. Until then, the disease remained a perplexing scourge, responsible for more than 100,000 deaths in the United States.[13] Immigrants were often held liable. When an epidemic broke out in Philadelphia in 1793, the disease was identified as a German affliction, "Palatine fever," on account of the many victims in the city who had immigrated from that part of Germany.[14]

PUCK.

THE KIND OF "ASSISTED EMIGRANT" WE CAN NOT AFFORD TO ADMIT.

Augusta was hit by two severe outbreaks of yellow fever in the nineteenth century, in 1839 and 1854. The 1839 epidemic was especially serious, infecting up to a quarter of the town's population and ultimately killing 240 residents. Nearby seaports like Savannah and Charleston saw serious outbreaks year after year, while Augusta escaped on most occasions with no more than a handful of cases. The cause of these outbreaks and how the disease propagated remained obscure. "Yellow fever usually commences its work insidiously, and spreads from point to point, without any such premonition as might be available for escape," local physician L. A. Dugas remarked in the *Southern Medical and Surgical Journal*.[15]

The epidemics were an especially potent challenge for Augusta because the town was an emerging nucleus of medical science. The Medical College of Georgia, one of the first medical schools in the United States, was founded in Augusta in 1828. The *Southern Medical and Surgical Journal*, which reported regularly on the epidemic fevers of the nineteenth century, was established in Augusta in 1836 and was edited by the principal founder of the medical college, Milton Antony. Antony himself was one of four Augusta doctors who contracted and died of yellow fever while treating patients in 1839. On a marble tablet still visible today at the Medical College of Georgia, he is described as "a martyr to humanity and the duties of his profession, during the fatal epidemic of 1839."

By 1854, when yellow fever struck Augusta once again, taking 110 lives, the medical establishment had a clearer sense that the disease had come there from elsewhere. "It is well established," Dugas noted, "that it can be carried about from place to place, by ships, steamboats, closed railroad cars, and indeed by any conveyance in which a certain quantity of the pestilential air may be transported."[16] When the disease surfaced in a number of nearby port cities in 1876—Charleston, Port Royal, Savannah, Brunswick—local officials mandated a quarantine on all rail passengers and other travelers coming to Augusta from those cities. Violators were pursued and were liable for hefty fines or even a jail term.

As such measures became more prevalent, debates ensued regarding their necessity. Was it needlessly cruel to deny people the ability to flee a deadly disease? Georgia Board of Health representative and Augusta native Henry Fraser Campbell posed this question to the American Public Health Association in Nashville in 1879.[17] With words that can only be described as prophetic, the physician compared what he had seen during earlier epidemics to what had since developed in the name of quarantine:

> Looking then into the history of the past, and comparing it with the present tone of public feeling towards refugee cases of yellow fever in healthy inland communities, we cannot fail to discover a most marked and contrasting change. Instead of the welcome and refuge and nursing and tender care extended in the past, all travelers during the season of an epidemic, however distant, have become now by statute—by sanitary statute—objects of suspicion marked for exclusion unless they can purge themselves of the abhorred *taint* of having come out of the infected region, while any one so unfortunate as to be attacked with the disease in his flight had better die by the wayside than be allowed to enter and diffuse poison in the pure atmosphere of a healthy town.

Campbell argued that the disease was carried from place to place by noxious elements in the air, rather than by contagious contact from person to person. We know now that he and other experts of his time were mistaken, that the deadly fever was indeed contagious, and that there were no "atmospheric germs" simply to air out as a way of resolving an epidemic. Nevertheless, it is striking to consider the depth of commitment the physician sought to nurture on behalf of those shut out for the sake of protection, those who would "suffer and perish, outcasts by the wayside, in sight of the inhospitable and garrisoned households of fear-stricken strangers"—not least because this sympathy had limits of its own, governed by a racial logic.

In Augusta, Campbell notes, first in 1839 and then again in 1854, "twelve hours did not elapse after the declaration of the epidemic, ere, as we may almost literally assert, the entire white population had removed to a safe distance out of the limits of the infected atmosphere." They decamped to the wooded hills to the west of town, the public official noted, leaving behind the Black families who made up nearly half of Augusta's population at the time. A terse note from Campbell parried any questions that might arise: "The colored people were little or not at all liable [affected] in these epidemics." And yet we know this was not the case.

On November 12, 1839, the Augusta *Chronicle & Sentinel* resumed publication as a daily newspaper after a two-month suspension. The epidemic had been that serious; "the hand of Death has wrought many gloomy chasms in its enterprising and business population," the editors wrote on the paper's front page. What followed were the names of 205 white men, women, and children who had died of yellow fever since the epidemic began that August: local residents; natives of Ireland, England, and other American states; physicians like Dr. Milton Antony and Dr. Isaac Bowen; a painter, a printer, many boys and girls. Here's how the accounting ended:

Mrs. Caroline F. Gunther,	Germany
Adeline Martin (6 years old),	Resident
Sanders Walker,	"
Simeon Walker,	"
Mrs. Martha Shaw,	"
Benjamin Sims,	"
Larry Hoy,	Ireland
Hezekiak Bailey,	Resident

Master Charles Ogden,	"
Jacob Danforth,	"
Mrs. Gay,	"
Matthew Nelson,	"
Mr. Rush,	"
And thirty-five negroes.	

Those Black victims went altogether unnamed, in the city's newspaper of public record and even, as I learned, in the death registry of the city cemetery.

It's hard to say what happened in the chaos of those months, especially among Augusta's enslaved population, likely as many as 3,000 strong.[18] It would take many more years for the fundamental relationship between the transatlantic slave trade and the spread of yellow fever from West Africa to the Americas to come into focus. "When the slave trade first began," as Molly Crosby observes, "every European country that profited from the purchase and sale of Africans would soon see a yellow fever epidemic."[19]

None of this was known or acknowledged in nineteenth-century Augusta. Here, the physicians of the antebellum era relied on enslaved people to look after their domestic needs, even to secure the cadavers that made possible their medical knowledge.[20] The international webs of money and power that brought both prosperity and disease to the city remained obscure in their vision of public health. Anxieties hinged on the incursion of a foreign enemy, rather than the forms of exploitation that made this possible in the first place.

It wasn't just the gravity of yellow fever that inspired dread. It was also what it did to the body, the way its victims came apart. Observers of the nineteenth-century epidemics reported on its strange and unsettling symptoms in gory detail. There was the "black vomit" that victims threw up violently, so much so that the disease was often known by this name. "The peculiar offensive-ness of the perspiration, on one or two occasions," wrote one doctor in the *Southern Medical and Surgical Journal*, reporting on his experience of the 1854 outbreak in Augusta, "struck me promptly with sensations of repug-nance, and made me dread its approach."[21]

Yellow fever is a viral hemorrhagic fever, known, like other diseases of this kind, for its gruesome ability to make the body bleed from many places at once, as if disintegrating and losing its basic cohesion. The illness still claims tens of thousands of lives each year, primarily in Africa. The fear that it once inspired in the United States, meanwhile, has been seen most vividly in recent times with another hemorrhagic fever, Ebola. Named for the river in Zaire where the disease was first identified in 1976, Ebola became synonymous with acute biological terror for many Americans. A CNN commentator named it "Fearbola" in 2014.[22]

The outbreak that began that year claimed the lives of over 11,000 people, nearly all of them in the West African nations of Liberia, Sierra Leone, and Guinea. In the United States, there were a total of eleven patients treated for Ebola, two of whom died. "Ebola poses no substantial risk to the US general population," the CDC declared that August.[23] And yet there was a widespread sense of alarm, even panic. "What we're seeing is a catastrophic health crisis in West Africa, and an epidemic of fear here," Anthony Fauci observed, serving at the time as the director of the National Institute of Allergy and Infectious Diseases.[24]

In 2014 that mood was as palpable in Augusta as anywhere else — even more so, in fact, given the many local healthcare workers who had provided medical aid in West Africa; the American soldiers sent there to help with the epidemic from nearby Fort Gordon; and the proximity of the CDC and the Emory University Hospital in Atlanta, where an American nurse infected with the virus had been sent for treatment.

"People were so terrified," an Augusta pediatrician told me, recalling conversations she had that year with local parents. "What if it comes here? Should I take my kids out of school? How will we protect them?"

Late that October, a young patient at the Augusta University hospital was asked to remove the orange and black CAUTION tape decorating her hospital room door for Halloween, because other patients were worried that she had Ebola. Just north of the city, an anesthesiologist of Senegalese origin was tracked down by county health officials to ensure he didn't have the disease; they were summoned by the local motor vehicle office, where he was seen to cough when he'd come to pick up new license plate tags.[25] And an anonymous contributor to the *Aiken Standard*, published across the Savannah River from Augusta, had this to say about those who might violate their Ebola quaran-

tine: "I think if they try to go out the front door of their house, and the author-
ities are there, they should shoot them down. I guess then we won't worry
about it anymore."[26]

Without a doubt, the vehemence of these concerns had to do with much
more than the severity of a possible outbreak. There was also its West African origin, the idea of racial chaos and degeneracy coming into the United
States. "Considering that much of augusta looks like third world west africa,
ebola should feel right at home," one Augusta resident wrote at the time on
Facebook. With President Obama in the Oval Office, meanwhile, there were
many who asserted that the government had shown far more concern for
African victims of the disease than for its dangers to American citizens. Lest
we forget, "Obola" was one caustic nickname for the president that year, as if
he were a virus himself infecting the body of the nation.[27]

What to do in the face of such threats but to try and shut the door? Calls
for total and immediate quarantine were in the air once again. Donald Trump
took to Twitter dozens of times that year to demand an immediate halt to all
flights from Ebola-infected countries into the United States, even those res-
cuing stricken American aid workers. Otherwise, he warned, "the plague will
start and spread inside our 'borders.'"[28]

It was in this climate of acute anxiety that Rick McKee penned that border
cartoon in 2014. The ominous question that gives it force — "Mind if we tag
along?" — is posed by three runaway microbes trying to sneak across the
border: one light green and knobby like a little dill pickle, another that looks
like a spiky blue ball, and the third shaped like a purple worm with a knot in
its tail, carrying that bundle marked "disease."

"That purple one is Ebola, I think," someone posted on the cartoonist's
Facebook page. "Ding ding! Give that man a prize!" McKee wrote back.

"I don't have a fear of disease," the cartoonist had told me. But when I
looked back at the drawings he had made that year, I could see that Ebola
was much on his mind: there were the doctors in full-body yellow protective
suits exiled to Liberia; the Georgia governor emitting a cloud of deadly germs
from his mouth as a political aid stood by in another yellow protective suit,
reporting on a mysterious outbreak, an "unethical epidemic" in state government; and the kid trick-or-treating on Halloween in yet another yellow suit
and gas mask.

"And what are you supposed to be?"

"Under quarantine."

The clumsy suits were good fodder for a humorist, as was, no doubt, the larger climate of panic. But there was also a warning in these drawings, as with his reply to a critic who called the border microbe cartoon "fearmongering, a badge of honor for conservatives."

"It's not ignorance but common sense," McKee replied, "to make sure we are not allowing diseases to spill unfettered across our border. It's why we have legal immigration and checkpoints at airports." Weighing all of this, I felt we had to meet again.

"We call those pieces talkers," McKee explained when I showed him the Ebola cartoons at the *Chronicle* office a couple of days later. "When I draw a cartoon, I try to find the thing that people are talking about. I'm sure it was on everybody's mind, during that time."

"There's being cautious about one thing as opposed to something else," I acknowledged. "But how do you know you're not overreacting?"

"I thought it was an outbreak, an epidemic. At the time, we didn't know we were only going to have a handful of cases. Something as visual and shocking and frightening as Ebola, when you don't know you're only going to have a handful, it's a scary prospect."

"Are we overgeneralizing about these folks though?" I asked, bringing up the border cartoon again. "You see someone walking down the street with brown skin, you don't want people looking at them thinking, *There goes a walking talking disease.* But that's the power of the image, it helps make associations. And sometimes the things we do get weaponized, made to serve purposes we may not intend."

"I agree," McKee replied. "People are being demonized. But I think you're trying to intellectualize what is basically evil, racist hatred. It's always been there. Now it's seeping into the mainstream. You're giving them too much credit if you try to get into their heads."

Just a few weeks before McKee and I met, his 2014 border cartoon went around once again on Twitter, shared this time as a warning by a self-styled #TrumpGirl. "They don't come here alone," she wrote. "They bring all kinds of ICK with them. So that dishwasher in your local restaurant? How is THAT tasting?" Paired with two nauseous emojis spewing green floods of vomit, the cartoon was retweeted nearly three hundred times on just this one occasion.

People had sorry-looking emojis of their own to commiserate with, warning against restaurants, takeout pizza, even salad — sharing measures they'd taken to boost their own immunity. And, as always, there was a measure of solace in such vigilance.

"I have not washed my dishes the last 3 years," a diehard #MAGA fan from Nevada declared, daring readers to take her regimen of self-exposure to germs seriously. "I was preparing for this invasion. I urge all Americans to do the same, it is not too late."

———————

On the last day of January in 2020, Rick McKee put out a Groundhog Day cartoon: a sketch of Punxsutawney Phil cowering within his burrow, vowing to remain inside as the daily news brought an ominous headline to his neck of the woods. "Coronavirus Spreading."

"I called it," McKee told me when we caught up by phone one afternoon that April. "It'll be a long time before we come back to any sense of normalcy."

Over the following months of the pandemic, the cartoonist produced dozens of coronavirus-related drawings. One off-color cartoon implied that it was a perverse fondness for bat meat in China that had landed the United States in this predicament. But, for the most part, these images seemed to suggest something altogether different. It was no longer a matter of shielding the country from a foreign danger of contamination. The illness was already here, a green miasma of spiky particles hanging in the air, sickening people not simply with a virus but with the denial of its reality. For the stock figure in these cartoons was a white man in a red MAGA cap, belly hanging below the hem of a "Don't Tread on Me" T-shirt, and an open mouth oblivious to the viral particles swirling around him — a body, in other words, heedless of its own porous borders, disregarding the need for boundaries. More than a biological infection now, the disease had become Trumpism itself, and it had fully possessed its host.

"It's baffling, completely mind-blowing," McKee told me when we spoke again in the spring of 2021. "I don't understand it. It's like we're living in an alternate universe, an episode of the *Twilight Zone*. A few of us are watching, and it's like they've all been . . ."

"Infected!" I interjected.

"Exactly." We talked about the paradoxes that seemed to have caught hold of Republican politics in the era of Trump. McKee felt that the pandemic had borne out his earlier alarm about open borders, the protective function of border security. How then to explain why so many on the right had come to reject the seriousness of the coronavirus as a threat? "You've got to throw out your rulebook, what conservatives do believe, what they used to believe," McKee reflected. "Can I even say that I'm a conservative anymore?"

To my eyes, many of his cartoons remained harsh, sometimes even cruel. We talked about a drawing he'd published that March, amid the news of another surge of undocumented migrant children at the southern border. In this cartoon, the border is no more than a dotted line. President Biden is at the wheel of an ice cream truck plying the northern side of the line, as a swarm of eager children rushes in from the south. Biden is befuddled, as though he can't recall that he's driving a truck full of sweets with the words "Immigration Policies" stamped across the hood. "What's with all the kids?" he asks.

When we talked, I pointed out to McKee that thousands of people were still being turned away at the border each week without even a hearing, with

Rick McKee/*The Augusta Chronicle*

the specious public health reasoning of the Trump administration's Title 42 policy still in effect. There was also the larger question of what we owed migrants from Central America, given the economic devastation and political chaos they had endured, as well as the role of the United States in fomenting these troubles.[29] "Don't we have a moral responsibility to help them out?" I asked.

"I'll be accused of being heartless," McKee acknowledged, speculating that many asylum seekers were coming to the United States with ambition, rather than desperation. But he also struck a different tone I was surprised to hear, given the tenor of our previous exchanges. "Helping the situation there, so people want to stay where they are, is better than building a wall," he told me, talking about the value of foreign aid and other ways of tackling root problems of economy and politics in Central America. "That would be in our national interest. We're a global society now, we're all interconnected. The pandemic has put an exclamation point on that."

In *On Immunity*, her book-length meditation on ideas of disease and well-being, Eula Biss underscores the fundamental interdependence of each body with the bodies of others. "We are protected not so much by our own skin," Biss writes, describing the lessons of herd immunity, "but by what is beyond it. The boundaries between our bodies begin to dissolve here."[30] For so many of us, the coronavirus pandemic seemed to have brought home this truth: that immunity from harm is ultimately a collective matter. Whether the body of a person or the body of a nation, hard lines between inside and out present an impossible and unlivable ideal. The fact remains, as Biss suggests, that we "owe our health to our neighbors."[31]

NINE

LIVING WITH EXPOSURE

HUDSON RIVER VALLEY

The appeal of an impervious shield has spanned the distance, in the United States, between terrestrial and molecular levels. Take, for example, the small character that often appeared in the early promotional materials for Teflon produced by chemical manufacturer DuPont. In the top-left corner of each issue of the *Journal of Teflon* that DuPont published in the 1960s, you would find a little figure composed of linked rings and strands, a person whose head and torso looked to be made from the atoms of carbon at the heart of the Teflon polymer, and whose limbs led out like the pairs of fluorine bound to each of those carbon atoms.[1]

Here was "Mr. Teflon," as one internal marketing memo put it in 1957, one who could be given "a personality of its own."[2] This personality comes through most clearly in the demeanor maintained by that little character throughout the pages of DuPont's promotional pamphlets. Whether lounging in a pan of boiling water or casually grasping a bolt of electric current, whether lifting a barbell or swinging a basket of fresh eggs, whether diving into a lake or patrolling with a rifle, this molecular person approached all things with the same jaunty and intrepid spirit, the smile never dropping from its face.

Portraits of Mr. Teflon appear throughout an introductory article published in the July 1961 issue of the *Journal of Teflon*, one aiming to explain "Why Teflon Fluorocarbon Resins Behave as They Do."[5] The article describes the chemical structure of the polymer molecule, the way its fluorine atoms are arranged to "form a tight, protective cover over the chain of carbon atoms" at its heart. It is this structure, the article pronounces, that explains why the substance is so indifferent to the shifting circumstances of the surrounding world: why it is able to "resist attack" by heat and other chemicals so successfully, why it repels attachment to other things so effortlessly. "This sheath of fluorine atoms may be likened to a smooth, impenetrable shield."

Dwell on the easy promise of an image like this one, this idea of a smooth and impenetrable molecular shield, and you can't help but think about the tenor of American life during those Cold War years. The 1950s and 1960s saw the development of a nuclear culture in the United States, anthropolo-

Extreme chemical inertness

Courtesy of the Hagley Museum & Library.

gist Joseph Masco observes, one that asked American citizens to avoid panic and to keep their emotions under check, even as they were invited, again and again, to envision the total annihilation of their homes and neighborhoods. These tensions amounted almost to a "psychotic contradiction," Masco writes, "an everyday life founded simultaneously on total threat and absolute normality."[4] No wonder the appeal of a miracle barrier, one built to withstand any possible threat.

"How can we best and most dramatically demonstrate the properties of Teflon?" a DuPont marketing team reflected in a freewheeling brainstorming session held at the Hotel Du Pont in downtown Wilmington in 1956.[5] To be sure, many of the 171 different ideas floated during the meeting and recorded in the minutes had to do with the slipperiness of Teflon, the effortless cleaning and handling that the new material promised. Still, it is striking to consider how many of these suggestions zeroed in on the promise of defense, the idea of a shield to defend a body against the wildest fantasies of attack and torture:

25. Build a mechanical man of Teflon and let him walk through a roaring flame.

33. Show a photo of a Teflon figure that has been in a well known volcano like Vesuvius for a year.

58. Have a picture of a gasoline fire and show a figure in the fire.

78. Show what happens to Teflon after it's hit by a 16" shell from a Navy battleship.

88. Exhibit a figure that has been through the last H bomb test of Teflon.

106. Exhibit a figure that has been in a blast furnace in a steel mill for 4 to 8 hours beside one that has not.

133. Immerse it in a bucket of acid.

166. Exhibit a mine-car made of Teflon after it has been retrieved from a fall, perhaps into the Grand Canyon, loaded with lead ore.

Imagine something capable of surviving all such trials; imagine people too equipped with such material, surviving all such trials as well. With Teflon, as DuPont would promise consumers when its Teflon-coated cookware hit the marketplace, "sticking problems just glide away." Hence the calm and reassuring tone struck by company spokesman Larry Livingston in a series of televised commercials for DuPont's chemical inventions that aired in the 1950s. One advertisement followed Livingston as he walked to a demonstration table and picked up a bread tin coated with Teflon. The tin, it seems, was spotless after 1,258 loaves baked without a single drop of grease, all on account of that invisible and impossibly slick wall of film.

"Someday, you ladies may have a lot of things coated with Teflon enamel," the company spokesman suggests in the ad: "rolling pins, measuring cups, even that glue plop . . ."—and here he blinks his eyes dramatically and makes to swallow loudly, adding, with a warm smile, the words he meant to say instead: "glue pot."

"Maybe I need a Teflon-coated throat," he adds, beaming warmly yet again.[6]

DuPont was founded in 1802 as an explosives manufacturer. With its tremendous profits during the First World War, the company drew condemnation as a "merchant of death." In the years thereafter, DuPont rebranded itself as an enterprise devoted to American well-being, focused on making "better things for better living, through chemistry," as it insisted over many decades of sponsored radio and television programming and concerted advertising.[7] This "better living" depended on the imagined promise of plastics like Teflon and other synthetic materials, new ways to shelter the space of everyday life from nagging problems and destructive forces, to secure the body from the troubles and dangers of the world outside.

This optimism has long assumed an ominous charge. Plastics are literally inside us now, in a grim realization of that fantasy of a Teflon throat that DuPont broadcast in the 1950s. Tiny fragments of plastic material can now be tracked in everything from pilsner beers to wild-caught fish.[8] Perfluoroalkyl substances or PFAS chemicals—a class of compounds that includes Teflon and thousands of other synthetic chemicals—have been identified in the bloodstream of 97 percent of the American population and are likely present in the drinking water consumed by more than 200 million residents of the United States.[9] PFAS are widely known as "forever chemicals" because of the toughness of their structure and their resistance to molecular breakdown. With a toxicity measured in parts per *trillion*, these industrial chemicals have even been found in the tissue of hundreds of wild animal species in scattered places around the globe.[10]

These new realities force us to rethink how we imagine the body: less as an individual container to shield and protect than as a meeting ground for many different relationships of implication and exposure. Our bodies have a wider ecology that enfolds the landscape and its history, as scholar Michelle Murphy observes: "Our bodies . . . are a manifestation of something bigger, that stretches outward to water, air, ancestors, and other beings, that stretches backwards to messy histories."[11]

These histories carried by our bodies now have an indelible industrial imprint, due to the unavoidable nature of modern contaminants. "We are enmeshed in these chemical infrastructures," Murphy notes, calling on her work on industrial pollution in the Great Lakes region to evoke "the vastness of our chemical relations, relations that extend far out from our skin." But these bodily burdens also reflect a deep inequality when it comes to pollution and its consequences, as Murphy adds. "Embodiment is a collective binding of profoundly uneven relations of porosity to exposure: my vulnerability to injury is entangled with your comfort."[12]

What does it mean to attest to such exposure, to struggle for bodily well-being in a spirit of collective justice rather than retreat? Imaginations of the fortified body rest on the idea that individual Americans must do what they can to secure their own health. But the truth is that bodily well-being is a collective condition. This chapter focuses on the efforts of clean water advocates in two small towns of New York's Hudson River Valley—Hoosick Falls and Newburgh—two of many places around the country that are struggling with PFAS chemical contamination of their water supplies. The work of local residents and activist leaders in these places shows how protection can be pursued as a matter of mutual responsibility.

"It's in everything," people in the town of Hoosick Falls in upstate New York will say about Teflon. And when they do, they speak from a unique kind of personal experience. For many decades, factories in this place on the banks of the Hoosic River—an important tributary of the Hudson—used Teflon to make everything from molded gaskets to thread seal tape, circuit boards to missile parts. "We were the capital of Teflon," the town's elderly historian Phil Leonard recounted to me one February afternoon in 2017.[13]

Hoosick Falls isn't far from the Vermont state border, and my brother Karthik was teaching art at the time at Bennington College. The armory building on Church Street in Hoosick Falls, once a base for the New York National Guard, had since been turned into a community center, and my brother had rented out some space in the turret of the castle-like structure for an art studio. He introduced me to Aelish Nealon, who led a youth center and community organization also headquartered in the same building. Nealon, in turn, connected me with a number of local residents willing to talk with me about the industrial past and present of the town.

Over a few days in 2017, I learned how closely Teflon had been woven into the fabric of local life. In the zenith of its manufacture there, people who worked in the plants would carry home sheets of Teflon-coated fabric to line the shelves and drawers of their own houses. They would use these Teflon sheets to protect the ovens in their kitchens and to bake cookies for children at home. They would saw open the giant leftover casks that held the raw material to make buckets and rain barrels for their gardens. If you worked at one of these plants, as so many in the town did, you'd get a tangible sense of the material's appeal.

"You spill something, and the water beads on it," a man who worked for a decade in one of the factories recalled. "You put acid on it, nothing happens. You pound it, nothing happens. If people were cooking with it, you figure it had to be okay."

For much of the twentieth century, Hoosick Falls was an industrial boomtown, boasting numerous hotels, car dealerships, and department stores, and factories making tools, valves, insulation, and paper. In the 1980s, many of the plants began to close down, as they did in so many northeastern cities. Ornate buildings at the heart of a once-thriving downtown linger on as empty brick shells. Many families have moved away. Still, decades after the industrial heyday of Hoosick Falls, its legacies persist within the bodies of residents in alarming ways.

John Hickey had worked at the Saint-Gobain Performance Plastics plant on McCaffrey Street for thirty-two years when he died of kidney cancer in 2013. His son Mike and their family doctor began to suspect that local industries had something to do with talk of many unusual cancers. Mike Hickey had the water from their kitchen tap tested, finding that it had high levels of a chemical called perfluorooctanoic acid, or PFOA. At the time, the chemical was an essential component in the manufacturing of Teflon products, and like others in the hamlet, the plant on McCaffery Street used PFOA to make Teflon-coated fibers. In other states, Hickey gradually learned, DuPont was being sued for toxic releases of PFOA.[14]

Subsequent tests revealed that the Hoosick Falls municipal water supply was contaminated with the chemical, along with many other local wells. The seriousness of the problem owed a great deal to the material properties of PFOA and the way it was managed. The chemical is difficult to scrub from airborne emissions. It was used in the form of a fine powder that would build up on the uniforms of plant workers, only to be taken home and washed into pipes and lawns. Sacks and barrels that contained the material were dumped at the landfill and in other places that went untracked. One of the most troubling aspects of PFOA is its persistence in the environment and in the bodies of those who ingest it, even passing from mother to child through pregnancy and nursing. People in Hoosick Falls began to compare the crisis to the lead disaster in Flint.

Residents I met talked about their exposure to PFOA in a striking manner. "I'm 50," someone might say, meaning not their age but instead the presence of PFOA in their blood, measured in parts per trillion (ppt). At the time, the Environmental Protection Agency had set a health advisory standard of no more than 70 ppt of PFOA in public drinking water supplies, a standard that has since been lowered to a maximum contaminant level of just 4 ppt.[15]

Because so little is understood still about the chemical and its many hazards, people in places like Hoosick Falls have had to wrestle with unnerving mysteries. One night at a local bar, I met a teacher who was playing cribbage. All of his children had tested with high numbers, and one of them, a fourth grader, was still wetting her bed at night. The teacher didn't know if this was a developmental delay or an effect of the chemical, known to cause kidney problems. "We were feeding our kids poison all those years, that's what gets me," he said.

In 2017, the EPA added the Saint-Gobain Performance Plastics factory on McCaffrey Street to the Superfund National Priorities List of the country's most hazardous waste sites. But fresh problems continued to surface unexpectedly. At a town meeting that February, a company executive from Honeywell disclosed a new source of pollution from one of their defunct factories in the hamlet. Testing the groundwater for PFOA, they discovered a narrow plume of VOCs—volatile organic compounds—seeping through the groundwater from the site of a factory that had been closed for more than twenty years and razed fully to the ground. The company wanted permission now to test for vapors in the homes of those who lived along the path of that plume.

"We'll seal off the floor, or vent under the slab so it doesn't seep into your house," the executive said at the public meeting, trying to assure residents that they could still live in their homes as they always had. But people found little solace in such promises. "Shame on the company for using chemicals that are dangerous, then disposing them in so sloppy a way—not okay!" someone called out angrily at the meeting, which ended with people shuffling out of the community hall in weariness and uncertainty once again.[16]

Such circumstances have led many residents of this rural region to assume a newly activist orientation with regard to questions of bodily and collective health. "Their confrontation with PFOA has keyed them in to the wider struggles against contamination today" observes David Bond, a professor at nearby Bennington College who has developed a community-based research program focused on the local PFOA water crisis. "The largely white, working-class communities of Hoosick Falls and Bennington have hosted mothers from Flint, Michigan; sent care packages to the water protectors at Standing Rock; collaborated with high schoolers from East LA working on drinking water issues; published op-eds in communities around the United States that have discovered PFOA in their water; and reached out to communities around similar plastics plants in India and China."[17]

While I was in Hoosick Falls, I met with one of these local activists—Loreen Hackett of PFOA Project NY. When the water crisis broke, Hackett took black-and-white portraits of her young grandchildren, each holding a sign declaring the level of PFOA in their bloodstream: 142 and 117 ppt. The photographs of these winsome children, stark and unsettling, quickly went viral.[18] "My family, we're poster children for PFOA exposure," Hackett told me when we met for a conversation at her house one morning. She had extremely high levels of the chemical in her own blood, despite never having worked in one of the factories.[19]

"Doctors have called me a walking immune disaster for years," Hackett said, recounting how she'd been forced to retire early on disability some years ago. Her youngest daughter, who was twenty-four at the time, had also developed similar problems from a very young age. "It basically feels like Hiroshima in my abdomen," the young woman said sardonically, ducking in from the kitchen while her mother and I were talking.

Hackett and her daughter lived in a small apartment just down the street from the Saint-Gobain plant, one of the few that remains open and operating today. Hackett recalled how ash from the plants would settle like snow on the roofs of the town when she was a child. She and other kids would swim each summer in a pond that tested for PFOA at 1,000 parts per trillion as late as 2017, several years after DuPont had suspended the use of the chemical in Teflon manufacture. Given the chemical's slow but steady rate of decline over time, in the water as in the blood, how much exposure would Hackett have gotten over the years? "Think back and it would drive you nuts," she told me.

We sat in Hackett's living room, surrounded by potted plants and framed family photos dating back to the hamlet's boom time. Her laptop was cued to a live feed of a New York state legislative session on public health. Hackett's hands shook in frustration as she talked about these sessions. Like many there, she felt that state and local officials had downplayed the danger in their drinking water, trying to reassure rather than seeking to resolve. "From day one, you'd think we were wearing overalls, carrying a six-pack of Bud with a straw hanging out of our teeth, the comically stereotypical hick villager without the intelligence to understand the science," Hackett said, her eyes flashing as she described what it was like to testify before state health officials in Albany. "They didn't see us coming."

She sent me into the kitchen when we took a break from watching the section together. "Help yourself to some coffee." It struck me as a warm and inviting space, a jovial plaque—"Instant Human, Just Add Coffee"—hanging from one of the wood plank cabinets above the countertop coffeemaker. Beside the machine though, was a tell-tale sign of what had happened to domestic life in this small town: a gallon jug of Best Yet bottled spring water, with many more piled up in cases stacked beside the back door.

A state-of-the-art water filtration system had recently been added to the town's municipal water supply, "probably the cleanest water in the country now," as some in the town had said to me. Hackett, though, refused to drink from the tap without knowing that the filters could handle the range of chemicals possibly present in their water, in this place dense with the remnants of heavy industry. "I just want to know when I can drink from the damn faucet or give my kids or grandkids a drink of water," she told me that day in 2017. "Our water isn't *fixed*, like some people say. We are drinking poisoned, filtered water."

When Hackett was first tested for PFOA in 2016, the chemical level in her bloodstream was among the highest in the township. By the time we caught up once again seven years later, traces of the chemical in her body had slowly subsided but remained higher than 95 percent of the American population, as she recounted. She'd given up on holding out against the tainted and purified local water supply. "I can't get away from the stuff," she told me. "How hard do I need to keep trying to lower my level? It's stressful to do this every day."

By now regulatory agencies had identified thousands of discrete PFAS chemicals, of which only twenty-three were being monitored and tested. Every month, meanwhile, brought news of another staple product where PFAS residues had been found.[20] "It's in our makeup," Hackett noted. "It's in peanut butter, spaghetti sauce, shaving cream, diaper cream. It's in menstrual products, toilet paper. They're finding it everywhere, but nothing is labeled."

Some countries in Europe have begun to consider a ban on all nonessential uses of PFAS. But here in the United States, where the chemical industry dominated the regulatory system, protection from these contaminants seemed to be a dangerous illusion. "It's all chemicals," Hackett mused. "Is there even water in the water anymore?"

———

Water, that vital necessity and the substance most essential to our bodies, has become a source of great anxiety in many places around the United States. "The water from our taps today justifiably is regarded as safe by most people," environmental scholar James Salzman writes.[21] Nevertheless, the bottled water industry has managed to capitalize on widespread unease about the quality of public water supplies in the United States. American consumers now buy an astounding 75 billion disposable bottles of water each year, each a tiny enclosure of an essential resource, a shelter made for one.[22] Meanwhile, as interest and investment in shared public infrastructure lags, people are often left to subsist on contaminated public water supplies or forced to rely instead on such bottled alternatives.

In the fall of 2017, I attended a trade show in north Texas for the International Bottled Water Association. I registered for the conference as an academic observer, curious about how the industry made sense of itself. I was struck by the buoyant and combative tone that many participants projected, including bottling company executive and Ohio Republican politician Lynn Wachtmann, who had just become chairman of the association. "The activists are alive and well," he declared on the convention's main stage, which he had ascended to the strains of a loud guitar tune, but the industry would persevere "to fight back and beat down our enemies. With our combined efforts, we will continue to grow bottled water."

As one might expect at a bottled water convention, neat rows and clusters of fresh plastic water bottles were everywhere and free for the taking. Nearly everyone seemed to have a little bottle in hand, as if this was a basic necessity, a matter of vigilance, taking charge of your need for water wherever you went. I saw that people there tended to keep their bottles closed, screwing on the little plastic caps with every small sip. Trash containers were available at every turn to dispose of empties. I was struck by the resonance between this evident faith in a sealed bottle and a larger culture that celebrated the self-contained and invulnerable body.

One evening I spoke with a middle-aged white man in a brown suit who worked for a water conditioning company in west Texas. I had noticed his habit of crumpling up each disposable bottle into a little ball when it was empty, and I asked him about this gesture. "I like to put things away," he told me, describing how he'd throw these crinkled balls of plastic into the back of his SUV while he was driving. I couldn't help but imagine them piling up in heaps, a traveling signpost for the mountain of waste that all of us were building together.

To be sure, those who spoke at that convention usually insisted that their bottles were an alternative to sugary soft drinks, rather than a rejoinder to the tap. Still, as I wandered for a few days through the cavernous hallways of the center, I found that horror stories about dirty faucets and public fountains were almost inescapable. Everyone I spoke with disavowed the purity of what they called "public water." A Niagara company representative told me that he'd never drink from the tap at home, hadn't used a drinking fountain since he was a kid. "They're gross, disgusting!" he told me with a crinkled nose. "You just don't know what's in it, or on it."

Elsewhere in the exhibition hall, a small company from New York was marketing water filters. I was struck by their display, which featured a large-scale illustration of a stream of blue water running through a tall filter: brimming on one side with microbes and particles of many shapes and colors, and completely clear of these little bodies on the other. The representative on duty sported a bright purple tie and a lavender shirt to match. Walking me through their filtration process, he avowed that he'd never let his nephews and nieces put their mouths near a public drinking fountain. "I wouldn't drink that shit!" he told me with a goofy grin. "Believe me, if you've seen what I've seen, you wouldn't either."

The market was one that seemed to thrive on such insecurity. One morning I attended a talk about water and the health of the body. Cognition, mood, resistance to disease, even longevity — all these things could be compromised by minor levels of dehydration, the speaker insisted. Thirst was no reliable sign; by the time you felt it, your body already had less water than it needed. "You could, right now, be mildly dehydrated," the lecturer said, looking out from the podium with a small plastic bottle in his own hand. He would stop now and then for a dramatic sip, a little pedagogy, no doubt. And as he went on, I began to hear the crinkle of plastic here and there in the room, almost like a nervous reaction, people in the audience sipping from the tiny mouths of their own bottles. One woman got up to grab a handful of bottles for her table. Others stockpiled them as they headed out the door.

Public drinking fountains were switched off across the country in 2020 when the pandemic struck. But they'd already been disappearing for years, and whether they will return remains uncertain.[23] The clear liquid locked within a typical PET (polyethylene terephthalate) bottle may be no cleaner or safer than what comes out of public fountains or faucets; bottled water is regulated so loosely that its quality is difficult to judge.[24] Yet, with such water, many Americans have come to believe again in the safety of a resource untouched by the wrong people, a dark contemporary echo of the segregated fountains of the Jim Crow era. And as with that era, there remains a stark divide between those who can secure safe water for themselves and those who cannot.

———

The city of Newburgh rises above the western banks of the Hudson River, about a hundred miles south of Hoosick Falls. An important nucleus for industry and commerce in the nineteenth and twentieth centuries, this city has also grappled with the legacy of shuttered factories and the remnants they left behind. More than three quarters of the population is Black and brown by heritage: descendants of those who came for work in past decades from the South and elsewhere, and more recent migrants from Mexico, Peru, Ecuador, and other countries in Central and South America. The lead-lined pipes that comprise more than 40 percent of the city's water service lines have posed an enduring public health predicament for Newburgh's diverse residents.[25] Then in 2016, just a couple of years after the PFOA crisis broke in Hoosick Falls, residents of Newburgh discovered a new and related industrial contaminant in their own drinking water.

The city sourced its drinking water from a surface reservoir called Washington Lake on its western outskirts. Further west and further upstream from the reservoir is the Stewart Air National Guard Base. In early 2016, New York state officials identified high levels of another hazardous PFAS chemical—perfluorooctane sulfonate or PFOS—in the stormwater draining from the base into local waterways and eventually the reservoir.[26] Associated once again with a range of serious health problems, the chemical was a key component of the "aqueous firefighting foam" that had been used on the base for many years in training exercises and accident response protocols; it turned out that 4,000 gallons of the chemical had even been spilled by accident on the base in 1990.[27]

Newburgh's city manager declared a state of emergency in 2016, and the city began drawing its water from a different local pond, and later, with financial support from the state of New York, from the Catskills Aqueduct that supplied New York City. Newburgh has a new water treatment plant in place that includes an active carbon filter system to remove PFOS from its water supply.[28] But the airbase continues to use aqueous firefighting foam laced with PFAS chemicals, as do hundreds of other military bases around the country.[29] And after decades of ingesting contaminated water, Newburgh's residents have been found to carry high levels of several PFAS chemicals—including PFOS—in their blood.[30] "We don't see why the city of Newburgh, why us residents should carry the burden of filtering the toxins from the base," argues Ophra Wolf, one of the founders of the Newburgh Clean Water Project. "The base needs to stop the toxins from coming down the hill."[31]

The Newburgh Clean Water Project (NCWP) is a grassroots organization of volunteers who have led the local fight for clean water. As in Hoosick Falls, activists with the organization have mobilized around a more expansive picture of bodily health and environmental well-being. "The earth is really suffering because of all the advancements we've made," Gabrielle Burton-Hill—an African American civic leader and another founder of the NCWP—observed when we met in Newburgh in early 2023. "We're just disconnected all over the place, with each other, with the earth, with the community," she added, describing her environmental and social activism as a work of renewing connections.

We met at a creative and co-working space on Broadway called Grit Works. The space served as a base for workshops in community facilitation and restorative justice, using a method of dialogue circles developed by another local organization, the Restorative Center, to which Burton-Hill also belonged.[32] With these circles, which Burton-Hill was trained to lead, "people speak from the heart, not from the head," she told me. The approach was meant to encourage people to take part in charged conversations in a spirit of vulnerability and trust. "It's a space where we don't have to put up any walls or facades," the activist explained.

In 2017, the NCWP kicked off their organizing for clean water with a series of circles called "I Am Water." Participants were encouraged to reflect on their own intimate relationships with water: where they had first learned to swim, what they drank and cooked with, the waters of the womb from which they had come into the earth, water as the substance of their living bodies. "We had to start with our own bodies before going to the body of water itself," Burton-Hill explained to me. I found myself struck by the profound truth in what she said. Body and environment are inextricably tied together, as a common medium of well-being.

For environmental justice communities like Newburgh, this a hard-won lesson. "In a community that is already disproportionately impacted by other environmental exposures," as epidemiologist Erin Bell, who is leading a study of PFAS and public health in Newburgh and Hoosick Falls has observed, "we are concerned that these exposures might have a greater impact than they otherwise would."[33] Burton-Hill's own daughter was hospitalized for seven days when she was eighteen months old so that doctors could address the alarming levels of lead that had been found in her bloodstream. Her granddaughter was born without a left forearm, possibly related, as Burton-Hill sees it, to the environmental poisons the family had absorbed.[34] "If clean water is a human right, why isn't the government providing that for its citizens?" she asked me pointedly.[35]

Burton-Hill was a warm and engaging presence. The word "LOVE" ran along both sleeves of the pullover she was wearing when we met in Newburgh, and as we walked around together, she greeted others who passed by in an effusive manner. Still, I could feel the caution with which she had learned to live. She took me to a nearby market to buy a gallon jug of Poland Spring water to rely on as we spoke. And she admitted that after decades of dealing with the lead in their pipes and the other contaminants that had since surfaced, she struggled with trusting the city's tap water, even with the new water treatment systems in place.

"Six months from now, it'll be some other thing," Burton-Hill speculated about that water. And she also conveyed the heavy burden—personal and financial, but also moral and environmental—of having to live with such conditions of environmental neglect, and the distrust and further damage they provoked. "We stopped drinking the water because of the lead. We started buying plastic bottles, causing more harm to the planet. How many bottles have we put into the community?"

An Air National Guard base was established west of Newburgh as an institution for national defense. The firefighting chemicals leaking into the local water from that base and from countless other military facilities around the country were designed once again with protection in mind. On account of that contaminated water, people in such places have come to rely on bottled water and other alternatives, also in the name of safety and security. At a larger and collective scale, however, it is increasingly difficult to live with the consequences of all these decisions. And as we see in places like Newburgh and Hoosick Falls, the burden of unlivable circumstance is starkly unequal, felt deeply by some and hardly at all by others.

The future of Newburgh's water remains muddied and uncertain. The city is locked in litigation with many parties including the Department of Defense. The Stewart Air National Guard Base has been listed as a New York State Superfund site, required to follow mandatory cleanup protocols, and a Restoration Advisory Committee—including representatives from the National Guard base, local government officials, members of the NCWP, and other local community representatives—has been established to guide the slow process of environmental remediation.[36] With financial support from the state of New York, Newburgh continues to tap drinking water from the aqueduct connecting the Catskill Mountains to New York City. And even if means are devised to filter PFAS definitively from the city's local water supply, a cascade of other problems has erupted on the lands around the base.

Newburgh is a compact city inhabited mostly by residents of color. The city is surrounded by an independent town—also, confusingly, named Newburgh—with a population of comparable size living on ten times the land area; it is much wealthier and mostly white. Newburgh city draws its water from the landscape of Newburgh town: lands belonging to the town form the catchment area for the surface reservoir that holds the city's water. And here, aside from the concerns posed by the local air base, patterns of commercial and transportation development over the last few decades have compromised the quality of water running through this watershed in countless other ways.

I got a vivid sense of this predicament one morning in a tour around the watershed with Chuck Thomas, a member of the Quassaick Creek Watershed Alliance and the chair of Newburgh city's Conservation Advisory Council. He took me by car through a sprawling terrain of big-box retail complexes and commercial warehouses, massive buildings strung along the I-84 and I-87 interstates and other major thoroughfares. These roadways crisscrossed what had once been a rolling landscape of family farms interspersed with wetlands, their open space lost to the acreage of parking lots, real estate sub-divisions, and asphalt corridors. The Newburgh Clean Water Project has been organizing around these developments as well, fighting new retail and com-mercial projects and holding regular watershed tours to bring home the en-vironmental significance of this terrain.[37] But the city's clean water advocates have little purchase on the decisions made by the Newburgh Town Council. Local zoning regulations and land use laws have failed to recognize the eco-logical interdependence of upstream and downstream communities.

Still, as Thomas showed me, the water is everywhere—tucked out of sight yet flowing ineluctably downstream, through the paved streets, grassy lawns, and sprawling parking lots of these developments, toward the res-ervoir that holds the city's contaminated supply and then the Hudson River beyond: vegetated swales and streamlets lodged between the parking areas of adjacent constructions; narrow channels of water running between and even underneath the shopping complexes; a puddle that may have been some solace to a deer marooned between two daunting streams of traffic; a small pond jammed between an interstate and a new Walmart, harboring redwing blackbirds, a red-tailed hawk, even a pair of white swans, the raucous call of blue jays still audible over the vehicular din beyond.

I was shaken by what we saw: the landscape of oil-fueled commerce that collected the water that those downstream were meant to drink and live with. "Doesn't it break your heart?" I couldn't help but blurt out as we drove.

"It does," Thomas replied. "Watersheds are incredible resources. Look at all the life they support." But he also told me that he was a believer in the sci-ence of water filtration and watershed management. "I want it clean. If noth-ing else, we're dumping it into the Hudson River from here, and it spreads into the world from there."

It felt as profound as a Gestalt shift, exploring this urbanizing landscape with Thomas that morning. Seen one way, this was just another site of subur-ban sprawl and highway-driven development, its looming warehouses cater-ing to every need that people in this country had learned to have—including, no doubt, packaged water and other bottled drinks. But seen again with such water and the nature of its movement in mind, the environment was some-thing else altogether: a place to gather up and pass along the substance most necessary for all the life bustling around us. Individual human bodies locked within the wheeled mechanical bodies that took them in and out of this place might have the freedom to come and go as they wished, but they could not shake this ultimate truth: there was a larger body responsible for their well-being, the landscape of an earth that needed protection as well.

Ronald Zorrilla, founder of a local urban environmental organization called Outdoor Promise, put it plainly when we met later that afternoon. "Imagine our veins getting blocked," Zorrilla said. "We're clogging our arteries, giving ourselves a heart attack." Zorrilla invoked an ecological body as he spoke, far bigger in scope and significance, encompassing the individual needs and boundaries that we tend to take for granted as embodied beings.

The lessons of such perspective may be sought in many ways, including the nature of the Hudson River itself at this point. The Hudson here is less a river than a tidal estuary, its waters heading out and coming back many times each day, always bringing other things in their wake. Looming over the river just south of Newburgh is Storm King Mountain, where a power plant proposed in the 1960s galvanized the modern American environmental movement.[38]

The tides of that history return with every new struggle both here and beyond, as with the tides of the river and even the walls of the body itself. Nothing can be cast definitively beyond. Things we relinquish tend to return. And there is a justice yet be found in that ebb and flow.

PART IV
WALLS OF THE MIND

TEN

MASKED REALITIES

SOUTHERN MICHIGAN

On March 11, 2020, the World Health Organization declared that the accelerating global outbreak of COVID-19 had become a pandemic. On the same day, my university suspended all in-person classes, and we plunged headlong into a new reality of distant and uneasy life. One year later, the virus still ran rampant in Brazil, Mexico, and many other countries. A devastating second wave of infection was just beginning in India. But the United States finally seemed to be turning a corner. I received my own first dose of a vaccine at the Baltimore Convention Center on March 11, 2021. "Feels pretty momentous," I wrote to an acquaintance in Michigan as I sat through the mandatory fifteen-minute observation period, adding a selfie with the map-printed face mask I had taken to wearing. "It was exactly one year ago that our university shut down."

Frank wrote back almost immediately from his small town in southern Michigan. "Momentous, yes. But not for the reasons you subscribe to. Compliance, control, and capitulation. I truly detest pictures with face diapers on.

Seriously, I do. At your age are you seriously that scared of this? Really? I've never had one day of fear from the virus. Not one."

It was less fear that brought me there than a sense of responsibility, especially for the more vulnerable people in our daily orbit. I felt lucky to have gotten an appointment, and I found the operation that morning impressive and efficient. The convention center had been repurposed as a field hospital, and they were now vaccinating over 2,000 people each day. Cordoned lines ran around and within that cavernous space, with staff well-versed in the procedures they were following, systems in place to check in and register, and chairs spread widely to maintain physical distance. Frank noticed all this too, in the background of the photo I sent him.

"The chairs spaced apart behind you are truly laughable to me," he wrote. "You should have taken me up on my offer and come out here and witnessed how other people lived. Why would I get a vaccine for a cold that I'm 99.9 percent sure to survive? This entire fiasco is almost a joke." He told me about a funeral he had just attended in his town. Two fifths of the well-wishers had declined to wear face masks. "Hugging, shaking hands, everyone mingling. Almost like a real free America . . . almost."

Frank was a businessman, with a handful of restaurants in Michigan and Indiana. He was hardly a heedless and wanton soul, having cobbled together some financial security after many years of struggle. He was seriously worried about things I hardly ever thought about: the danger that Islamist extremists could bring to his small town in southern Michigan, or the violent elements that might infiltrate the country through the southern border of the United States, more than 1,500 miles away. If these were indeed serious concerns, as Frank insisted, why wouldn't a pandemic inspire the same spirit of vigilance? As Trevor Noah put it in the spring of 2020 in a *Daily Show* segment about pandemic face masks—and President Trump's own refusal to wear one: "No, Mr. President, it's not a mask. It's a border wall for your face."[1]

There is something peculiar about the deep opposition we have seen, in American conservative circles, to face masks, vaccines, and other forms of pandemic protection. Why would a politics so keen on safety—"more attuned to external threat and internal contamination," as Ross Douthat observed in an interesting column for the *New York Times*—react to the coronavirus with such flippancy?[2] We have seen how ideas of safety and security manifest themselves in many kinds of physical and figurative walls in the contemporary United States, from the scale of the individual body to the nation as a whole. But there's no reason to expect that these boundaries will always line up neatly with each other. COVID-19 slipped into and spread throughout the United States on account of a different kind of barrier running through the full span of American life—what we might describe as a *wall of mind.*

As we now know, Americans have profoundly different ideas about what is simply real, ideas that sometimes verge on the irreconcilable. These notions depend on walls of the mind: the stubborn boundaries of idea and information that work to enforce particular points of view, that make it possible to commit oneself fully to a private reality, as if each of us was stranded on some island of idiosyncratic thought. Such divides may seem fleeting and intangible, but they are just as hard as anything made of brick or concrete. As Governor Jim Justice of West Virginia said in the spring of 2021, with the same phrase used by countless public officials wrestling with COVID-19 vaccine refusals in much of the United States, "we have hit a wall."[3]

How are such walls of the mind built up, and what would it take to bring them down? I first got to know Frank (as I call him) during fieldwork in the Midwest in the summer of 2017. We kept in touch over the years, corresponding often by text during the first year of the pandemic. Throughout those months, Frank maintained a steadfast refusal to wear a face mask, which he described to me as a muzzle, a slave mask, a face diaper, and an embodiment of tyranny. We traded countless heated messages, arguing over the basic facts of the virus. Neither persuaded the other of anything in these debates. But I did come to appreciate, over time, why our differences of opinion were as deep as they were and the foundations that anchored our rival judgments.

Frank and I face each other across the chasm of polarization, the growing tendency to disparage those across the political aisle as enemies and villains.[4] Vaccines and face masks have been made into highly partisan commitments, making it hard to see those who choose otherwise as anything but senseless and unhinged. Throughout the pandemic, situations of structural neglect and exploitation kept vaccines out of reach for many poor people of color in the United States. But the "red state" problem with vaccines—stubbornly low rates of vaccination in the states and counties with the broadest white Republican base—represents something else: less hesitancy than outright refusal.[5]

These patterns of refusal are so consequential that the excess death rate due to the coronavirus pandemic in the United States has been as much as 76 percent higher for Republicans than for Democrats.[6]

Many may find it tempting to take such data as evidence of a "pandemic of the unvaccinated," endured by heedless people elsewhere living out the consequences of choices they might not make themselves.[7] The mistrust and disdain are corrosive, the temptation to turn away all too inviting. Still, as the gravity and endurance of the pandemic suggests, our fates remain hitched together, even when we can't stand talking to each other. The consequences of the choices that others make will continue to haunt us all.

The 1776 pamphlet by Thomas Paine that spurred the American Revolution was one that trusted in the value of *common sense*, that a reader faced with its facts and arguments would "divest himself of prejudice and prepossession," would accept the invitation to "generously enlarge his views beyond the present day."[8] These are perilous times to place such faith in the judgments of our compatriots. And yet, as ever, we may have no choice but this faith.

Frank and I are each committed to ways of living that the other finds reckless. Frank prides himself on being an American capitalist, and scoffs at the idea our economy might promote climate change, right-wing political violence, or impossible degrees of inequality. I, meanwhile, no doubt fit his stereotype of the oblivious college professor, lecturing privileged kids about utopian futures while freedoms crumble around us. Over the years, Frank and I have had passionate quarrels about the truth of the pandemic, the outcome of the 2020 presidential election, or what happened at the Capitol on January 6, 2021, on a day when Frank too had come to protest in Washington.

Everything seems to conspire against the very possibility of our conversing. What dialogue is possible when the basic truths of reality itself seem so tenuous and debatable, and when the gulf between rival perspectives becomes a matter of life and death? Such moments of closure are dispiriting but also edifying. Dialogue may have little promise when our most essential collective institutions seem to tear us asunder. But the pursuit of such conversations can at least bring home how much work there is to do. We ought to try and grasp them as carefully as possible: when exactly they manage to work, when they might begin to break down.

Frank and I first met in 2017 at FreedomFest, an annual libertarian conference and conservative cultural festival in Las Vegas, billed as "the world's largest gathering of free minds."[9] The event was sponsored in part by the Atlas Society, an organization dedicated to preserving writer Ayn Rand's intellectual legacy. I quickly gathered that many there prided themselves on contrarian viewpoints, no matter how awkward their social implications. "Envy is the root of all evil," a young woman declared to loud cheering, during one panel on Rand. "Let's face it," the CEO of the Atlas Society added, a big gold $ brooch pinned to her dress in homage to the writer: "Social justice is envy, their way of making a virtue out of a vice."

There were a fair number of young people wandering through these hallways, like the college students wearing black "Less Marx, More Mises" T-shirts in honor of the Austrian free market economist. Many voiced candid suspicions of politicians, financiers, and professors like myself. The conference also drew older men and women, some of them wearing red MAGA hats. "There's so much think about," a seventy-three-year-old real estate broker told me after one panel, a button denouncing political correctness pinned beside the Republican Party patch on his backpack. "At my age, you've got to keep your mind active. This is food for the soul."

For me, FreedomFest was a difficult place for such freedom of thought. To be sure, you could see Ayn Rand go head-to-head in spirited debate with a powdered Ben Franklin under the spotlights of the main stage at the Paris Las Vegas resort. But I often felt like I'd landed amid the cogs of a political entertainment machine, greased with plenty of wealth and glitz. "All the smarter, funnier people are on our side now," Greg Gutfeld of Fox News joked one day, and indeed, "the left" was a pervasive specter, constantly conjured up and dismissed as a worthless antagonist. There was also the sense of doubt that an emphatic individualism could insinuate into any encounter. "They're all hawking, they're all selling," one elderly attendee warned as we walked out of a marquee session together, advising that I ought not to trust what was just said.

Frank and I wound up sitting next to each other at a few of the conference sessions. I was struck by his friendly demeanor and his candor. Ayn Rand's

Atlas Shrugged, he volunteered, was the best book he'd ever read: "I remember reading it and thinking, *This is exactly what I am.*" After a rambling hour of keynote musings by William Shatner one evening, we walked over to a hotel bar, getting caught up in a good-natured verbal duel that lasted many hours and many rounds.

It quickly became obvious that we hardly agreed on anything. I was disturbed by the conference speakers who ridiculed the idea of a livable minimum wage. He talked about the high school kids who worked for him in southern Michigan and high wages as a ticket to inertia. I asked the bartender for a drink without a straw, explaining I was concerned about disposable plastic. "I love plastic," Frank responded with a mischievous smile.

Frank had been a wrestler in high school, and clearly both of us enjoyed the verbal jousting. We kept in touch. Later that summer, I visited his town for a few days and learned more about his life. Frank's father had been a tool and die maker at an auto plant. Unable to afford college, Frank floated around for a few years, working oil fields in North Dakota, selling vacuum cleaners in Texas, keeping bees with a friend. A restaurant he started finally took off; now, in his fifties, he was still opening new places and putting his earnings into new properties.

"I've got shit everywhere," he said with a self-deprecating laugh as he drove me around his town. "I think it comes from being poor. It's like Monopoly—you just want to collect what you can before you lose it all."

Later that afternoon, we settled into a long conversation on the back porch of his cabin beside the local lake. The stark differences between us became quickly apparent once again. I was worried about neglected and mounting ecological crises, a dark imagination of what lay ahead. Frank, meanwhile, pulled out a copy of *Abundance: The Future Is Better Than You Think* from a bookshelf.[10] "Let's not forget that a rising tide lifts all boats. Entrepreneurs have lifted all of us up."

He picked up the cell phone lying on the table between us. "This is the greatest tool in the world. It's a business in my pocket. Look what it's done for Africa, the poorest of the poor. You can get every piece of information in the world on this little thing. Do we need libraries anymore, in every little town in America? Isn't that a waste?"

"But this is why we have institutions of learning," I shot back, alarmed. "They've got editors and librarians that we've decided to trust, to weed out the nonsense. Don't we need that? Can we really just trust people to figure it all out on their own?"

"I don't know if we can trust anybody, if we can trust any side," he responded. "They're all so invested. Who's the librarian? Is it a leftist, a rightist, a libertarian? At the end of the day, you really don't know what's in the mind of someone, right?"

"That's just it," I said. "If we've become so mistrustful of common sense, if everything begins to look so ideological that we can't even trust how a library is curated, how on earth can we see eye to eye? You trust your platforms, I trust my platforms, we see completely different things. How can there be common sense when we don't have a sense of things in common?"

"I don't know," Frank laughed. "You do say something that makes sense. I love that phrase, *common sense*. You don't have to be a genius, you don't have to be a scholar. But if you come over here and live in your own bubble, if you don't learn the language, if you get by your entire life, how does that help us communicate?"

We switched phones for a few minutes, looking at each other's Facebook feeds. Scrolling through them, you would think we lived in parallel universes. I had news of polluted water in the Gulf of Mexico and a sanitation campaign in India. He had alarming reports on sanctuary cities and the stifling of free speech on college campuses. The very sense of what was happening in the world—whether worrisome or worth celebrating—was starkly different on these screens.

"Personalization filters serve up a kind of invisible autopropaganda," Eli Pariser notes in *The Filter Bubble*, "indoctrinating us with our own ideas, amplifying our desire for things that are familiar and leaving us oblivious to the dangers lurking in the dark territory of the unknown."[11] Facebook used to call it "the wall," the space where each user's personal stream was posted and displayed. Though that term has now fallen by the wayside, I had the strong feeling, looking at Frank's newsfeed that afternoon, that social media still worked this way, like a wall or barrier between one private reality and another.[12] No wonder we disagreed so much.

As the coronavirus pandemic took hold in the spring of 2020, my Facebook feed grew dense with confusion and alarm. Frank's did too, but for different reasons. I anxiously tracked the development of an international crisis; Frank pieced together evidence of an unfolding "plandemic."[13] That March and April, I shared certain things that came my way via social media: on the collapse of public trust in the United States; on mutual aid and the politics of care; on the situation in India, Vietnam, and elsewhere. Day by day, meanwhile, Frank passed along skeptical claims about the gravity of the pandemic, jokes and memes about liberals, laments about people turning against their neighbors and giving in to irrational fears.

The internet and online social media and information platforms do more than change the contours of the reality we see. As researchers have shown, these platforms have been rewiring our brains, changing the neural networks of our minds and the way we think and act. "As the time we spend hopping across links crowds out the time we devote to quiet reflection and contemplation, the circuits that support those old intellectual functions and pursuits weaken and begin to break apart," writer Nicholas Carr observes in *The Shallows: What the Internet Is Doing to Our Brains*.[14] Stark emotional appeals drive traffic on profit-seeking media platforms, but they can also transform the basic sense of what the world demands of us.

In those intense and uncertain early months of the pandemic, Frank was especially furious about the restrictions imposed by Governor Gretchen Whitmer in his home state of Michigan. That April, he drove into Lansing with thousands of others, jamming the streets around the capitol for hours. One of the first anti-lockdown protests in the United States, "Operation Gridlock" in Michigan foreshadowed more violent events to come: an armed occupation of the statehouse and even a foiled plot to kidnap the state's governor.[15]

"It was the worst traffic I've ever seen," Frank chuckled on the phone, two days later.

His business had shifted to takeout sales, but others were folding, and he foresaw an economic disaster. "I'm good with 200,000 people dying," Frank told me flatly that day, insisting that a depression would bring more pain.

Over the next few months, we argued regularly by text. I tried to convince him the virus was serious, that masks were meant to protect others more than oneself. I showed him the sign my family had put up in front of our house for Halloween: "No Masks, No Candy."

"That's sad, perpetuating the fear," Frank replied, sending a different image my way: a sketch of an enslaved eighteenth-century Afro-Brazilian woman named Anastacia, mask over her mouth and a collar around her neck, an offensive image that has circulated widely as an anti-masking meme.[16] "That's what we did to slaves to show who controlled whom."

A middle-aged white man, Frank often used such language to decry mask mandates: being shackled, muzzled. "Your side enslaved me and my family."

"It's hardly the same," I had to say. I wrote to him about the history of racism in the United States, describing things that even my own Indian American immigrant family had endured. "Slavery is not a metaphor. It was a historical fact with effects that echo today."

"You know exactly what I mean," Frank replied. "It is humiliating. It is emasculating. And it's all based on a lie."

I found what he said preposterous and disturbing, a brazen assertion of white privilege. But his claims were anchored in a steady stream of right-wing media pronouncements that lent them legitimacy. Conservative politicians had even turned George Floyd's dying words—"I can't breathe"—into an anti-masking gibe.[17]

Floyd's harrowing last words catalyzed one of the biggest solidarity movements in the history of the United States.[18] But elsewhere, social media was working to inoculate people like Frank against the power of these words, sowing indifference instead of concern: an inability to register the experience of others unlike oneself.

"I need the boot off my neck," he kept telling me.

One evening that winter, Frank sent me a video message from a small town in northern Indiana: dozens of men and women packed indoors at the sports bar, not a mask in sight. I felt a pang at this glimpse of their easy laughter. One of my father's closest friends had just died from the virus in another small town not far from there. He'd served that community for forty years as a doctor and had most likely contracted the disease from one of his patients, who were often reluctant to wear face masks.

When I shared the story, Frank was undeterred. "People die. I've never been afraid of it. I know it's coming."

I was feeling hurt and a little combative myself, and I started throwing facts and statistics back at him. "People are playing Russian roulette with the lives of their own neighbors, in the name of freedom, and the numbers show the price," I shot back.

Frank remained defiant. "Freedom is more important to me."

————————

The morning after Election Day in November of 2020, I checked in with Frank. "How are you feeling this morning? Get any sleep?"

"I'm feeling terrible Anand," he replied. As he saw it, the theft of a presidential election was picking up speed. "I'm so sick of the left and the media. And I'm embarrassed that half the country could vote for more welfare, 'free' this and 'free' that."

His reply was eye-opening. "Mirror opposites, the frames of reference in our respective communities," I wrote back. "My social media feeds are full of people expressing shame about the other side, that half the country would appear to support racism, xenophobia, sexism, and white supremacy."

We each shared evidence from sources that we trusted: me from the *New York Times* and the *Washington Post*, he from the *Gateway Pundit* and the *Bongino Report*. "My frame of reference is correct," Frank insisted. "Your side is not." And on it went.

"When distrust of one's fellow citizens pervades democratic relations, it paralyzes democracy; it means that citizens no longer think it sensible, or feel secure enough, to place their fates in the hands of democratic strangers," political scientist Danielle Allen writes in *Talking to Strangers*.[19] But there is also recourse, she argues, in the cultivation of what she calls "political friendship," founded on "the recognition of a shared horizon of experience" and a commitment "to prove oneself trustworthy to fellow citizens."[20]

I've heard many a tirade from Frank over the years about "handouts" and the welfare state, but he has also demonstrated generosity time and again in his own way. He's flown out from Michigan at the drop of a hat to help distribute food to hurricane victims, or to stack sandbags against an impending flood. He's dismissed the risks of a coronavirus infection, but also donated thousands of dollars to small restaurants ailing under lockdown.

Knowing that there are people instead of monsters on the other side doesn't tell us anything about how to live with them. The fissures run deep, and the Capitol invasion in January 2021 should warn us that such bridges may prove a dangerous illusion. Still, there's something to be said for the value of such mutual understanding: if not to come to some agreement, then at least to grasp the roots of those convictions in the rhythms of other lives.

New organizations like Braver Angels have sought to work in this spirit, drawing on techniques from couples therapy to foster conversation between people who identify as liberal and conservative.[21] As Frank and I stumbled over impasse after impasse in the weeks after the 2020 presidential election, I suggested lightheartedly that we participate together in one of their workshops. "I am in no mood to reconcile with people that called me every pejorative in the book," Frank retorted gruffly. "That we must heal as a nation—what utter BS."

Soon after the pandemic lockdowns began, Frank got a yellow rattlesnake tattoo, along with that familiar rallying cry, "Don't Tread on Me." His social media posts grew angrier than I'd ever seen them. He was convinced that the panic over the virus was manufactured to perpetrate political fraud and steal the presidency from Donald Trump.

On January 6, 2021, Frank and a friend drove to DC for Trump's #StopThe Steal rally. "I will never stand at a 4th of July parade and pretend to be free again," he wrote me on the way. The next morning, he joined thousands of others at the rally, which he described as "massive, and peaceful." Instead of marching to the Capitol, he headed back to Michigan.

We'd been glued to a screen at home, watching what unfolded with horror. "This is the seat of government. It looks like an insurrection at the capitol," I texted.

"Maybe an insurrection is what it's gonna take," he shot back.

Frank wouldn't condone the violence at the Capitol. But he also wanted me to understand why people were so angry. "Treat me like a child, you expect me not to be pissed?!"

"Every day is a punch in the face with you guys," he added a few days later. "From f-ing straws, to sodas, to not smoking in my own restaurant, to seat belts, to threatening my guns, to forcing me to wear a mask . . . Every f-ing day, it's something else with you guys."

With what he said, the difference in our perspectives snapped sharply into focus. For Frank, the storming of the Capitol was retaliation: the outburst of a populace long under siege, struggling against a power constantly wielded in the name of care. From his standpoint, the uprising at the Capitol was less a violent eruption in the midst of peace than an aggressive response to ongoing forms of domination. As he saw it, people like him had been victimized, were fed up. And with all the influential conservative voices on his side — posts he kept passing along — nothing I said could shake this conviction.

"We just want to live our f-ing lives and be left alone," Frank told me.

Who did he have in mind when he used that word, "we"? How broad was that community? So much seems to depend on the lines we draw, what we feel we owe to others within and beyond those boundaries.

"I'm good with dividing the country," Frank declared. "One side gets the west and one side gets the east. We are self-sufficient. Your side is not."

"Whether it's capital or labor, land, air, or water, we're stuck together, left and right," I replied. "We do in fact need each other."

This became, for us, a familiar impasse. I'd tell Frank that we need to learn how to live together, that the country and planet need this. "I'm over this," he'd retort. "I'm going to build my little hamlet."

For many, the pandemic has revealed the porous nature of our bodies and lives: the invisible ties between one and another, the need to do well by others. For others, as we have also seen, it has affirmed the value of keeping apart, entrenching the deep histories of property, segregation, and isolation that secure white well-being in the United States.

"Why is this correspondence worthwhile for you?" I asked Frank a few days after the assault on the Capitol. "We spend so much time writing to each other. Why do you bother, if folks like me feel like such a problem to you?"

"Just clutching at straws," he responded. "Trying to open up eyes, mostly to no avail."

Ayn Rand's 1943 novel *The Fountainhead* culminates in a packed courtroom on the outskirts of New York City. Architect Howard Roark is on trial. He is charged with dynamiting a building he had sketched out himself, because its design was bent far afield from his original vision. The building, as it happens, was a low-income public housing project. "To the majority of us it will appear monstrous and inconceivable," the prosecutor declares.[22] The defendant objects in a long and impassioned soliloquy, explaining why he found its evolution so intolerable. He is acquitted by the jury and invited to rebuild what he has destroyed, this time exactly on his own terms. What does the victory stand for, in this nakedly allegorical tale?

"Man cannot survive except through his mind," Roark argues on the stand. "From the simplest necessity to the highest religious abstraction, from the wheel to the skyscraper, everything we are and everything we have comes from a single attribute of man—the function of his reasoning mind." And yet, Roark goes on, "the mind is an attribute of the individual. There is no such thing as a collective brain. There is no such thing as a collective thought."[23]

In Rand's novel, iconoclast Roark is a creator, perhaps the very paragon of a creator. The high walls he raises as an architect stand for "the heroic in man," the vast span of human ambition rising up to dominate nature and the earth. All these powers can only ensue, however, from a personal character completely aloof from the highs and lows of social life, an "iron conviction . . . which cannot be influenced by anything and anyone on the outside."[24]

Here, the path of the true individual seems to depend on a complete blindness to the will of others, a total absence of mutual regard. As Rand put it, Roark is "a man so impervious to compulsion that he became a kind of compulsion himself."[25]

Ayn Rand also saw herself in these terms. Rand came "to believe that her individual effort had solely shaped her ideas and driven her work," historian Jennifer Burns writes in her biography of Rand, *Goddess of the Market.*[26] But, as Burns shows, the truth of Rand's life and work could hardly be so simple. From the New York Public Library staff who sourced her books on architecture to the friends and acquaintances on whom these literary characters were modeled, from the fellow writers who helped her work through creative blocks to the amphetamines that Rand like others took for momentum, *The Fountainhead* took shape in a profoundly collective world of intellectual and creative life.

Fiction itself is hardly the province of isolated minds, Rand herself acknowledged. "Spreading our ideas in the form of fiction is a great weapon," the writer noted to a merchant friend shortly after *The Fountainhead*'s release: "it arouses the public to an emotional, as well as intellectual response to our cause."[27]

From a contemporary vantage point, these words have a prophetic quality. The fever pitch of partisan politics today is driven by stories that often have the most tenuous connection with reality. I learned this myself in the fall of 2021, in sharing the story of my conversations with Frank in the form of an essay for *The Guardian*.[28] Within three days of its publication, more than half a million people had read the piece. Reactions were startlingly different, and often quite virulent. Someone took the time to type and mail an anonymous threat from the Midwest to my campus address in Baltimore. Readers on the right condemned the essay as patronizing and untrue. Readers on the left excoriated me for my indulgence of Frank. The words were what they were, but like a Rorschach inkblot, people found in them profoundly different things.

Meanwhile, Frank and I had also stopped talking. For months, we had texted daily, even several times a day now and then. He faulted me for cozying up with the "totalitarians." Still, he was willing to keep up with our exchange, which eventually spanned more than 25,000 words. Then something changed when I shared some of the writing I was working on, an early draft of the essay about our conversations that I eventually published in *The Guardian*. "Being called a racist and a misogynist just about does it for me," he told me, among other things. And though I tried to explain that I was seeking to convey exactly this difficulty, the challenge of seeing oneself and one's own perspectives from a radically different point of view, it was clear that this exercise appealed much more to me than to him. Just like that, he stopped writing to me.

Now and then on social media, I would run across memes that Frank posted about the pandemic. Amid the daunting new surge of COVID-19 cases that summer of 2021, he shared a simple way to protect yourself from the spread of the virus: just plug your ears to block out the news. Like many, he remained steadfast in his refusal to wear a mask or take the vaccine. He'd probably had the illness and overcome it already, he would sometimes say, tough like the former president he revered. Things that I found alarming—harsh words for public health officials, disruptions of school board meetings, harassment of store workers trying to enforce pandemic restrictions—

looked to him like assertions of freedom. He and I felt very differently about such matters, but we had lost the ability to share those differences with each other.

In our exchanges, Frank would often rail against cities like Baltimore, insisting that liberal public officials and citizens like me had let them crumble. But now, as I write these words in the spring of 2023, three years after the start of the pandemic, the evidence suggests that his rural region in southern Michigan has suffered more from the disease than my city. Overall life expectancy remains much higher there than in Baltimore, due to structural conditions of social and racial inequality. Yet, with vaccination rates remaining quite low in that part of Michigan, the mortality rate for COVID-19 is 17 percent higher in his county than in the city where I live. In an adjacent rural county in southern Michigan, where Frank has another restaurant and spends much of his time, the coronavirus mortality rate is 45 percent higher than in Baltimore.[29]

Given all of this, I hope we and other people in our respective places stay well. For masks and vaccines acknowledge something Frank was reluctant to admit in all our exchanges: the truth of our vulnerability, our capacity to wound and be wounded by others. I don't know if he and I will ever talk again. And yet we remain exposed to each other's whims and disdains. One way or another, we'll have to figure out what to do with each other's company.

ELEVEN

TURNING RIGHT AND LEFT

SOUTHERN CALIFORNIA

The alt-right Breitbart News Network is headquartered in a nondescript office building on San Vicente Boulevard in West Los Angeles. The building was less than a mile away from where we lived for much of 2017, and I drove or biked past it countless times. There was no signage outside that brick building with dark tinted windows. Nor was there any evidence of the company's presence in the lobby inside.

That year, Breitbart had become one of the most influential conservative outlets in the country, and I was profoundly curious about what went on inside the building—the hashtag #war on the boardroom door, for example, that journalists had reported seeing.[1] But there was no obvious way to approach the company for a visit, or for the beginnings of a conversation.

Eventually, a mutual acquaintance put me in touch with one of Breitbart's senior editors. "I am out of town at the moment, visiting my early hominid ancestors, *homo conservitus*," the editor joked in reply. I was surprised by his lighthearted tone and his jest about anthropology. He offered a half-hour meeting at a nearby café, requesting that the conversation be off-the-record and asking what I hoped to accomplish in our meeting.

"As an anthropologist, my method is to canvass firsthand perspectives and contrary points of view on topics that people would otherwise tend to take for granted," I replied. "I would like to interview you briefly regarding your sense of Breitbart's role in shaping public opinion in the country at present," I wrote, an earnest entreaty in what felt like an unexpected opening for dialogue. "Lastly, I have read intriguing reports about your #war room and would like to give, in my own writing, if possible, a brief sense of what your operation looks like from the inside, to better situate and contextualize the stories that one finds on the website."

Soon enough, I learned that I had pushed too far. "There is no way I can discuss what goes on 'inside' the company, especially as we have never met," the editor wrote back. "To me that is a red flag, and I am afraid I have to cancel our meeting." Dozens of journalists sought him out each day, he added, "and most of them have malevolent intentions, either political or commercial."

The turn in tone was swift and unexpected, and there was no going back. A wall had gone up, impossible to scale. "That was a bad week," he finally conceded a few months later when we crossed paths briefly at FreedomFest in Las Vegas. "We were getting threats. We had a bunker mentality." But we never had another chance to talk.

I've since replayed this exchange many times over in my head. Was there malice in what I wrote? I'd clearly come across as far too eager. And you don't have to be an anthropologist to know that social life always has the potential for overstepped boundaries and defensive reactions. How to make this feel more like a friendly knock on the door than a home invasion?

"I'm at war with the mainstream media because they portray themselves as objective observers of reality when they're no such thing," the late Andrew Breitbart wrote in his memoir, *Righteous Indignation*. The book by the founder of the Breitbart News Network reads like something between a bemusing coming-of-age story and a hard-nosed primer for cultural insurrection, taking on the task of grasping, as Breitbart puts it, "the architecture of a world that I resided in but couldn't see completely: the Democrat-Media Complex."[2] How is our sense of reality shaped by such media? And what does it mean to try to look beyond them?

This challenge is particularly interesting in Breitbart's case because of where he grew up, in one of the bastions of America's liberal elite, the glitzy suburbs of West LA. And it brings into focus, therefore, a larger mystery: the question of how people form their views of the world and their sense of political necessity. For despite its reputation as a liberal utopia, Southern California has long been a crucial fount of American conservatism.[3] Both Reagan and Nixon have their presidential libraries there. The Claremont Institute is a highly influential center for conservative political thought, while many prominent media personalities on the right—Matt Drudge, Hugh Hewitt, Dennis Prager, Ben Shapiro—launched their careers in the Los Angeles area. Stephen Miller of the Trump administration grew up in the People's Republic of Santa Monica, as this famously left-leaning coastal enclave is sometimes known, while Steve Bannon honed his political instincts in the notoriously liberal circles of Hollywood.

California is, according to Alex Marlow, Breitbart's editor in chief, a "huge laboratory of, essentially, leftism."[4] His readers from the state often lament their political isolation, while those from elsewhere fantasize about a different kind of border wall altogether: one that could isolate California from the rest of the country. How had this environment become a seedbed of American conservatism? The situation demands a "political epidemiology," as *The Intercept* has put it, an effort to identify the soil in which stark ideas take root.[5]

Accounts of ideological divides in the United States fall back too easily on the distinction between coastal cities and flyover country, a generalization that fails to account for the many local and sometimes surprising engines of political conviction.[6] These contexts matter a great deal, for everyday environments and circumstances of life shape political commitments to a profound degree. Familiar impasses in the United States stem from more than a difference in political viewpoint: there are tangible differences at work in the lived commitment to categorical walls and hard lines of thought, habits of life and mind that can make disagreements seem intractable. All of this came into focus for me in Los Angeles in the spring and summer of 2017, when an old friend and I tried to work out together why we disagreed so much.

———

In Los Angeles, I was on a trail that led close to home. My father took a job at the Veterans Administration hospital there in the summer of 1980. With the zeal of immigrants for education and opportunity, my parents scraped together enough to send my sister, brother, and I to a pair of prestigious prep schools, since merged into a single institution — the Harvard-Westlake School. As it happens, it was from this school that Alex Marlow would graduate in 2004, a few years after my younger brother. And he wasn't the only alum from Harvard-Westlake to join the staff of Breitbart; reporter Julia Hahn (class of 2009) wrote a number of incendiary dispatches on immigration and Islam before heading into the White House with Steve Bannon in 2016. Was this anything more than a coincidence?

Political polarization is an effect of social and personal identity, scholars like Lilliana Mason have shown: the groups that people identify with, and against. When lines of affinity and antagonism overlap with each other, it becomes more difficult to cross them. This is especially true now on the American right, which is increasingly white, Christian, and rural in orientation, as Mason observes.[7] But similar dynamics may also unfold in liberal outposts like Los Angeles, as Peter Maass — another Harvard-Westlake alum — suggested in a profile of Julia Hahn for *The Intercept*: "People don't like to be told what to think, so it shouldn't be a surprise that an atmosphere of doctrinaire liberalism might produce reactionaries who delight in defying the dogmas that seemed so repressive when they were growing up."[8]

Harvard-Westlake's upper-school campus is slung onto the northern slopes of the Hollywood Hills, not far from the film and television complexes of Studio City. When I returned to the campus in the spring of 2017, more than a quarter century after I'd graduated, I was struck by the stunning views of the San Fernando Valley and the mountains to the north. Why hadn't I noticed before? The air was probably hazier then. I'd also spent most of those years looking down instead of up, having quickly learned in junior high to size up my peers by the logos on their shoes, always pricier than the Kmart sneakers my frugal parents picked out for us.

Coming back after a long time, I paid a visit to the school archives, curious to see what Marlow's senior yearbook page looked like. I found a sober young man looking back at me from one corner of the page, surrounded mostly by close-up portraits of a kitten. He'd named favorite concertos by Tchaikovsky and others, and his list of "Life Top Ten" began with (1) God, (2) Family, and (3) Baseball. Of all those who had graduated with him that year, Marlow was the only one who'd posed for his class picture in a sport coat and tie.

"That doesn't surprise me," one of my old teachers said when we met for lunch a few days later. It was a wonderful surprise to find her and a few others still teaching at the school. Marlow had passed through all of their classrooms. "He had a very traditional style to him, very courteous, a much more mature way of talking and sounding and acting than other kids," another teacher recalled. "He was a throwback in a way."

All of them felt there was much less political discussion and debate on campus now, with conservative students far less inclined to speak up than before. "Maybe they withdraw to their corner of the internet?" one teacher speculated as we sat around one of the hexagonal tables of the cafeteria courtyard.

"It's a fine line," another added. "If you push too hard, the kid's not going to feel safe in the classroom anymore. You want to open up their eyes a little, or push them to articulate how they're feeling, but you can't go too far because, well, they're young. They're adolescents, they take things very personally, they're very sensitive. If they think you hate them, that's just going to shut everything down."

This is something, of course, that all of us tend to do, especially in the face of intense convictions and heated disagreements. Over the years, I had side-lined my own childhood friends who leaned conservative. It was only after the election in 2016 that I began to feel sheepish about this and tried to rekin-dle some of those bygone friendships. I was glad when an old friend from LA reached out on Facebook that December. "Hi Anand, can't believe we're not FB friends," he wrote, tacking on a warning as well: "Please don't judge my politics, LOL."

Armen had lived up the street from my family in Encino, and we'd car-pooled together to school for many years. We sat side by side in the front row of Dr. Peet's homeroom in seventh grade, trying not to snicker at his graphic lessons in sex ed. Armen still lived in LA, and had just launched a small legal firm of his own. His Facebook feed revealed someone who relished a dirty martini and a good cigar, not to mention a bit of online jousting, the chance to thumb his nose playfully at liberal friends. We began to meet up for lunch near his office downtown. We enjoyed arguing with each other, and it was a way to figure out how we'd diverged so much.

Like me, Armen was no outsider to the educated elite of the country. But as we started to hang out again after many years, it became clear that our sense of the world was shaped by very different facts. I was worried that year about climate change and the fate of the Paris Accord, which the United States had just repudiated, concerns that didn't seem to register with him at all. Meanwhile, he would bring up events and scandals I could hardly recollect: the "reset" button presented by Secretary of State Clinton to Russian Foreign Minister Lavrov in 2009, or the Tea Party groups targeted by the Internal Revenue Service during the Obama years.

"Are you serious? Oh my God, how do you not know that?" Armen would ask each time something like this came up. "This is what shocks me about living in separate bubbles. One of the most common things you see conservatives saying is, *Look at this big fucking deal, and it's on page A38 of the New York Times, the paper of record.* You hear that all the time."

"Do you remember where you heard about the IRS going after the Tea Party?" I asked him.

"That's the problem with our bubbles," he replied. "It was all around me."

"And it wasn't around me at all," I added, laughing.

His black hair was thinning now, and mine was getting grayer by the month. How had we gotten to this point of mutual incomprehension, growing up around the corner from each other in the 1980s? On the radio, conservative commentators were speculating that the political chasm in the country verged on civil war. Armen agreed that it was serious. "I think we're coming apart at the seams, as a country," he said soberly.

We were talking over lunch that afternoon on Ventura Boulevard, the long and typically gridlocked artery through the San Fernando Valley that we used to take to school each morning. "I was an oddball. I never quite fit in," Armen recalled. His family had emigrated from London to Los Angeles when he was ten. They were Armenian by ancestry and Christian by faith, from a community that had settled centuries ago in Iran. He lived now in the suburb of Glendale, an Armenian American stronghold, and his children went to an Armenian school.

"He was always a traditionalist, very loyal," his mother told me a few weeks later at Armen's spacious split-level in the Glendale hills. She and her husband greatly admired Reagan and Thatcher, and they had made this known as the family would watch TV together each evening in the 1980s. "I was a Republican before I was a conservative," their son recollected. "I knew they were the good guys, but I didn't know why."

I had my own idea of the good guys back then, but to be honest, I thought I knew exactly what made them so: they, like me, simply knew better. Dan Quayle made a cameo on my senior yearbook page—"Verbosity leads to unclear, inarticulate things"—along with some well-worn radical quotables. "World, get a clue," I'd declared, capping off this smug parade.

Armen, meanwhile, grew up as a hard-core fan of heavy metal, and a song called "Media Overkill" by the Scorpions got top billing on his senior page, where he reproduced some of its lyrics about being watched and controlled by powerful media forces. Paging through that 1990 yearbook, we laughed at how contemporary these lyrics felt now, conservative diatribes against the mainstream media and all. Armen didn't remember sharing these words as a political gesture. "The Scorpions were my favorite band—I grew up with them," he said. Still, the problem of media influence got him vexed even now. "Why are they mostly left-wing? Think about it. It's the biases that push people in certain directions. Most people go into media wanting to change the world. Conservatives don't want to change the world. That's the whole point of being conservative."

In the late 1980s, while we were still in high school, Armen discovered Rush Limbaugh. It was almost by accident—a friend had been teasing him for his political views by calling him "Rush," and Armen finally searched out his radio show on KFI. He began to listen in earnest the next summer, as he spent day after day filing papers for a small law firm that had just set up shop in an empty office building. "There was nobody else in there with me, and I would just turn on the radio and listen to him. Otherwise I'd get bored."

"So what was it about him that appealed to you?" I asked. I had no idea he had been listening to Limbaugh at the time.

"He was funny, and I was learning what it meant ideologically to be conservative."

"What do you mean by that?"

"Back then what he was saying was so different from everything else around me. Being conservative was a kind of counterculture. It was a completely different way of looking at things. It was one that I agreed with. It made me realize that the points of view I was exposed to were very left-wing. Maybe everything around me was biased in a way."

"I learned a lot from that; it set me on a course," he added. "In fairness, after I started listening to him, I got more ideological. It became a bigger part of my life."

Armen stopped to pull up rushlimbaugh.com, chuckling at one of the lead headlines on the site: "Pathological CNN Is Making Professor Dershowitz Go Bald."

"See, this is why I like Limbaugh," Armen said, looking up from the screen. "He'll say outrageous stuff like that and make you laugh. Rush is over the top, but he may be the most influential man on the American right."

———

In the early 1990s, not long after Armen and I had graduated from high school, Ronald Reagan described Rush Limbaugh as "the number one voice for conservatism" in the United States.[9] At the time, Limbaugh (who died in 2021) already reached an audience of 14 million listeners weekly via hundreds of radio stations around the country. The ascent of conservative radio personalities like Limbaugh depended to a great degree on the suspension of the fairness doctrine by the Federal Communications Commission during the Reagan years, which had mandated that radio stations present politically balanced programming. There was also a matter of style, for the dominant figures of Limbaugh's generation were "entertainers first, conservatives second," as historian Nicole Hemmer has observed.[10] "They found a way to make their work profitable and popular, ensuring that the conservative message reached every pocket of the country."[11]

A few days after Armen and I had spoken at that restaurant on Ventura Boulevard in 2017, I spent a morning listening to Limbaugh's three-hour show on "The Patriot" radio station in Los Angeles, 1150 AM. Between promotions for window blinds and cybersecurity software, and brief segments from Fox News—"we report, you decide"—Limbaugh inveighed against "global warming malarkey," the deceptive schemes of former FBI Director James Comey, and the "nonstop mindless raw hatred" aimed at President Trump.

The media were responsible for this, Limbaugh said, reiterating an abiding theme in his shows. But so were American universities, "creating literal mind-numbed robots" rather than critical thinkers. Here was a more insidious Russian influence on American public life, beyond any election meddling. "The Russians are constantly attempting to infiltrate, and they have succeeded. Why do you think there are so many Communist college professors?"

I burst out in spontaneous laughter when I heard these words on the radio. But when Armen and I listened together to that part of the radio show later that afternoon, his reaction was markedly different. "He's referencing something factual here," he told me: a Soviet financing of American academia during the waning years of the Cold War. "There are more Marxists than Republicans in academia," Armen quipped. "Everybody on the right talks about that."

He promised to dig up an article that would substantiate this history, which I found unbelievable. But I was less curious about the facts in this case than our respective habits of interpretation. It struck me once again, as it often did in our conversations, that Armen paid much more attention than I did to categorical divides, to distinctions between one kind of thing and another: the fundamental difference, for example, between left and right.

On another occasion, we wound up talking about a story on *60 Minutes*, about an undocumented restaurant owner deported back to Mexico after many years in Indiana, and the misgivings his wife and friends had felt in voting for Trump.[12] To me, this was another tragic story indicative of the times. Armen, though, saw it as "a classic left-wing hit piece," a "bullshit tugging at the heartstrings" with a highly unusual story, purely to make a political point. He was vexed because the story disguised its manipulative intent: "If you want to be *left*, that's fine, but don't sit there and tell me, *Oh, we're not left.*"

For Armen, there was also the basic issue at stake, the legal categories governing who rightly belonged where. "The law says he has to be deported," he insisted. "That's what the law says. If you don't like it, change the law!"

Both his family and mine had emigrated to the United States in the late 1970s. And yet we saw this immigrant story in starkly different terms. I was caught up in the intensely personal drama of betrayal and expulsion. Armen was more interested in classifying and categorizing its actors, their deeds, and the storytellers who put those events into circulation.

Over time, I began to see that there was a consistency to this difference, in how we responded to such news. Each of us had different facts at our disposal. But over and above these differences were the ways that we tended to frame these facts and their availability—whether we were debating immigration, marijuana, climate change, or policing, Armen's pointed sense of "the left" kept surfacing. Every position could be recast as a partisan political commitment, as an instance of that politics, rather than a real and specific concern about the world.

Political psychologists have found patterns of this kind in studies of ideological orientation in the United States. "What we recognize as political conservatism is driven by a higher degree of cognitive and perceptual categorization," Everett Hudson Young argued in a 2009 study at Stony Brook University.[13] To be sure, everyone depended on categories to make sense of the world, Young acknowledged. But his extensive survey and experimental work with over 500 respondents in New York and Florida suggested a relationship between political tendency and the strength of those categorical divides in mental life. Conservatives were more likely to think with "impermeable walls" rather than fuzzy distinctions and associations, working intuitively with more "clear-cut boundaries" between one kind of thing and another.[14]

I think about what Armen once told me, chortling about the struggles of his liberal friends to keep their principles in line: "The fifteen-year-old teenager in me does love to see the wild gyrations of my friends on the left sometimes." As political psychologist John Jost notes, "heightened epistemic motives to reduce uncertainty and ambiguity and attain a sense of order, structure, and closure may favor the adoption of conservative attitudes."[15]

A stronger commitment to sharply defined distinctions, such as the very difference between left and right: this is one way of making sense of the Father's Day gift that Rush Limbaugh was hawking on the radio that June of 2017—a car magnet emblazoned with the crest of the Limbaugh Institute for Advanced Anti-Leftist Studies. There are also the hard lines of the automotive environment itself. An automobile on the road is like a bubble among bubbles, an environment to shelter particular ideas. And the audience for talk radio is mostly automotive, dominated by in-car listeners tuning in alone.[16] "The format blossomed at a time when American society had become more isolating," historian Brian Rosenwald observes, as "suburban sprawl drew neighbors far apart and ensured more time spent alone in cars."[17]

It is worth considering how these various elements might build on top of one another: a personal tendency to think in hard lines and firm boundaries; a political climate of intense divisions; a media discourse that magnifies and supercharges these divides; a social life bricked into individual homes, far-flung suburbs, and private automobiles, affording precious little scope for exposure to contrary points of view. Think of the feedback loops that can take shape between these various levels of division, forming what the political theorist William E. Connolly calls a "resonance machine," a network of related feelings feeding and intensifying each other.[18]

You can begin to appreciate how Southern California might work as an accelerant for a tempestuous politics, like the wildfires that race so often through its chaparral canyons.

————

After graduating from high school in 1990, I went off to Massachusetts to study at Amherst College, while Armen enrolled at Claremont McKenna, a notably conservative Southern California liberal arts college founded by Republican businessmen in the early twentieth century. Armen wrote his senior thesis under Harry Jaffa, a political philosopher who guided the establishment of an influential conservative think tank, the Claremont Institute, in 1979.

When William Voegeli, an editor for the think tank's *Claremont Review of Books,* was asked to speak to the Lincoln Club in the spring of 2017, Armen offered to take me along as a guest. It was difficult to pass up this chance, as the Lincoln Club was the foremost Republican political action committee in California.

Rarely had I set foot on such hallowed political ground. What, though, to wear? The invitation specified "business attire," but as a professor who didn't give a lot of thought to dressing well, I wasn't sure what this could mean.

With Armen's advice, I rented a dark suit and cut my hair. I borrowed a pair of black shoes from my dad and checked to make sure my fingernails were trimmed. I must have been on the right track, I learned when I met my friend at the door that day. "You look like the president of a Republican Club," he told me with a dry laugh.

The event was held at an elite private social club in downtown Los Angeles. "Stuffy," Armen observed, as we made our way toward the dining room, past the ornate fixtures along a dim and thickly carpeted hallway. We were seated by chance beside a portrait of the mining magnate Harvey Mudd, one of the founders of Claremont McKenna. It was the fifth of May, Cinco de Mayo, and the waitstaff, polite and decorous, had plenty of margaritas on hand.

Speaker Voegeli had recently published a book called *The Pity Party: A Mean-Spirited Diatribe Against Liberal Compassion*, a title that drew laughs from the well-heeled crowd: mostly older, almost all white. He spoke at length about the enigma of Trump's electoral victory the previous fall, its surprise for the conservative intelligentsia and its implications for their movement. The victory was partly due, he said, to the clustering of Democratic votes in supermajority areas like Los Angeles County. "Our registered Democratic friends seem not to like us that much and wish to avoid our company," Voegeli joked, "and whether or not it hurts our feelings, it seems to hurt their electoral prospects."

But, he added, "it's not just a physical distance between red and blue America; there's a psychic and philosophical distance as well." The left, he suggested, was increasingly antagonistic to "the idea of comity, of respect for others' opinions, the notion that in this big country we need to find ways to get along, to live and let live." And this, Voegeli argued, had a lot to do with the theories to which the left subscribed, peculiar canons of thought that insisted that "there is no justice, there is no nature, there is simply power, and people either take it or they don't."

At one point, Voegeli made a joke about professors, apologizing in advance to any that might have been there by chance in this club of attorneys, bankers, and business executives. If I had spoken out, I might have asked if the situation was as stark as he painted it, for many of the liberals I knew — professors, even — shared many of the values that he lauded. At the time though, it seemed better to listen. And what I heard again and again were the rumblings of a war I had no idea was raging, at least not on the terms being articulated there.

Many people I knew were angry, yes, but their ire was mostly focused on concrete targets: Trump, the Republican Congress, regulators who cozied up with lobbyists. Here, though, the enemy seemed far more expansive and un-graspable, *the left*, whatever that was, bent only on realizing itself. How could the response to its machinations be anything but anxious? My friend Armen posed one of the last questions that afternoon at the Lincoln Club. He hadn't voted for Trump himself in 2016, and he was concerned about the difficulty of remaining a sincere conservative, between a new president who'd made a "head fake" in their direction and a left making its decisions, as he saw it, on purely instrumental terms. "Do we face the same danger, of conservatives looking at the world that way?"

"Yes," whispered the elderly and bespectacled woman sitting beside me. She was a retired banker and a longtime member of the Lincoln Club. When she learned I was a professor, she told me how unsettling she found the campus environment at UCLA these days, close to where she lived in West Los Angeles, packed with so many strange-looking and unpredictable char-acters. As she saw it, even Fox News was becoming unreliable in their report-age, a tad bit "lefty" now and then; she'd taken to watching the One America News Network instead.[19]

———

Armen had joined us as that retired banker and I stood chatting at the close of that event in 2017, along with an investment banker sporting an elephant tie. "Welcome to the resistance," my old friend had joked that day. But in the years that followed, like many other conservatives in the United States, he grew more disillusioned with the Republican Party.

"I believe I'm still a genuine conservative, but the Republican Party no longer is," Armen eventually told me in the months leading up to the 2024 presidential election. He expressed a sense of disgust at the party's blind fealty to Trump, its opportunistic populism, its abdication of a commitment to law and order. And many conservative media outlets, as he saw it, had been taken over by "entertainers" with no loyalty to matters of principle. "Now I find myself politically homeless," he confided.

What Armen said struck a chord with me as well. I had long struggled with the question of how to identify myself politically, whether liberal or socialist or anarchist or green, or something else altogether. I'd had many moments myself of strident and often contemptuous certainty over the years. But I had also been granted a certain kind of education in *un*certainty, in the value and importance of grappling with what to think and do in the absence of clear coordinates.

There was all that I had learned as an anthropologist at large in the world, in countless situations where I didn't quite belong.[20] There were also more specific lessons in politics that I had absorbed, such as the "Introduction to Political Science" course I had taken in my first semester at Amherst College in 1990, a few months after Armen and I had graduated from high school. As it happened, philosophies of home and belonging anchored that undergraduate course taught by the American political theorist Thomas L. Dumm, an experience that left me with questions with which I still wrestle today, more than thirty years later.

"Home, in our contemporary democracy, is comprehended as a private place, a place of withdrawal from the demands of common life, a place of fixed meaning where one is protected from disorientation, but also from the possibility of democratic involvement," Dumm writes in a chapter of his 1994 book *united states* that brought into focus many of the problems we had explored in class a few years prior. "Hence one might say that democratic life requires one to overcome the fear of homelessness, to develop the courage to leave home (embracing another fear) without knowing when or whether one will return."[21]

Decades later, these words feel prescient, and even more relevant to the challenges of a more tenuous moment. I remain uncertain as to where that open road may yet take myself and others in this fraught American polity of ours. But I'm grateful for the company of old friends like Armen, however vexing it can be to consider where they might like to go.

TWELVE
SHEDDING WALLS

COLUMBUS, OHIO

When life or death issues take on the quality of a pitched and relentless battle, the consequences can be wrenching. On July 1, 2022, the *Indianapolis Star* reported that a ten-year-old rape victim had been forced to travel from Ohio to Indiana for an abortion. A ban on all abortions after six weeks of pregnancy had just taken effect in Ohio, in the wake of the Supreme Court's shocking decision to overturn *Roe v. Wade*. Many observers, including President Biden, took the news story as a grim forecast of horrors to come. Outlets like Fox News and the *Wall Street Journal*, meanwhile, dismissed the account as implausible, even a lie or hoax.[1] These protests subsided once the case was confirmed by reporters from the *Columbus Dispatch* in Ohio, but the Indianapolis doctor who performed the procedure on the young girl remained in the crosshairs of conservative critics. The attorney general of Indiana accused the doctor of using the child's trauma to "push her ideological stance," as if the doctor were the wrongdoer in this case.[2]

Such impasses are alarming and dispiriting, especially when lives are on the line. All the more reason to pay close attention to genuine openings when they arise, often unexpectedly. Take, for example, the menstrual equity movement, committed to a cause—remedying the profound inequalities of access to period products faced by those who menstruate—that has come into focus as a public policy concern only in recent years. Progressive measures to address "period poverty" have been passed by many state legislatures in the United States—often quite conservative ones—in the same years that issues like reproductive rights have met with serious restrictions. There is so much at stake in making sense of these developments.

"We've gone from zero to sixty, periods as a whisper or insult to the initiation of a full-blown, ready-for-prime-time menstrual movement," Jennifer Weiss-Wolf notes in *Periods Gone Public: Taking a Stand for Menstrual Equity*.[3] Advocates have called attention to the serious and sudden challenges that menstruation can pose for students, for the poor and unhoused, and for those who are incarcerated. And the campaign to end the "tampon tax"—the sales tax levied on period products—has prompted legislation in dozens of states around the country, with nineteen states lifting this tax between 2016 and 2023.[4] In many of these instances, campaigners have motivated abrupt shifts in public concern and commitment.

In Ohio, Akron Representative Greta Johnson first introduced H. B. No. 272—"Exempts feminine hygiene products from sales tax"—as a menstrual advocacy measure in the summer of 2015. "Feminine care products are not a luxury; they are a healthcare necessity," she stated at a press conference in the Ladies Gallery of the Ohio statehouse in Columbus that June.[5] For two years, Johnson tried to get the bill through the Ways and Means Committee, to no avail. "They were clearly uncomfortable," she recounted to me, describing how these lawmakers—almost all men—looked studiously away or down at their phones as she spoke of the hardships that those stranded without such products might endure. The committee tabled her bill without a single question from legislators. Soon thereafter, Johnson resigned her seat in the House of Representatives and returned to Akron. "I was tired of all the patriarchal bullshit."

Not much changed politically in Ohio over the next few years. Republican lawmakers continued to dominate both houses of the state legislature. And yet, when the tax exemption for menstrual products was introduced once again in 2019—co-sponsored this time by Democrat Brigid Kelly and Republican Niraj Antani—the measure passed almost unanimously through both the Ohio House and Senate, before being signed into law by Republican Governor Mike DeWine in November 2019.[6] What made the difference this time around? "Relationships are everything," Representative Kelly told me when I asked her this question a few years later. "It's important to get to know people," she explained. "I know this is something important to you. Here's something I'm working on. Is this something that we could do together?"

Kelly's words suggest the importance of building common ground, a value that often surfaces when it comes to changing minds.[7] This ambition may seem naïve, even dangerous in situations of stark and intractable polarization, because it suggests the idea of becoming a collaborator across enemy lines. "The notion that we can find some type of common ground on social media today may seem like a pipe dream," sociologist Chris Bail acknowledges.[8] And yet, as Bail observes in his recent book *Breaking the Social Media Prism*, there is a great deal of neglected potential even in "learning to communicate in the language of the other side."[9]

Walls of the mind anchor the isolated spheres of thinking and imagination that make it so difficult to agree about what is even happening, or why it matters. As with any wall, however, their integrity also depends on the commitment to maintain that isolation. Create spaces for more open and meaningful interchange, and these barriers may start to come apart. This is a lesson that the menstrual equity movement knows well—what it means to shed such walls.

———————

The 2017 Women's March was one of the largest public protests in the history of the United States. On January 21st, the day after Donald Trump's presidential inauguration, something like 4 million people took to the streets in Washington, DC, New York City, Los Angeles, and hundreds of other American cities and towns, protesting the election of Trump and its possible consequences for the lives and bodily well-being of the country's women.[10] The triumph of an openly misogynistic candidate invited indignation and anger, as did looming threats to reproductive rights. Many took the vision of a nation secured by hard and unyielding walls as an affirmation of a masculine ideal of the body.

Hence the many playful retorts made by marchers to the stern-faced politics of protection that impelled Trump's campaign: the edgy visual puns in the pussyhats knitted and worn by thousands of women and the verbal jabs in the signs they were carrying.

One of the most popular slogans in the marches took direct aim at the signature promise of the Trump campaign: "Shed Walls, Don't Build Them." The motto was a favorite on social media and in the press on the protests. It cropped up in dozens of major American cities, in smaller places like Chattanooga and Boise, and in sister protests abroad in Ottawa, London, Edinburgh, Berlin. These words on the signs—"shed walls, don't build them"—were almost always paired with a picture of female reproductive anatomy: uterus, vagina, ovaries, and fallopian tubes. This uterus, sometimes, was smiling. Often the ovaries were shaped like fists. On many of the posters, a fallopian tube was turned up instead of down, that ovary raised like a fist with a middle finger extended, as if making a gesture of abdominal defiance. The organs in these drawings often trailed droplets of blood, tangible reminders of the endometrial walls that a menstruating person sheds each month. These were pictures that embraced the reality of a porous individual body.

The slogan, meanwhile, also affirmed the truth of an interdependent society. The women's marches brought together women and allies concerned not only about women's rights and reproductive rights, but also the politics of social welfare, racial justice, environmental protection, sexual orientation, and immigration. Their unprecedented turnout, researchers have shown, was "the direct result of the effective mobilization of various individuals and organizational constituencies that were motivated by intersectional issues," beyond the limits of any individual identity or specific political concern.[11] Photographs from the marches attest to these bridges. Those carrying "Shed Walls" signs walked alongside others lofting slogans like "Here and Queer," "Hear Our Cries," "Equality Hurts No One," or "Jesus Was a Brown Refugee." Others nearby called attention to movements for abortion rights, migrant rights, native sovereignty, Black Lives Matter, climate change, and many other issues, including kindness as such.[12]

The "Shed Walls" slogan was coined by a handful of feminist activists based in Columbus, Ohio. These young women worked for a small startup company called Aunt Flow, dedicated to making menstrual products more widely available in public facilities and for underprivileged women and girls. They had already been campaigning against the basic conceit of "feminine hygiene," the way that familiar euphemism implied that there was something dirty or shameful about menstruation. Then, in the early days of January 2017, they announced a new campaign against social barriers, an invitation to become "a voice of acceptance for those who feel like they're silenced." The call to shed walls went out via Instagram and other social media on January 8th, accompanied by a line drawing of a female reproductive system. In less than two weeks, the idea was everywhere.

Later that summer of 2017, I had the chance to meet Claire Coder, the company's twenty-year-old founder, and Lindsey McEntee, who served at the time as their COO ("chief ovulation officer"). They were operating back then out of a warehouse on the outskirts of Columbus. They showed me boxes of organic cotton tampons that they sold on a one-for-one subscription basis, each box purchased financing the donation of another box to a woman in need. Their business plans were innovative and energetic and had already won the attention of magazines like *Forbes*, *InStyle*, and *Teen Vogue*. How did they get from menstrual equity work to a campaign against walls more generally?

"There's nothing obvious about the relationship between a uterine wall and a border wall, a wall of tissue and a concrete wall," I pointed out. "It's peculiar, isn't it? And yet, you made the connection in a way that people picked up all over the place. How did this happen?"

The phrase came to mind, Coder and McEntee explained, while they were working one evening around the rickety dining table in Coder's apartment. They were thinking about the election, what kind of impact the new president's words and decisions might have on them and other women. They started to play around with ways of responding to Trump's coarse and aggressive language about women's bodies. "To me, it's an act of defiance," they said. "I'm a woman, and I menstruate, and I'm not afraid to talk about it."

The month before we met, Coder had appeared on the cover of the Columbus city magazine *614*, for a special feature on the city's young entrepreneurs and activists. The magazine photographs captured the energy and enthusiasm that she conveyed in person. There again was her exuberant smile, radiating from someone with deep pink paint splashed all over her white clothing. There was something about the juxtaposition of her smile with the rosy color dripping from her torso and down the legs of her pants; the photos spoke of a brash assurance, a willingness to defy convention. Indeed, Coder had left college to pursue this mission.

"Do you think there's a relationship between the menstrual taboo," I asked her, "and the kind of intolerance that prompts calls for a border wall?"

"I look at it a little metaphorically," she told me. "You build a wall around your communication style. *We're gonna put up this wall. We're not crossing it to talk about menstruation. We're not crossing it to talk about abortion.* You build that wall and pretend that everything on the other side doesn't exist. You don't cross it to talk about any of these really difficult topics that need to be talked about."

It was this kind of wall that the young women of Aunt Flow encountered most often. Talk of menstruation provoked discomfort, sometimes even a visceral revulsion. Asking people, especially men, to heed these bodily walls quietly shed each month meant asking them to confront other walls as well, implicit boundaries around what they were simply willing to think about. There was the entrepreneurship judge, for example, who heard Claire Coder deliver a pitch for support of Aunt Flow's work. "Aside from the fact that this is utterly gross," he told her, "you're really solving a problem."

Disgust, like anger and fear, says much about the nature of a social milieu. Disgust is a defensive reaction, erupting when boundaries are trespassed, working to secure, on a physical and emotional level, the integrity of those lines once again. "Disgust is associated with a set of moral and political judgments that fall on the more conservative end of the political spectrum," political psychologists David Pizarro and Yoel Inbar observe.[13] This is, in other words, a deeply political emotion, one that implies strong commitments to certain ideas about the body, its borders, and its rightful place in public life.

Whenever an action provokes revulsion, such commitments snap sharply into focus. More than any other feeling, disgust illuminates the walls many people live with and take for granted, and what it would mean to try and shed them. Changing someone's mind is never just a matter of rhetorical persuasion. The strongest opinions have something like a visceral quality to them, as if they pulsed through the blood and gut. Anyone hearing those opinions has to wrestle with the ebb and flow of these sensations, with feelings of anger and fear, desire and disgust.[14]

Artwork by Sharon Teuscher. Courtesy of Aunt Flow.

This challenge shaped even the design of the logo for Aunt Flow's "Shed Walls" campaign, the original drawing that inspired so many participants in the women's marches. Here again was a reproductive tract, but one composed of thin lines and few details. On either side of the ovaries were three black droplets of ink, radiating outward like vibrant rays of matter. This was a body less leaking than gleaming, one that seemed to celebrate its ability to spill out into the world.

"You want to catch people where they are," explained Sharon Teuscher, the maker of the image. She was a freelance artist and a recent graduate of the Columbus College of Art and Design. She said that the picture had to get people to consider the slogan, without recoiling instinctively in anger or disgust. "If they instantly look away, they won't read the message, or absorb what you're trying to express," Teuscher said.

———

Aunt Flow shared a Columbus warehouse with a few other small startup companies. A young woman floating a skin care enterprise ducked into the doorway at one point while Coder, McEntee, and I were talking, holding up a corkboard with the words "SEND NUDES" laid out in strips of masking tape. Her company was working out a new slogan, for nude faces in their natural states. The space felt open and irreverent, emblematic of what we often read about the ethos of young startups. You could think of Claire Coder in such terms as well, as a freewheeling Gen Z entrepreneur. But her childhood added layers to this picture.

Coder grew up in Toledo, Ohio. Her mother was an art therapist, "super-hippie, a liberal wahoo," as she put it. Her father, on the other hand, was an avid conservative. "Every day, we would listen to Rush Limbaugh on the way to school in the morning, and I would fall asleep to Sean Hannity each night," she recalled. She remembered coming home one afternoon from elementary school with one of the pencils that the teacher had given out to each student in the class. Her father took one look and shook his head. "Fucking handouts."

Eventually, her parents split up, each worried about what the other might say to their only child. "Claire, you need to question what you hear on the radio," her mother urged. And she did ask questions, especially when she began to participate in mock trials in high school. "That's a fallacy, fact check!" she'd tell her dad, which he never liked.

All the same, Coder admitted, she grew up leaning conservative, especially in fiscal matters. Donald Trump's background as a businessman even appealed to her at first, though she eventually decided, she told me, that he was a "loony." Growing up, she often tagged along to the shooting range with her father and kept an NRA bumper sticker on her car for years before finally removing it. "I figured it would save my car from being vandalized."

All these details really struck me, as I had taken Coder to be a straight-forward liberal, given the kind of work she did. What floored me even more was her father's zealous support for Aunt Flow. He had stickers for the organization on his Yamaha motorcycle and his Ford F-150 truck. He had taken to wearing the "Flow Bro" T-shirt designed for Aunt Flow's male allies, the motto "Don't Be Self-Conscious About Being Socially Conscious" written in pink across the back. The more I heard about him, the more I felt I had to meet Steve Coder in person.

I had the chance just a few days later, at a Starbucks outside of Toledo. A land surveyor, Steve was still in his work boots and surveying gear that afternoon, just off from a day of work for a new retail development nearby.

Single now at the age of sixty-one, he seemed to appreciate the company. "Sometimes you feel like you've gotta get out more, like you've been too closed in," he mused at one point, as we talked on the patio over a pair of coffees.

Without a doubt, Steve was proud of his precocious daughter. He had many stories to tell about her enterprising talent as a child—the smallest girl on her softball team, he recounted, Claire would somehow manage to get on base, even if just a bunt. He chuckled at the "Let's get it in your face" spirit of her menstrual equity campaign. He confessed that he'd never really registered the euphemism "Aunt Flow" until Claire chose it for the name of her company; in his experience, menstruation was more along the lines of "I know what it is, but I don't want to talk about it." And yet here he was, with an Aunt Flow sticker on the back of his truck out in the parking lot, so candid and enthusiastic about his daughter's business in tampons.

What about that slogan of theirs that went viral, "Shed Walls, Don't Build Them"? The way he talked about it, Steve didn't seem too perturbed by illegal immigration to the United States; in any case, as he saw it, "the wall is more of a metaphor" in conservative circles. He thought of the Aunt Flow slogan as a clever way to promote the company, describing the startup venture and its "buy one, give one" model of tampon donation as a capitalist enterprise. "She's providing things through a vehicle that is basically a conservative idea," he told me.

As much as he insisted on all this, however, Steve's involvement with Aunt Flow took his own thinking in unexpected directions. Take, for example, what he did at the Doo Dah Parade in Columbus that summer of 2017. Billed as an annual celebration of "liberty and lunacy," the parade turns High Street each Fourth of July into a public stage for zany antics and free-spirited discourse. That year, there were the Marching Fidel Castros, as always. There were the women in red *Handmaid's Tale* robes and white headgear, twirling yellow uterus flags that borrowed the motto of the Tea Party movement, "Don't Tread on Me." There were the Sean Spicer impersonators, the Border Patrol officers with leaf blowers, and the bike chariot bearing a modern-day Darth Vader, a dark lord who kept reminding the crowds "Alderaan = Fake News."

And here too, in the midst of all this—among the ghouls and zombies, the ghostbusters and avenging heroes, those sporting rainbow gear of all kinds—were Claire Coder and her father, representing Aunt Flow. Steve had on his "Flow Bro" T-shirt over a pair of black jeans, carrying a big sign with the handwritten slogan "TOILET PAPER is FREE. Why not TAMPONS." Those clustered along the sidewalks of High Street would have seen a tall white man in glasses and a shaved head, chanting, until his voice grew hoarse: "Periods are real! Tampons are real!"

A few days later, I learned from Steve, he was back at the surveying office in Toledo, sitting around with a few other guys from the company, talking about what they'd done over the long weekend for the Fourth of July. Coder had told them about the parade, getting really animated about Aunt Flow's business model, which the other men, mostly middle-aged, were curious about themselves. "We spent half an hour talking about tampons," he recalled. Then there was a hush, as it suddenly struck them how odd this was.

"I looked around and said, 'I hope Detroit is playing tonight,'" Coder told me, and they were back again to safer ground, back onto, as he put it, "the man's soil."

Coder, meanwhile, kept pushing these boundaries. It turned out he had once gone so far as to write to a senior executive at Toledo's conservative talk radio station, the one that Claire had grown up hearing, telling them that his daughter, "an impressive young local entrepreneur," was in town and willing to talk about her menstrual products company on-air. "This doesn't really fit our audience, but we wish Claire the best," the executive replied. Steve persisted, pointing out that his daughter would be appearing soon on *Ellen*. A curt reply came back just a short while later. "Our target audience will remain just as uninterested."

The menstrual taboo is known as a widespread phenomenon. But, as anthropologist Alma Gottlieb has observed, the taboo has meant very different things in different places.[15] Western cultures still evince the idea of menstruation as shameful and polluting, even a curse. But many other cultures associate menstrual blood with mystical properties and sacred power, contrary meanings and associations that can be mobilized by activists to powerful effect. As Gottlieb writes, "menstrual politics offer powerful options for women simultaneously exploiting and exploding menstrual taboos in support of broad social justice movements."[16] The menstrual movement has often done this by defying the ways that taboos and other conventions organize communicative space, introducing stories of personal experience and bodily detail where you wouldn't expect to find them, where they would not seem to belong.

"We will talk about periods openly and proudly," Gen Z menstrual activist Nadya Okamoto declares in *Period Power.* "We will organize and talk about cycles and period products and menstrual health through megaphones on stages, and advocate for the Menstrual Movement to rooms full of initially uncomfortable listeners, who can then go on to do the same thing. BREAK THE SILENCE."[17] In 2014, Okamoto founded the menstrual equity organization PERIOD, while she was still a junior in high school. Like Aunt Flow and other allied efforts, PERIOD has become a highly influential presence in the broader landscape of #periodpositivity, with hundreds of student-led chapters around the country. Follow that hashtag and you'll find posts starkly different from the typically scripted and sanitized presentations of self that social media platforms like Instagram often encourage. These organizations are staking out space instead for frank depictions of bodily fluids and processes, engaging with accidents both sensitively and humorously, sharing stories of both the pain and joy of menstrual being.

A student-led PERIOD chapter at Ohio State University in Columbus played a crucial role in the eventual repeal of Ohio's pink tax in 2019. At the age of nineteen, Anusha Singh, founder of the OSU campus chapter, testified to lawmakers at the Ohio statehouse in favor of that repeal. Like Greta Johnson and other women advocates on the issue before her, Singh also met with disdain and discomfort when she spoke on the topic to a legislative committee composed almost entirely of older men. "Many of the men refused to make eye contact with me and looked down at their iPads. Some of them started blushing, or even squirming in their seats. A few of them even rolled their eyes at me from across the room," Singh later recounted in a TEDx talk from Columbus.[18] And yet, as we know, the campaign against the pink tax found startling success that legislative season in Ohio, due in part to the energetic rallies, petitions, and media outreach that the movement pursued, but also to the alliances they managed to build this time around.[19] I reached out to Singh to understand better what had changed that year.

When we met via Zoom in the spring of 2022, Singh was serving as a national campaign lead for PERIOD, and as a community and social impact specialist for Aunt Flow. On the wall behind her desk were mementos from her organizing work at OSU and from the National Period Day that she and other activists had staged in October 2019. Stacked against another wall were a few boxes of Loopholes, a playful breakfast cereal that menstrual equity organizations have developed to encourage federal action on period poverty — every box of strawberry-flavored cereal is also packed with tampons and pads, a lighthearted way of making these products eligible for assistance under the federal Supplemental Nutrition Assistance Program.[20]

"As students, we wanted to do something, but we doubted the power of our voices," Singh, a former neuroscience major, recalled. "None of us had PhDs in menstruation studies." What they did have was abundant passion for the issue and many personal stories to share. They advocated for better access to period products at OSU, bringing in student leaders and others as "menstrual equity champions." When they got involved in the larger effort to repeal the statewide pink tax in Ohio, they were startled by the lack of momentum on the legislation, which had gotten stuck once again in the House Ways and Means Committee.

"For so long, we were in our own bubble at college, very openly petitioning for this issue," Singh told me. "It felt so different to be in a different reality, with predominantly older white men who do not feel comfortable discussing these issues. But we persisted. We held press conferences, we organized several ourselves." Ultimately, she said, reflecting on the success of the campaign, "it makes me feel very hopeful, because it shows the power that young people also hold in influencing some of the older generations to care about this issue."

"How do you work with the defensiveness that you encounter, that reflex to reject?" I asked her. Framing was critical, Singh explained: student activists had to learn how to appeal to the interests and imagination of Republican lawmakers. They framed the issue as a matter of tax relief, the easing of an undue burden on families. They spoke of medical necessity, the unfairness of taxing tampons as luxury items, rather than gender justice. Advocacy for women's rights in general — say, "This is how we're going to smash the patriarchy" — wouldn't get them very far. Instead, they invited men with authority to imagine what specific women in their lives were going through: "it affects daughters in Ohio, it affects sisters, wives — using that language really helped us in our messaging."

This strategy forced some difficult choices. The menstrual equity movement has come to acknowledge that menstruation isn't solely a matter of women's experience, as transgender men and non-binary individuals can also menstruate. With this reality in mind, PERIOD activists at OSU sought at first to have period product dispensers installed in all university bathrooms, for women and men alike. When they found themselves caught in a social media firestorm, they scaled back to a pilot plan for a limited number of women's and gender-neutral bathrooms, then organized over time to extend access to all women's and gender-neutral bathrooms.

At the statewide level, meanwhile, activists deliberately gave the Republican co-sponsor of the pink tax repeal bill, Miamisburg Representative Niraj Antani, a platform to advocate publicly on behalf of the measure — at the inaugural National Period Day rally on the steps of the Ohio statehouse, for example, on October 19, 2019. Activists from Planned Parenthood were upset by this decision, Singh recounted, because of his staunch opposition to abortion rights. "But we knew it was essential to pull him in," she told me. "We needed him to pass the menstrual equity legislation," and they felt that the passage of reproductive justice legislation in the future would require the kind of cultural change represented by such measures for menstrual equity.[21]

I reached out to Antani on several occasions, to no avail. But his Democratic co-sponsor on the pink tax repeal measure, Representative Brigid Kelly of Cincinnati, was kind enough to make some time to talk with me. She described the "serendipitous" nature of her partnership on the bill with Antani — "he hates taxes." She told me how they worked to bring other Republicans on board as well, with a far more diverse set of advocates in its favor than in previous legislative sessions: the students from OSU, and progressive organizations as before, but also Girl Scouts, other elected officials, even Ohio Right to Life.[22] The measure was eventually folded into a bill that granted income tax deductions to teachers, lawyers, and lobbyists, passing unanimously through the Ohio House before clearing the Ohio Senate 30–1 on October 23, 2019, four days after the Period Day rally that menstrual equity activists had staged on the statehouse steps.[23] "It's not a partisan issue," Kelly told me. "It's not about Democrat or Republican, urban or rural; it's about helping people live healthier and more productive lives."

Republican "Flow Bro" Steve Coder said something similar about the pink tax repeal: "it's not a liberal or a conservative issue. You're not going to charge people a tax on food. There are certain things that just make sense." He, like many others in Ohio, had come to a place where the measure seemed like straightforward common sense. What else might find such agreement? For, as Kate Clancy argues in *Period: The Real Story of Menstruation,* "a liberatory period future does not in fact focus just on periods and period experiences. It casts its eyes upon the power structures that stigmatize and marginalize menstruating people."[24]

Building toward such futures will be a difficult challenge, especially with the cascade of troubling news in recent years. *Roe v. Wade* was overturned by the Supreme Court just a few weeks after Representative Kelly and I spoke in June 2022. Ohio Governor Mike DeWine signed the controversial "Heartbeat Bill"—banning all abortions after six weeks of pregnancy in the state, with no exceptions for rape or incest—just a few months before approving the pink tax repeal.[25] Even when it comes to issues like menstrual equity and period poverty, there is so much more to be done. As Claire Coder has observed, "eliminating the tax may not impact the people that need products most," such as those who rely on public assistance for food and other necessities.[26] A federal menstrual equity bill to ensure access to period products in federal buildings, schools, workplaces, prisons, and homeless shelters has been stalled in Congress since 2019.[27]

Progress on such issues may well require the common sense that Steve Coder invoked, a shared understanding of what is reasonable and necessary, what a given situation demands. By no means is this a simple ambition.[28] The very possibility of common sense, as the philosopher Hannah Arendt observed in *The Human Condition,* requires the existence of a common world, a shared reality, "the presence of others who see what we see and hear what we hear."[29] Already in the 1950s, Arendt foresaw how "conditions of radical isolation, where nobody can any longer agree with anybody else," could reduce people to fully private beings, "deprived of seeing and hearing others, of being seen and heard by them." Such was the case in circumstances of political tyranny, she observed, but also with "the unnatural conformism of mass society," where each individual is "imprisoned in the subjectivity of their own singular experience."[30]

Conditions of collective life in the contemporary United States bear out Arendt's grim warning, as I've tried to show in this book. Walls at home and on the road, shielding the body from exposure and the mind from uncomfortable ideas: these are symptoms of an atomizing politics of fear and suspicion, yielding circumstances of isolation and neglect rather than the safety and security they promise. But security itself can be imagined and pursued otherwise if anchored in a sense of common fate, as the writer and organizer Astra Taylor suggests in *The Age of Insecurity: Coming Together as Things Fall Apart*. "The simple recognition of our mutual vulnerability—of the fact that we all need and deserve care throughout our lives—has potentially revolutionary implications," Taylor writes. "Indignation at the way insecurity is fostered and exploited under capitalism can help strengthen existing movements and galvanize new ones, coalescing powerful coalitions with the capacity to expand and fight for collective forms of security based on compassion and concern instead of desperation and fear."[31]

The walls that divide are difficult and real. But they do have the tendency to crack and fissure, as activists from the menstrual equity movement and beyond have shown. Work with others to chip away at those cracks, and another side can come into view. You can begin to imagine a shared and encompassing world once again, maybe even begin to rebuild that world in unlikely company.

"It's about meeting people where they're at," as Anusha Singh put it. "You don't want to drive them away."

CONCLUSION
LIFE BETWEEN THE LINES

Boundaries are ubiquitous and essential in human cultural life.[1] But they don't always have to take the shape of walls. Organizer and facilitator Prentis Hemphill has reflected on the interpersonal and psychological dimensions of this distinction. One can set boundaries as a way to care for oneself and others, pursue healthy relationships, and navigate the vulnerability that such relationships will bring. Walls, on the other hand, represent a refusal to relate altogether. Walls take "the risk of connection to be too high to engage," Hemphill writes; "they have a way of keeping you captive when they were once designed to keep you safe."[2]

The argument may seem metaphorical when extended to social and national life at a larger scale. But as we've seen throughout this book, the politics of national borders and social boundaries often tack between reality and metaphor, the physical and the psychological. "The defense that walls establish against siege works the fantasy of impermeability into a psychic politics in which the enemy is figured as raiding, invading, coming to take or plunder

215

what is rightfully the nation's own — its safety, security, peaceful or prosperous way of life, its jobs, its wealth, its First World privilege," Wendy Brown notes.[3] We need ways of imagining our collective existence that resist this hard logic of division, that don't fall back on a hard and inflexible line between life inside and the world outside.

I had the chance to pursue this problem together with students at Johns Hopkins University one semester in 2019, when I taught a seminar called "The Idea of America." We absorbed the insights of Chicana cultural theorist Gloria Anzaldúa, who suggested, in her work on cultural identity on the southern border of the United States, that "to survive the Borderlands / you must live *sin fronteras* / be a crossroads."[4] We read from a book of refugee fiction edited by the Vietnamese American writer Viet Thanh Nguyen, who argued that in "making borders permeable, we bring ourselves closer to others, and others closer to us."[5] We also took part in a virtual 3D tour of the Mashantucket Pequot Museum led by endawnis Spears and Chris Newell, founders of the Akomawt Educational Initiative, a Connecticut-based organization seeking to center Native American perspectives and experiences in museum education. "Our cultures have been here tens of thousands of years and have a deep understanding of this land," Spears reminded us, "very contrary to one that does not let people move across our continent, especially Indigenous people."

The virtual tour was part of an Akomawt presentation called "Illegal Immigration: The View from the Land." The idea was to approach contemporary questions of migration from the standpoint of the continent's most enduring inhabitants, rather than from the perspective of much more recent European settlers.[6] Spears and Newell took us through a life-sized diorama that modeled everyday life in a Pequot village in the sixteenth and seventeenth centuries, describing the ancestral stories of migration that animated people's understandings of themselves, and the practices of seasonal movement that kept them attuned to a living land. Spears noted that it was the violence of the colonial encounter that led to the raising of palisade walls around such villages in the seventeenth century, a newly stark distinction between inside and outside space, "structuring a village that is separate from the landscape, separate from Mother Earth."

A more fluid relationship between domestic space and the world beyond was reflected in the composition of early Pequot homes, and even in contemporary Indigenous homemaking practices, the native educators suggested. Doors had been made of deerskin, offering cover but no firm latches. Still today, Newell said, people allowed for an "Indian knock"—a visitor knocking once and walking into a home, without waiting for someone to let them in. "Privacy is not something that you covet necessarily because you need the help of the community to survive," he observed. "That bond shows itself in the way that doors open and close."

Recent years have underscored the significance of this insight, as the pandemic took a terrible toll on marginalized communities of color in the United States, most especially native communities already dealing with the consequences of centuries of dispossession and abuse.[7] For the Anishinaabe and Ukrainian writer Patty Krawec, this circumstance represents a failure of collective responsibility, a repudiation of the sense of accountability that being in good relation demands. "How can we find a way to live in the knowledge that we are all related? How can we become better kin?" she asks in a recent book, *Becoming Kin*.[8] One way to practice this responsibility, she has argued, is through endeavors in mutual aid, "working together to develop ways to meet each other's needs, while organizing against the system that created the need for that aid in the first place."[9]

Over the last few years, movements for mutual aid, racial justice, and cultural solidarity have brought Americans together in important new ways, redrawing the line between stranger and kin. These movements call attention to the structural conditions of American indifference, working to bring more radical commitments to care into the rhythms of collective life. Such mobilizations for racial, environmental, and gender justice, I've argued in this book, have much to teach us about how to take down the walls we live with now. They reveal crucial ways of working against the patterns of division and retreat that run through ordinary American life, the hard lines that have made living with the difference of others so challenging.

While the stories in this book have taken me to far-flung places, these possibilities are readily apparent right here in Baltimore, where my family and I have lived now for close to two decades. Many observers, including Trump, have depicted the city as a dystopian embodiment of all that is wrong with the contemporary United States.[10] Baltimore is a difficult and troubled city in many ways, especially for those most burdened by its economic and social inequality. "The Baltimore metropolitan area created the template for urban apartheid nationwide," as scholar Lawrence Brown has noted, serving as a seedbed for noxious strategies in urban segregation for more than a century: "Baltimore reveals the sophistication of structural violence deployed in city ordinances, real estate practices, mortgage lending, code enforcement, municipal budgets, zoning laws, urban planning, urban renewal, and urban redevelopment."[11]

These machinations have had an enduring legacy, reflected in the deeply unequal lives of the city's residents: in highly uneven access to educational and economic opportunity and exposure to harms like gun violence and environmental pollution, in average lifespans that vary by up to twenty years from one neighborhood to another.[12] Justice and reparation may take generations to fulfill. At the same time, there is some hope in the record of local experiments in convivial living, efforts to sketch what a more just and responsive practice of living together with others could begin to look like.[13] Home and road, body and mind: we may yet find a hardening of these walls and lines, or the resources to dream and build beyond them.

———

Pursuing this book has taught me how much turns on the immediate circumstances of our lives. With this lesson in mind, let me share something that happened one December night on my block in Baltimore, a couple of years ago. Hanging out at home that evening, we suddenly heard a loud crash. We thought at first that something big had fallen inside the house. Could the cat have pulled down a bookshelf or something, we wondered.

But nothing had happened inside. Looking out our front door revealed the most unfathomable sight. A car lay sideways on our narrow street, its steel roof facing us, with the hazy outlines of someone inside visible through the glass. Like many of our neighbors, we rushed to the car to ask the driver if she was okay. She assured us that she was fine, and a few of us held the vehicle steady as she clambered out through the sunroof.

The young woman was driving a Subaru Forester SUV, and the situation brought home how much of a bubble in the world such a vehicle was. Something had distracted her while she was driving, and she had veered one way then lurched back, the big wheel of her vehicle riding up along the side of another car parked on the street, toppling the Forester sideways.

The driver was shaken up but looked mostly unharmed, which seemed itself a miracle. She told us that she was on her way home from a late shift at work. Her own phone was smashed, and she couldn't remember anyone's number to call. But on our street, she found company. Many people on the block had heard the crash and came out to help. Those who were walking their dogs at that late hour also stopped to offer aid. We brought out a chair for the driver to sit on while she waited for the police and fire department. Someone gave her a blanket to keep warm. We made her tea, and a teenager who lived down the street brought her a cup of hot chocolate. "You look like you need a hug," she told the young woman, and offered one.

Many of us were with her until well after midnight that night, while the police and fire department came and went, and the tow truck hauled her car away. Neighbors helped sort the personal belongings that had spilled onto the street and stayed on to clean the glass and other debris from the asphalt. Meanwhile, someone walked the driver over to a friend's place.

The driver's SUV was designed to shield her from a dangerous world. And with all the metal tubing snaking around the exposed underside of the vehicle, it truly looked like an alien pod come crashing to earth. It seemed to have dropped out of nowhere into our neighborhood that night. But the driver wasn't alone where she had landed. She found company and care on that streetscape at night, and it mattered deeply that she did.

I'd like to think that someone who has had an accident like this on our block would have met with such a response no matter when or where it had happened. We are lucky to live on a walkable street with a civic sensibility and a thriving front porch culture, where people are likely to encounter— and often nod and acknowledge—others they don't know on a daily basis. But it is also the case that for so many of us here, the years of the pandemic turned our lives further toward the common streets, alleys, and trails of the neighborhood we shared. Space was held on the asphalt for daily walkers and occasional block parties. Birthdays and long weekends were celebrated out in the open on front lawns and porches. Halloween brought neighbors together to plan one-way trick-or-treating routes and strategies to deliver candy from a distance. All this came to matter at a moment as unexpected as that December night.

New forms of mutual aid — assistance with groceries, community initiatives in public health, collaborative modes of parenting — took shape in our neighborhood of Wyman Park as with so many other places during the early months of the pandemic. But there were also more radical initiatives elsewhere in the city that transformed the spatial coordinates of home and belonging, like the B'more Community Fridge established in the fall of 2021 and managed month by month by a dedicated team of volunteers and donors.

The fridge has a place in a local ecosystem of public resources, lodged in an alleyway off North Avenue beside community garden Hidden Harvest and drawing electricity from Bluelight Junction, an adjacent community dye garden and educational facility. Painted vibrantly with an image of okra and purple corn at first, later a goldfinch munching on sunflower seeds, the fridge has stocked fresh fruits and vegetables, bread, snacks, and many other groceries.[14] A variety of other necessities — toilet paper, toothpaste, soap, menstrual supplies, COVID-19 test kits, and so on — have been kept in an adjacent pantry cabinet. All of these goods were free for the taking, shared publicly with a "take what you need, and give what you can" philosophy.[15]

Like other such resources established around the country, the B'more Community Fridge was created to address the rampant food insecurity in American cities, exacerbated by the pandemic and affecting Black and brown communities disproportionately. But as a founder of the effort, former Johns Hopkins University student Clara Leverenz noted, the outdoor resource also served as a means of deepening social relationships at a moment of intense isolation. "The fridge has been a real connector," she observed.[16] Christina Calhoun, another core organizer, suggested that "at the end of the day, everyone understands sharing a meal, having a first aid cabinet, having a paper goods cabinet — that feeling of safety."[17] It is striking that in meeting that need for safety, these organizers looked beyond the domestic sphere, instead creating a shared space of belonging that turned the line between home and world inside out.

As we've seen elsewhere in this book, the pandemic was an occasion to confront the deep relatedness of individual bodies, even as we put strange new forms of distance between us. As medical anthropologist Julie Livingston wrote in 2020, "the coronavirus pandemic has laid bare a fundamental truth often ignored in American society: the human body is a relationship."[18] In a city like Baltimore, carrying a long industrial history and its complex afterlife, the relationships that make for both good health and ill health are manifest even in the air that people breathe.

The biggest stationary source of air pollution in the city is the BRESCO waste incinerator, located on an industrialized shoreline in south Baltimore. Thousands of tons of garbage from around the city and its surrounding counties are trucked there to burn each day. But incineration's effects on public health—asthma, lung disease, elevated risks of many cancers—are more evident among the low-income neighborhoods and communities of color close to this and other such facilities.[19] It was widely reported in 2020 that the air pollution pervasive in such neighborhoods was likely to heighten the risks of COVID-19 exposure for low-income communities of color.[20] And yet that year the city of Baltimore quietly renewed its contract with BRESCO for another decade, even while the pandemic brought a surge in the use of disposable materials and far less access to recycling services, as the city grappled with the limited availability of sanitation workers.

In the face of these developments, environmental justice activists in Baltimore redoubled their efforts to combat the tide of waste and pollution that city residents endured, releasing a "Fair Development Plan for Zero Waste" that same year. In the fall of 2021, activist leaders of the city's Zero Waste Coalition organized a speak-out on a public plaza in front of City Hall, calling on the mayor to help establish a community-led municipal compost facility as an alternative to the waste incinerator. People were invited to gather in a broad circle around a field of bright paper flowers planted into the grass, each of which carried a message like "Incinerator Pollution Kills," or "This Is Essential to the Health and Well-Being of All Baltimore Citizens!" This theme of a common embodied fate was dramatized by the structure of the speak-out itself, in which a ball of yarn was thrown from speaker to speaker across the wide circle of the gathering, becoming a web of crisscrossing strands that visually attested to the reality of interconnection.

I had the chance to help a little with that event at City Hall, along with students from a class I was teaching at Johns Hopkins in collaboration with one of the main organizers of the effort—the South Baltimore Community

Land Trust. We continued to work and teach together through the summer of 2023, bringing university students to a rec center in south Baltimore each week to collaborate on a number of environmental justice issues faced by local residents. The intertwined nature of communities that may not think very much about each other, or see each other at all, was an abiding theme in our engagements. Ray Conaway, president of the Community of Curtis Bay Association, spoke earnestly about this idea at a community meeting one February evening, when our students shared research findings about the environmental and social impact of a coal storage and transportation facility in that locality.

"When I was sitting back there viewing this, I just thought about one of my favorite quotes that I have to share," Conway said. "Dr. King, when he was in jail in Birmingham, when he wrote his famous letter from a Birmingham jail, said 'We are caught in an inescapable network of mutuality, tied in a single garment of destiny. Whatever affects one directly affects all indirectly.'" He spoke aloud one more line from Dr. King's letter as others at the meeting joined their voices to his, repeating together the words of that sentence as if to make its truth as tangible as possible: "Injustice anywhere is a threat to justice everywhere."

Moments like this were powerful lessons in the value of working against walls of mind, structures of unequal knowledge and privilege that denied the very possibility of such shared outlook and experience. In a city like Baltimore, universities and other educational institutions are also deeply implicated in such divides.[21] The pandemic years were once again an occasion to wrestle with this fact, as the physical closure of ivory tower institutions raised basic questions about other ways in which access to knowledge might be organized and exercised. Many of us within the academy began to experiment with more open formats for learning and interchange.[22] And in such work, there were important partnerships to be forged with local institutions equally interested in a less exclusionary circulation of knowledge.

I think of Red Emma's, for example—a radical bookshop and worker cooperative that kept a steady schedule of public conversations and events going during those isolating years, in person at their Baltimore venue and streaming live online. When the annual meeting of the American Anthropological Association was held in Baltimore in the fall of 2021, Red Emma's hosted a more public-facing panel discussion one evening called "Right to the City: Baltimore Activists Talk Back to Anthropology."[23] While the members-only academic conference itself felt rather devoid of people or collective energy, the bookstore that evening was packed with attendees, all carefully masked to ward off contagion. The social justice organizers and activist academics who spoke on the panel talked about the importance of creating and supporting intellectual spaces of a more radical character, beyond the walls of elite academic institutions.

Among these speakers was Shashawnda Campbell, an environmental justice organizer with the South Baltimore Community Land Trust and the activist with whom I had worked most closely in my own community-based teaching in Baltimore. Campbell talked about the ongoing struggling against incineration and hazardous industry in south Baltimore: the massive facility that she and other local students had rallied against being built near their neighborhoods while they were still in high school and the fact that urban waste streams draw together the lives of those who dwell spatially apart.[24] "All of your trash is burnt in these communities," Campbell pointedly reminded the well-meaning liberal audience.

The activist also had a lot to say about boundaries of thought: the forms of experience and perspective we are typically willing to take seriously as knowledge and other ways of being in the world that we tend to let slip too easily. "What happens in your community" is itself an essential form of knowledge, Campbell insisted, "and recognizing that it is affecting you, your community, your neighbors, your kids." Failing to see this meant erasing other communities and their histories, those who were polluted out of existence in cities like Baltimore, but also the vision they may have held for rebuilding the world otherwise. "Let's not think about knowledge in one way," she told us. "Don't miss the knowledge that's in front of you."[25]

———

Now and then over the last few years, when I've talked about this project, people have asked, sometimes quite candidly, why they should care. The question is no surprise. Dealing with circumstances of hopeless strife is hard enough wherever each of us is; having to imagine this situation all over again from a profoundly different standpoint—especially from another side in social or political terms — can verge on an almost unbearable burden. Attention to others can imply an indulgence of them, which is a lot to ask when they seem indifferent to one's own suffering. I've had these feelings myself. But I've also felt, as I've said when faced with this question, that I had no choice but to take on this project. For reasons both personal and professional in nature, the problems of others unlike me became my own problems.[26]

Political theorist Norman Geras addresses this concern in a 1998 book, *The Contract of Mutual Indifference: Political Philosophy After the Holocaust.*[27] In the book, Geras reflects on the ample evidence of those who went on with their lives in various European cities — watering plants, relaxing with children, quietly looking elsewhere on street corners and railway platforms — while the Jewish neighbors and families in their midst were rounded up and taken away in the 1940s. "How continue life as normal after having seen *that*?" Geras asks. "How, if you are not a stone or pile of dead wood or a cadaver?"[28]

This hardening of the self comes down to a kind of implicit moral contract, Geras argues, one of neither giving care to others nor expecting it in return, denying both the right to assistance in circumstances of need and the duty to give such aid. "A liberal culture underwrites moral indifference," he adds:

> For the principal economic formation historically associated with liberalism . . . is one in which it has been the norm for the wealth and comfort of some to be obtained through the hardship and poverty of others, and to stand right alongside these. It is a whole mode of collective existence. Not only an economy. A world, a culture.[29]

This too is evident once again in a city like Baltimore. The first municipal ordinance to regulate neighborhood residence by race in the United States was passed in Baltimore in 1910, a model for cities across the country. When the Supreme Court invalidated these laws a few years later, Baltimore builders pioneered the development of private neighborhood communities governed by restrictive covenants barring Blacks and Jews.[30] Among them was George R. Morris, a two-time head of Baltimore's Board of Realtors, who built many neighborhoods, apartment buildings, and golf and swim clubs with such covenants in place. A sign planted outside his Meadowbrook Swimming Club just north of the city read "PRIVILEGES OF THE SWIMMING POOL ARE EX-

TENDED ONLY TO APPROVED GENTILES."[31] As a private facility, the club was allowed to maintain this discriminatory policy for decades beyond the mandatory desegregation of public pools in the United States in the 1950s.

We were forced to confront this racist history as a family in the fall of 2016, like so many other American households of color dealing with the consequences of what Van Jones described as a "whitelash against a changing country."[32] It happened that both of our children were taking swim lessons at the Meadowbrook Swim Club, most notable by then as the home pool of the legendary Olympian Michael Phelps. Our eight-year-old son had been less than enthusiastic about his lessons that November, which we took at first as the sign of a challenge. But then he shared something on the way home one Saturday afternoon.

"You know why I sometimes don't want to go to the locker room at Meadowbrook?" he asked. It turned out that a group of teenagers had been talking near him as they changed. Within earshot of our son, one of them said to the others that he would have liked the club better "when they didn't allow coloreds or Jews here." And then again, a few weeks later, a different group of boys a little older than our son was talking in the same locker room about some other place with many white people and "no Muslims" at all, how good that other place had been, pointing out our child and making a face at him as they walked out.

We were shocked to hear these things. We too were witness now to the raging antisemitism and anti-Muslim sentiment of those months, running through the highest levels of national political discourse. Then there was that one word that I couldn't get over, that strange plural noun, "coloreds," coming from the mouth of our son in 2016, a brown child trying to make sense of life in the city where he was born. A truth all around us was suddenly revealed. The clientele at the swim club remained predominantly white. And the walls of the facility kept up a naïve celebration of its racist history, with detailed boards at every turn documenting its storied legacy; none of them mentioned the club's segregated origin, but it was obvious in photo after photo of a lily-white population at play. Though we had hardly paid any attention to those history boards, what they stood for snapped sharply into focus that Saturday afternoon: an exclusionary past was there to be reclaimed, and we couldn't get away from it ourselves.

These last years have brought many harsh reminders of the deep well of racial hostility at the heart of the American experiment, the righteous exploitation and dispossession that grounded the conquest and settlement of this long-inhabited continent. But the struggle for social justice endures at local and national and planetary scales, and the experience and insight born of these struggles will remain a crucial resource on the path ahead. For, as historian Robin D. G. Kelley has argued, movements for social justice

> do what great poetry always does: transport us to another place, compel us to relive horrors and, more importantly, enable us to imagine a new future. . . . In the poetics of struggle and lived experience, in the utterances of ordinary folk, in the cultural products of social movements, in the reflections of activists, we discover the many different cognitive maps of the future, of the world not yet born.[33]

And these are possibilities to be charted in many ways—even in the space of a once segregated pool.

For thirty-five years, from 1921 to 1956, Black residents of the city of Baltimore were allowed to use a single outdoor public pool: Pool No. 2 at Druid Hill Park. Much smaller than the whites-only pool at the same park, Pool No. 2 was a vital necessity for Black athletes in the city and a beloved space of recreation for Black children and adults alike. The city was ordered to desegregate its pools in 1954, shortly after three Black children in Baltimore drowned while swimming in natural waters more accessible to them than this one pool.[34] Pool No. 2 was closed soon thereafter and fell into disrepair, until a few decades later, in 1999, when the pool became the site of an extraordinary commemorative project by the renowned artist Joyce Scott.

Pool No. 2 exists today as a rectangular field of grass, framed by the original boundaries of the pool and the square ceramic tiles that lined them, with a full set of bright blue handrails reaching from the concrete pathway on every side down into the grassy surface of the long-gone pool. Scott has spoken of her intent to create "an art situation where people can go into space and hopefully be."[35] The formerly segregated pool—built as a box to contain the bodies restricted to it—now invites those who come by to cross back and forth across its lines, between the grass and the concrete around it, in and out of the space were the water once was. And this is what you might

find happening at Druid Hill Park any given day: people running or walking around the concrete perimeter of the pool, stepping down into the grass to exercise or lounge, taking its lines in a spirit of lighthearted play rather than as warning to keep in or out.

"I love that because of the grass you can walk across the water. I love that it looks like if you grab hold of the railings and step down you can plunge into a world beneath the earth," writer and playwright R. Eric Thomas has mused about this space.[56] And indeed, this small place in contemporary Baltimore has something crucial to tell us, like all of the experiments in a more engaged and responsive living that I've followed in this book. The seeds of a more livable world remain to be found beneath the boundaries of this one. And we may yet find it within our hands, and in our hearts, to nurture a space for them to grow.

ACKNOWLEDGMENTS

Life in the United States can be profoundly isolating, and all too precarious for so many. Work on this book taught me to seek perspective and even hope in conversation and relationship, often in the company of others with whom I thought I shared painfully little. This book grows out of exchanges over many years with hundreds of people from many walks of life. What made it possible were countless moments of unexpected camaraderie and kinship, despite the tensions so prevalent in the air, and the stark implausibility of some of these connections.

I came as a stranger to most situations in this book. The kindness that I encountered so often was itself a revelation. I have tried chapter by chapter to acknowledge those whose active help made it possible for me to explore and understand their respective scenes. I have also tried to write in a spirit of gratitude with regard to those whose stories feature here, even on occasions of stark and sometimes maddening disagreement. I want to thank all of them once again here: the people, often pseudonymous, whose stories lend life to this book. The very sense of my place and community in the world has been reshaped profoundly by our conversations.

Many others have supported this work in foundational ways. My research was supported by a Catalyst Award from the Office of the Provost at Johns Hopkins University, and a Practical Ethics Award from the Berman Institute of Bioethics, also at Johns Hopkins. I am indebted to the following institutions for giving me the chance to talk about this project and hone its arguments over the years: Carnegie Mellon University, Catholic University of Leuven, Central European University, the Centre for Development Studies (Trivandrum), Deakin University, Goethe University, Indian Institute of Technology (Madras), Johns Hopkins University, La Trobe University, Macquarie University, National Institute of Advanced Studies (Bangalore), New School University, Pompeu Fabra University, Queen's University Belfast, Rice University, Stockholm University, University of California–Los Angeles, University of Maryland–Baltimore County, University of Pittsburgh, University of Southern California, and the University of Washington. Presentations and discussions at meetings of the American Anthropological Association, the American Ethnological Society, the Society for Cultural Anthropology, and the Society for Psychological Anthropology were also pivotal in the book's development, as was an early public reading and conversation at the Bird in Hand bookshop in Baltimore.

I am profoundly grateful to the students at Johns Hopkins University who assisted with research and the conceptualization of this project: Jessie Croteau, Evan Kim, Robert Lee, Amadea Martino Smith, Ricky Poulton, and most especially Raychel Gadson, whose findings and insights have shaped the ultimate structure and message of this book in countless ways. I owe my deep gratitude as well to the students in many classes over these years—"Influx/Efflux" in the spring of 2018, "Vulnerability" and "Invitation to Anthropology" in the fall of 2018, "The Idea of America" in the spring of 2019, "Public Anthropology" in the fall of 2022, the "Environmental Justice Workshop" in 2022–23, and "Pollution" in the spring of 2023—for their insights on fragments and excerpts from this work, and most especially to Jane Bennett and Shashawnda Campbell for co-teaching "Influx/Efflux" and the "Environmental Justice Workshop," respectively, with me.

Two essays for *The Guardian* taught me what this book was about, and I'm deeply grateful to editors Jessica Reed and Poppy Noor for pushing me to develop my thinking and expression. The editors of *Sapiens* were also kind enough to publish an early essay from this project, and Emily Sekine was wonderful to work with on that writing. My gratitude as well to the editors of a Society for Cultural Anthropology series on "American Fascism"—Chris Nelson, Heather Paxson, and Brad Weiss—for publishing another excerpt from the project. And among the countless conversations and exchanges that yielded this book, I need to thank the following individuals for giving me the chance to work out ideas through public interviews, conversations, and podcasts: Shoko Yamada for *Ekrits,* Juha Kaakinen of *Housing First Europe,* Bret McCabe of *Johns Hopkins Magazine,* Suchitra Vijayan of *The Polis Project,* Kulasegaram Sanchayan of *SBS Tamil Radio,* and Albert Imperato of the *Vir Vulnerabilis Vir* podcast. Though we did not see our collaboration through to a published book, I am grateful to Katherine Flynn of Kneerim & Williams for her insights, encouragement, and interest in this project. And my most profound debt with regard to publication is owed to editor Dylan Kyung-Lim White at Stanford University Press, whose thoughtful and engaged presence has helped shaped this book in innumerable ways, from the narrative voice and arc to the very possibility of its title. I am grateful to the anonymous reviewers enlisted by the press, whose comments and suggestions improved the manuscript in many crucial aspects, and it's been wonderful working with the entire team at Stanford, including Austin Michael Araujo, Susie Chavez, Lizzie Haroldsen, Bridget Kinsella, Emily E. Smith, Melissa Jauregui Chavez, Adam Schnitzer, copy editor Jennifer Gordon, indexer David Luljak, and everyone else who pitched in.

I owe so much to the many colleagues and friends who read and shared reactions to drafts and excerpts from this project, talked with me about it as it came together and came apart, and offered counsel and perspective through its many challenges and frustrations. My gratitude to Bürge Abiral, Nat Adams, Chloe Ahmann, Musahid Ahmed, Rebecca Altman, Alessandro Angelini, Fred Appel, Ahilan Arulanantham, David Bond, Dominic Boyer, Darren Byler, Joseph Calamia, Kriston Capps, Sharad Chari, Lawrence Cohen, Nathan Connolly, William Connolly, Sophie D'Anieri, Lee Davis, Lisa Davis, Raj Dayalan, Jason De Leon, Mike Degani, Bob Desjarlais, Thomas Dumm, Bill Egginton, Melissa Evans, Brendan Feehan, Mayanthi Fernando, Angela Garcia, Ilana Gershon, Jim Gibbons, Brian Goldstone, Gaston Gordillo, Radhika Govindrajan, Akhil Gupta, Bernie Guyer, Jane Guyer, Niloofar Haeri,

Hahrie Han, Tobias Hecht, Heiko Henkel, Eric Henney, Cymene Howe, Eric Jackson, Michael D. Jackson, Priya Jagannathan, Jonas Johnson, Naveeda Khan, Jessie Kindig, Eben Kirksey, Dorinne Kondo, Jake Kosek, Nicole Labruto, Tommi Laitio, Darius Lakdawalla, Andrew Lakoff, Aja Lans, Panthea Lee, Jovan Lewis, Tanya Luhrmann, Nancy Lutkehaus, Scott MacLochlainn, Emily Martin, Stuart McLean, Maria Merritt, Sabine Mohamed, Charles Moore, Donald Moore, Cristina Murphy, Tahir Naqvi, Priya Nelson, Paul Nestadt, Chris Newman, Viet Thanh Nguyen, Habiba Noor, Tom Özden-Schilling, A. S. Panneerselvan, David Platzer, Debbie Poole, Valeria Procupez, Andrea Rackowski, Hugh Raffles, Maya Ratnam, Ashanté Reese, Joshua Reno, Elizabeth Rodini, Sarah Roth, Alaa Saad, Faraz Sanei, Roy Scranton, Becquer Seguín, Mona Shah, Ellen Sharp, Emma Snyder, Ragini Tharoor Srinivasan, Alexias Stafilatos, Karen-Sue Taussig, Jordan Tierney, Maria Vesperi, Kevin Vosen, Christine Walley, Alisse Waterston, Ken Wissoker, Zoë Wool, and Caitlin Zaloom. For those I may have missed inadvertently, my sincere apologies, and the gratitude you deserve.

A book that leans toward a more radical sense of kinship depends so deeply on the insight and support of my own. I want to begin by thanking my neighbors in Baltimore, for sustaining a community space that has taught me so much about conviviality. Karun and Uma both grew up here as children, and I owe so much to their company and imagination. Sanchita has asked many of the hardest questions about this project, and it could not have come together without her abiding encouragement, compassion, and radical vision. Her parents Devika and K. B. Nair have been so generous in their care and support. My first apprenticeship in American life came alongside my sister and brother, Vidhya and Karthik, and I am ever humbled by their kindness and wisdom. Lalitha and Ganesh Pandian immigrated to the United States just a few months before I was born, and my sense of what remains possible here and beyond owes everything to them. Thank you for bringing your openness of spirit to this country.

NOTES

Introduction

1. For another ethnographic account of the same convention, see Georgina Voss, "Welcome to the SXSW of Concrete," *The Atlantic*, March 3, 2017. https://www.theatlantic.com/technology/archive/2017/03/concrete-america/518502/

2. See Adam Serwer, "The Cruelty Is the Point," *The Atlantic*, October 3, 2018. https://www.theatlantic.com/ideas/archive/2018/10/the-cruelty-is-the-point/572104/

3. See, for example, Lilliana Mason, *Uncivil Agreement: How Politics Became Our Identity* (Chicago: University of Chicago Press, 2018).

4. This argument is synthesized in my 2022 essay in *The Guardian*, "Look Around You. The Way We Live Explains Why We Are Increasingly Polarized," *The Guardian*, January 16, 2022. https://www.theguardian.com/global/2022/jan/16/look-around-you-why-increasingly-polarized

5. As quoted in the film by Raoul Peck, *I Am Not Your Negro*, 2016.

6. Palpable here is "the ineluctable siren's call of a 'normal' that never existed in the first place — or rather, a normality that is inseparable from the death and ruin which that normality itself produced" described by Patrick Blanchfield in many trenchant essays on American gun culture, such as the one that includes this passage: "Death Drive Nation," *Late Light*, November 2022. https://late-light.com/issues/issue-1/death-drive-nation

7. Jamelle Bouie, "A Gun-Filled America Is a World of Fear and Alienation," *New York Times*, May 9, 2023. https://www.nytimes.com/2023/05/09/opinion/allen-texas-shooting-guns.html

8. Katie Reilly, "Schools Are Spending Billions on Safety Measures to Stop Mass Shootings. It's Not Clear They Work." *Time*, June 16, 2022. https://time.com/6187656/school-safety-mass-shootings/

9. Sarah Jones, "The Hardening of America: From Schools to Starbucks Bathrooms, a Pernicious Idea Gains Ground," *The Intelligencer*, June 8, 2022. https://nymag.com/intelligencer/2022/06/the-hardening-of-america.html

10. "Lowly, unpurposeful and random as they may appear, sidewalk contacts are the small change from which a city's wealth of public life may grow," Jane Jacobs observes in *The Death and Life of Great American Cities* (New York: Vintage Books, 1961), 72.

11. Cliff Kuang with Robert Fabricant, *User Friendly: How the Hidden Rules of Design Are Changing the Way We Live, Work, and Play* (New York: MCD Books, 2019).

12. Jake Blumgart, "What Will Become of Levittown, Pennsylvania?" *Bloomberg*, March 1, 2016. https://www.bloomberg.com/news/articles/2016-03-01/what-will-become-of-levittown-pennsylvania

13. See, for example, Ryan D. Enos, who argues that geographic separation encourages "the separation of people in psychological space and, ultimately, political space" in *The Space Between Us: Social Geography and Politics* (Cambridge: Cambridge University Press, 2017).

14. As Edward S. Casey and Mary Watkins note in *Up Against the Wall: Re-Imagining the U.S.-Mexico Border* (Austin: University of Texas Press, 2014), 119, "our government could not build such a wall at the border if we were not already living within metaphorical walls in our towns and cities, walls that separate citizens from noncitizens. The wall at the border snakes itself into our communities, dividing schools and classrooms, hospitals, and neighborhoods."

15. Nancy Rosenblum, "The Good Neighbor in a Time of Crisis," *HistPhil*, August 19, 2020. https://histphil.org/2020/08/19/the-good-neighbor-in-a-time-of-crisis/

16. "President Obama's Farewell Address," *White House Archives*, January 10, 2017. https://obamawhitehouse.archives.gov/farewell

17. Anand Pandian, "The Casual Menace of a Trump Rally," *Sapiens*, October 27, 2020. https://www.sapiens.org/culture/trump-rally-hostility/

18. "Debate: Baldwin vs. Buckley," *American Archive of Public Broadcasting*, June 14, 1965. https://americanarchive.org/catalog/cpb-aacip_151-snooz71m54. I

am deeply grateful to an anonymous reviewer of this manuscript for bringing these words to my attention.

19. Given the fraught nature of its subject, I use pseudonyms throughout this book, unless I am writing about those whose work and views are already public, or those who wanted to be described with their own names.

20 Rabindranath Tagore, "Gitanjali 35," in *Gitanjali: Song Offerings* (London: Macmillan, 1913).

21. I make this argument in methodological terms in *A Possible Anthropology: Methods for Uneasy Times* (Durham: Duke University Press, 2019).

22. My gratitude to Jason De León for introducing me to volunteers from the Tucson Samaritans. As De León reflects on the significance of the organization's care work, and the difficult challenge of remembering those effaced by the violence of American border policy, he writes "the desert has already started to erase this person, along with whatever violence and horror she or he experienced. This event will soon be forgotten before it was ever known": *The Land of Open Graves: Living and Dying on the Migrant Trail* (Berkeley: University of California Press, 2015), 27.

23. See Francisco Cantú's deeply affecting account of the psychic toll of Border Patrol work in *The Line Becomes a River: Dispatches from the Border* (New York: Riverhead Books, 2018).

24. "When groups live physically, socially, and emotionally separate lives, they are far less likely to empathize with each other," Michael Carolan observes in *A Decent Meal: Building Empathy in a Divided America* (Stanford: Redwood Press, 2021), 9.

25. Dean Spade, *Mutual Aid: Building Solidarity During This Crisis (and the Next)* (New York: Verso Books, 2020), 8.

26. Spike Carlsen, "The Forgotten Front Porch Is Making a Comeback," *Wall Street Journal*, September 26, 2020. https://www.wsj.com/articles/the-forgotten-front-porch-is-making-a-comeback-11601092860

27. Helen Rowe, "Is Temporary the New Permanent? COVID Street Experiments Open Our Eyes to Creating Better Cities," *The Conversation*, March 18, 2021. https://theconversation.com/is-temporary-the-new-permanent-covid-street-experiments-open-our-eyes-to-creating-better-cities-156591

28. See *The Care Manifesto: The Politics of Interdependence* (New York: Verso Books, 2020), by the Care Collective.

29. Mariame Kaba, "Yes, We Mean Literally Abolish the Police," *New York Times*, June 12, 2020. https://www.nytimes.com/2020/06/12/opinion/sunday/floyd

-abolish-defund-police.html. For more on this vision of a transformative justice, see Kaba's book of collected essays, *We Do This 'Til We Free Us: Abolitionist Organizing and Transforming Justice* (Chicago: Haymarket Books, 2021).

30. Paul Gilroy, *After Empire: Melancholia or Convivial Culture?* (London: Routledge, 2004), xi.

31. Amanda Wise and Greg Noble, "Convivialities: An Orientation," *Journal of Intercultural Studies* 37, no. 5 (2016): 423–431.

32. "The better power of the commons is to point to a way to view what's broken in sociality, the difficulty of convening a world conjointly, although it is inconvenient and hard, and to offer incitements to imagining a livable provisional life," Lauren Berlant suggests in "The Commons: Infrastructures for Troubling Times," *Environment and Planning D: Society and Space* 34, no. 3 (2016): 393–419.

33. Élisabeth Vallet, "The World Is Witnessing a Rapid Proliferation of Border Walls," *Migration Information Source*, Migration Policy Institute, March 2, 2022. https://www.migrationpolicy.org/article/rapid-proliferation-number-border -walls

34. See Álvaro Sevilla-Buitrago, *Against the Commons: A Radical History of Urban Planning* (Minneapolis: University of Minnesota Press, 2022).

35. Todd Miller, *Build Bridges, Not Walls: A Journey to a World Without Borders* (San Francisco: City Lights Books, 2021).

36. Audre Lorde, "Difference and Survival," in *I Am Your Sister: Collected and Unpublished Writings of Audre Lorde,* edited by Rudolph Byrd, Johnnetta Cole, and Beverly Guy-Sheftall (New York: Oxford University Press, 2009), 201.

37. There is promise still in the nurturing of contact, in situations that allow for "the perception of common interests and common humanity" between different groups of people, as social psychologist Gordon Allport put it in his influential 1954 book, *The Nature of Prejudice* (Reading: Addison-Wesley, 1979). Decades of work in "contact theory" have shown that meaningful connections can overcome feelings of anxiety and threat, softening social boundaries.

Chapter 1

1. Alina Dizik, "In These Gated Communities, Security Personnel Act More Like Concierges," *Wall Street Journal*, April 9, 2020. https://www.wsj.com/articles/in -these-gated-communities-security-personnel-act-more-like-concierges -11586444753

2. Rich Benjamin, *Searching for Whitopia: An Improbable Journey to the Heart of White America* (New York: Hachette, 2009), 1, 5.

3. In the residential development of Florida, the historian N. D. B. Connolly has

observed in *A World More Concrete: Real Estate and the Remaking of Jim Crow South Florida* (Chicago: University of Chicago Press, 2014), "real estate carried an inherent racial politics" (7), organized along the lines of distinctive racial enclaves. More generally in the United States, gated communities are more affluent and more racially and ethnically homogeneous than non-gated communities, Elena Vesselinov and Renaud Le Goix find in "From Picket Fences to Iron Gates: Suburbanization and Gated Communities in Phoenix, Las Vegas, and Seattle," *GeoJournal* 77, no. 2 (2012): 203–222.

4. "Racial segregation was built into suburban development from the beginning," historian Paige Glotzer notes in a study of pioneering ventures in suburban real estate development in the city of Baltimore, *How the Suburbs Were Segregated: Developers and the Business of Exclusionary Housing, 1890–1960* (New York: Columbia University Press, 2020), 1.

5. Edward J. Blakely and Mary Gail Snyder, "Divided We Fall: Gated and Walled Communities in the United States," in *Architecture of Fear*, edited by Nan Ellin (New York: Princeton Architectural Press, 1997), 97.

6. Setha Low, *Behind the Gates: Life, Security, and the Pursuit of Happiness in Fortress America* (New York: Routledge, 2004), 26.

7. Karen A. Danielsen, "How the Other Half Lives: Tenure Differences and Trends in Rental Gated Communities," *Housing Policy Debate* 18, no. 3 (2007): 503–534.

8. See, for example, Lynn A. Addington and Callie Marie Rennison, "Keeping the Barbarians Outside the Gate? Comparing Burglary Victimization in Gated and Non-Gated Communities," *Justice Quarterly* 32, no. 1 (2015): 168–192. "Despite the widely-held belief that gated communities are safer than their non-gated counterparts, little is known about the veracity of this assumption," the authors note.

9. Robert E. Lang and Karen A. Danielsen, "Gated Communities in America: Walling Out the World?" *Housing Policy Debate* 8, no. 4 (1997): 867–899. "In gated communities, with their privatized streets, recreation, local governance, and security, residents have less need of the public realm outside their gates than those living in traditional open neighborhoods," Edward J. Blakely and Mary Gail Snyder observe in "Forting Up: Gated Communities in the United States," *Journal of Architecture and Planning Research* 15, no. 1 (1998): 61–72.

10. Wendy Brown, *Walled States, Waning Sovereignty* (New York: Zone Books, 2014), 40.

11. US Census Bureau, *American Housing Survey*, 2021. These figures refer to "houses in subdivisions, multiunits, and mobile homes in groups of two or more." In Florida, however, the percentage of homes in such residential communities secured by community walls or fences climbs to 40 percent.

12. Rich Benjamin, "The Gated Community Mentality," *New York Times*, March 29, 2012. https://www.nytimes.com/2012/03/30/opinion/the-gated-community -mentality.html

13. National Association of Home Builders, *Housing Preferences of the Boomer Generation: How They Compare to Other Home Buyers* (BuilderBooks, 2016).

14. Robert Steuteville, "A Defining Moment for Gated Developments," *Public Square: A CNU Journal*, April 12, 2012.

15. Rowland Atkinson and Sarah Blandy, *Domestic Fortress: Fear and the New Home Front* (Manchester: Manchester University Press, 2016), 21, 131.

16 Bradley Garrett, *Bunker: Building for the End Times* (New York: Simon & Schuster, 2020), 3.

17. David E. Jacobs, "Environmental Health Disparities in Housing," *American Journal of Public Health* 101, no. S1 (2011): S115–S122.

18. Joint Center for Housing Studies of Harvard University, *The State of the Nation's Housing 2018*, 15. https://www.jchs.harvard.edu/sites/default/files/re ports/files/Harvard_JCHS_State_of_the_Nations_Housing_2018.pdf

19. Emily Yates-Doerr, "Why Are So Many Guatemalans Migrating to the U.S.?," *Sapiens*, October 25, 2018. https://www.sapiens.org/culture/guatemala-migrants -united-states/

20. Nicole Prchal Svajlenka, "Undocumented Immigrants in Construction," *Center for American Progress*, February 2, 2021. https://www.americanprogress .org/wp-content/uploads/sites/2/2021/02/EW-Construction-factsheet.pdf.

21. Candace Taylor, "Before Covid, Golf Club Communities Were in the Rough. Now They're Seeing Green," *Wall Street Journal*, December 9, 2020. https://www .wsj.com/articles/golf-club-communities-covid-11607528976

22. Tim Sullivan, Zonda, speaking during a February 9, 2021, session called "Designing Homes & Communities Beyond the Pandemic."

23. As was emphasized in a session on "Suburban and Urban Multifamily De- velopment in the Wake of Covid-19."

24. Sixty percent of respondents in this age bracket described access-control gates as an essential or desirable feature. See Rose Quint, *What Home Buyers Really Want* (BuilderBooks, 2021), A137.

25. Quint, *What Home Buyers Really Want*, 78–79.

26. On the post-pandemic boom in residential bunker construction, see Mira Ptacin, "Could Doomsday Bunkers Become the New Normal?" *New York Times*, June 26, 2020. https://www.nytimes.com/2020/06/26/realestate/could-doomsday -bunkers-become-the-new-normal.html

Chapter 2

1. For a critical cultural engagement with "the notion of the Midwest as a pastoral heartland, principally featuring agriculture and hardworking white farmers," an image resonant with the themes of this chapter, see Britt E. Halvorson and Joshua O. Reno, *Imagining the Heartland: White Supremacy and the American Midwest* (Oakland: University of California Press, 2022), 40.

2. Greg Grandin, *The End of the Myth: From the Frontier to the Border Wall in the Mind of America* (New York: Macmillan, 2019), 116.

3. Frederick Jackson Turner, *The Frontier in American History* (New York: Henry Holt, 1920), 15, 30.

4. Robert Bennett, "Tract Homes on the Range: The Suburbanization of the American West," *Western American Literature* 46, no. 3 (2011): 281–301.

5. Robert M. Fogelson, *Bourgeois Nightmares: Suburbia, 1870–1930* (New Haven: Yale University Press, 2007), 212.

6. Post on X (Twitter) by Donald J. Trump, July 23, 2020. https://twitter.com/realdonaldtrump/status/1286372175117791236

7. William H. Frey, "Biden's Victory Came from the Suburbs," *Brookings*, November 13, 2020. https://www.brookings.edu/research/bidens-victory-came-from-the-suburbs/

8. Andrea Vesentini, *Indoor America: The Interior Landscape of Postwar Suburbia* (Charlottesville: University of Virginia Press, 2018), 13, 12.

9. Vesentini, *Indoor America*, 11.

10. Michael Dolan, *The American Porch: An Informal History of an Informal Place* (Guilford: Lyons Press, 2002).

11. James Agee, "Knoxville: Summer of 1915," *Partisan Review* 5, no. 3 (1938): 22–25.

12. Jocelyn Hazelwood Donlon, *Swinging in Place: Porch Life in Southern Culture* (Chapel Hill: University of North Carolina Press, 2001).

13. "As a vehicle for upward mobility," Vesentini writes on the effects of air-conditioning, "coolness was thus inscribed in the same racial and class discourse that had led to the demise of the street, the lawn, and the porch as loci of public life. Finding release from hot weather outside one's house belonged in the urban past or specific groups, such as farmers, blue-collar workers, tenement residents, African Americans, and immigrant communities" (*Indoor America*, 124–126).

14. "November 4, 2019 Minutes," *Fargo City Commission.* https://fargond.gov/city-government/departments/city-commission/agendas-minutes/2019-minutes-video-archives/november-4-2019-minutes

15. Barry Amundson, "Neighbors Grumble, but Zoning Board OKs Duplexes in

South Fargo," *In Forum*, October 1, 2019. https://www.inforum.com/news/govern
ment-and-politics/4693713-Neighbors-grumble-but-zoning-board-OKs-duplexes
-in-south-Fargo

16. "November 4, 2019 Minutes."

17. "November 4, 2019 Minutes."

18. In the politics of urban American housing development, Katherine Levine
Einstein, David M. Glick, and Maxwell Palmer write in *Neighborhood Defenders:
Participatory Politics and America's Housing Crisis* (New York: Cambridge University Press, 2019), it is often the case that privileged "citizen participants use land
use regulations to buttress lawsuits, demands for parking and traffic studies, and
other claims that constrain housing development" (15–16), greatly complicating
efforts to make affordable housing available to city residents.

19. Barry Amundson, "City Commission Sides with South Fargo Residents over
Duplex Developer," *In Forum*, November 4, 2019. https://www.inforum.com/news
/government-and-politics/4755291-City-Commission-sides-with-south-Fargo
-residents-over-duplex-developer

20. City of Fargo, "2007 Growth Plan: Chapter 4: Growth in the Next 20 Years,"
55. https://fargond.gov/city-government/departments/planning-development/
land-use-zoning/future-growth/2007-growth-plan

21. City of Fargo, "2007 Growth Plan: Appendix One: Growth Projection Data,"
73. https://download.fargond.gov/0/fargo_growth_plan_2007_appendices.pdf

22. Lutheran Social Services of North Dakota was ultimately forced to close in
2021 due to the cost of its affordable housing program. In Forum Staff Reports,
"Lutheran Social Services of North Dakota to Close Its Doors; 283 Jobs Will Be Af-
fected," *In Forum*, January 15, 2021. https://www.inforum.com/community/luther
an-social-services-of-north-dakota-to-close-its-doors-283-jobs-will-be-affected

23. Jennifer Erickson, *Race-ing Fargo: Refugees, Citizenship, and the Transformation of Small Cities* (Ithaca: Cornell University Press, 2020), 129.

24. Erickson, *Race-ing Fargo*, 138.

25. "Stop Refugee Resettlement and Lutheran Social Services in North Dakota!"
change.org, August 10, 2015. https://www.change.org/p/cass-county-legislature
-stop-lutheran-social-services-in-fargo

26. Eric Klinenberg, *Palaces for the People: How Social Infrastructure Can Help
Fight Inequality, Polarization, and the Decline of Civic Life* (New York: Crown
Books, 2018), 11.

27. "Hukun Dabar for Fargo Mayor — My Story," *YouTube*. https://www.youtube
.com/watch?v=oXh1sdaubTI

28. Fargo has an "approval voting" system in place that allows voters to iden-

tify all the candidates they approve of, rather than selecting one alone. Mahoney won the approval of 65 percent of those who voted. Robin Huebner, "Support for Candidates Is Greater Than What Fargo Election Results Showed, Approval Voting Proponents Say," *In Forum*, June 17, 2022. https://www.inforum.com/news/fargo/support-for-candidates-is-greater-than-what-fargo-election-results-showed-approval-voting-proponents-say

Chapter 3

1. D. J. Norman-Cox, *Juneteenth 101: Popular Myths and Forgotten Facts* (independently published, 2020).

2. Laura Douglas, "Quakertown," Texas Historical Commission Subject Marker Application, Denton County, 2011. https://apps.dentoncounty.gov/website/HistoricalMarkers/PDFs/Quakertown-Undertold-Story-2010-Subject-Marker-Historical-Narrative-Denton-County.pdf

3. J. David Goodman and Edgar Sandoval, "Texas Will Place a Floating Barrier Between U.S. and Mexico," *New York Times*, June 8, 2023. https://www.nytimes.com/2023/06/08/us/texas-abbott-border-wall.html

4. bell hooks, "Homeplace (A Site of Resistance)," in *Yearning: Race, Gender, and Cultural Politics* (Boston: South End Press, 1990), 41–49.

5. Chelsea Stallings, "'Removing the Danger in a Business Way': The History and Memory of Quakertown, Denton, Texas," MA thesis, University of North Texas, 2015.

6. Karla Slocum, *Black Towns, Black Futures: The Enduring Allure of a Black Place in the American West* (Chapel Hill: University of North Carolina Press, 2019), 107, 131–132.

7. Douglas, "Quakertown."

8. Personal communication with Randy Hunt of Historic Denton.

9. Stallings, "'Removing the Danger in a Business Way.'"

10. "Interview with Alma Clark," Number 1636, University of North Texas Oral History Collection, September 29, 2006, 28.

11. C. Vann Woodward, *The Strange Career of Jim Crow* (New York: Oxford University Press, 2001), 44.

12. JoAnne Brown, "Purity and Danger in Color: Notes on Germ Theory, and the Semantics of Segregation, 1885–1915," in *Heredity and Infection: The History of Disease Transmission*, edited by Jean-Paul Gaudillére and Ilana Löwy (London: Routledge, 2001), 101–131.

13. "Rotarians to Get Out and Work for Park," *Denton Record-Chronicle*, March 26, 1921.

14. "Vote for the Good of the Order," *Denton Record-Chronicle*, April 4, 1921.

15. "Principles of Klan Defended by Speaker Before Large Crowd," *Denton Record-Chronicle*, August 5, 1922.

16. Jovan Scott Lewis, *Violent Utopia: Dispossession and Black Restoration in Tulsa* (Durham: Duke University Press, 2022), 132.

17. "City Park, One of Major Civic Assets of Denton, Lies Where Once Ramshackle Quarter Stood," *Denton Record-Chronicle*, June 29, 1939.

18. Stallings, "'Removing the Danger in a Business Way,'" 67–69.

19. "It is segregation that permits unequal access to public goods and services" in the United States, Jessica Trounstine argues in *Segregation by Design: Local Politics and Inequality in American Cities* (New York: Cambridge University Press, 2018), 2. "From the beginning, poor and minority neighborhoods received fewer and lower-quality services. They were less likely to be connected to sewers, to have graded and paved streets, or to benefit from disease mitigation programs" (2).

20. "Interview with Alma Clark," 14.

21. "Interview with Billie Mohair," Number 713, North Texas State University Oral History Collection, February 25, 1988, 21

22. "Interview with Euline Brock," Number 707, North Texas State University Oral History Collection, October 27, 1987, 55.

23. Richard W. Byrd, "Interracial Cooperation in a Decade of Conflict: The Denton (Texas) Christian Women's Inter-Racial Fellowship," *Oral History Review* 19, no. 1–2 (1991): 31–53. The organization was first known as the Denton Christian Women's Interracial Fellowship," but the word "Christian" was later dropped with the aim of being more inclusive.

24. "Interview with Euline Brock," 23.

25. "Interview with Dorothy Adkins," Number 705, North Texas State University Oral History Collection, November 17, 1987, 16.

26. "Interview with Trudy Foster," Number 706, North Texas State University Oral History Collection, November 17, 1987, 9–10.

27. One of these cards is on display at the Denton County African American Museum in downtown Denton.

28. "Interview with Dorothy Adkins," 4.

29. Byrd, "Interracial Cooperation," 47.

30. Carol B. Stack, *All Our Kin: Strategies for Survival in a Black Community* (New York: Harper & Row, 1974), 27–28.

31. "Interview with Billie Mohair," 13.

32. "Interview with Betty Kimble," Number 709, North Texas State University Oral History Collection, December 8, 1987.

33. Denton Public Library, "Foundation of Our History: The Repainting of a Mural on Robertson Street and the Importance of Their Voices," February 25, 2021. https://dentonlibrary.wordpress.com/2021/02/25/foundation-of-our-history-the -repainting-of-a-mural-on-robertson-street-and-the-importance-of-their -voices/

34. Denton Women's Interracial Fellowship, "Denton Women's Interracial Fellowship Monument," *Denton Women's Interraciall Fellowship.* https://www. dentonwif.com

35. My gratitude to Jessica Luther Rummel for sharing her research and insights with regard to the history of Denton's Confederate monument and its implications for contemporary racial politics in Denton and beyond.

36. *Historical Sketch of the Katie Daffan Chapter U.D.C.* (Denton: United Daughters of the Confederacy, 1918).

37. Apple Podcasts, *Confederate Monuments—Part 2: Black History for White People.* https://podcasts.apple.com/us/podcast/black-history-for-white-people/ id1514522005?i=1000488567486

38. bell hooks, *Belonging: A Culture of Place* (New York: Routledge, 2008), 7.

39. hooks, *Belonging*, 87.

40. Christian McPhate, "Will Southeast Denton See the Same Fate as Quakertown?" *Denton Record-Chronicle*, September 30, 2022.

41. Christian McPhate, "Southeast Denton Residents Draw Line in Sand, Meet with Developer to Fight Gentrification," *Denton Record-Chronicle*, November 11, 2022.

42. See also the two-part 2022 feature by Danielle Phillips-Cunningham, Alma Clark, and Betty Kimble, "Juneteenth Started in Texas. So Did This Black Town. Whites Destroyed It" and "White Racism Brought Down a Black Community. Will There Be Reparations?" *Washington Post*, June 18, 2022. https://www.washington post.com/politics/2022/06/18/juneteenth-quakertown-texas-black-race-white -supremacy/

Chapter 4

1. The new Tesla Cybertruck may be the apotheosis of this aspiration— advertised as bulletproof and described by Elon Musk as "the finest in apocalypse technology." See Alan Ohnsman, "The Business Case for Musk's Tesla Cybertruck Isn't Bulletproof," *Forbes*, December 8, 2023. https://www.forbes.com/sites/ala nohnsman/2023/12/08/the-business-case-for-musks-tesla-cybertruck-isnt-bul letproof/

2. Zifei Yang and Anup Bandivadekar, "2017 Global Update: Light-Duty Vehicle

Greenhouse Gas and Fuel Economy Standards," *International Council on Clean Transportation*, June 23, 2017. https://theicct.org/publication/2017-global-update-light-duty-vehicle-greenhouse-gas-and-fuel-economy-standards/

3. "The 2023 EPA Automotive Trends Report: Greenhouse Gas Emissions, Fuel Economy, and Technology Since 1975," *US Environmental Protection Agency*, December 2023. https://www.epa.gov/system/files/documents/2023-12/420s23002.pdf

4. For an early and influential critical account of these developments, see Keith Bradsher, *High and Mighty: The Dangerous Rise of the SUV* (New York: PublicAffairs, 2002).

5. Alexa St. John and the Associated Press, "SUV Sales Boom Has Erased Gains from Cleaner Car Tech, Upping Negative Environment Impact by More Than 30% over the Last Decade, *Forbes*, November 27, 2023. https://fortune.com/2023/11/27/suv-sales-boom-erased-gains-cleaner-car-tech-upping-negative-environment-impact-global-fuel-economy-initiative/

6. Lydia DePillis, "As GM's Lordstown Plant Idles, an Iconic American Job Nears Extinction," *CNN Business*, March 6, 2019. https://www.cnn.com/2019/03/06/economy/gm-lordstown-workers/index.html

7. Robert Channick, "While GM Idles Sedan Production, Chicago-Area Ford, Chrysler Plants Are Going Strong After Shifting to SUVs," *Chicago Tribune*, December 26, 2018. https://www.chicagotribune.com/business/ct-biz-ford-chrysler-jeep-auto-plants-chicago-20181203-story.html

8. Joshua Chin, "Mercedes-Benz to Stop Sedan Production in North America," *Automacha*, July 22, 2020. https://automacha.com/mercedes-suv-replacing-sedan-and-hatchback-production-in-north-america/

9. "Toyota Will Swap SUVs for Sedans at New U.S. Plant," *Gardner Business Media*, July 10, 2019. https://www.gardnerweb.com/news/toyota-will-swap-crossovers-for-sedans-at-new-us-plant

10. "The popular obsessions with safety and space, as embodied in the SUV, are euphemistic," Josh Lauer writes. "*Safety* is not road safety but personal safety, and *space* is not interior cargo space but social space, including the ability to traverse the most inhospitable terrain to sequester oneself from the hazards of modern civilization." See Lauer, "Driven to Extremes: Fear of Crime and the Rise of the Sport Utility Vehicle in the United States," *Crime, Media, Culture* 1, no. 2 (2005): 149–168.

11. "Traffic Safety Facts: Passenger Vehicles," *National Highway Traffic Safety Administration* (Washington, DC: US Department of Transportation, May 2017).

12. Michelle J. White, "The 'Arms Race' on American Roads: The Effect of Sport Utility Vehicles and Pickup Trucks on Traffic Safety," *Journal of Law and Economics* 47, no. 2 (October 2004): 333–355.

13. NHTSA fact sheets on pedestrian injury and death resulting from motor vehicle crashes define a pedestrian in terms that exclude children and others using such conveyances, that is, a pedestrian as "any person on foot, walking, running, jogging, hiking, sitting, or lying down who is involved in a motor vehicle traffic crash. These exclude people on personal conveyances like roller skates, inline skates, skateboards, baby strollers, scooters, toy wagons, motorized skateboards, motorized toy cars, Segway-style devices, motorized and non-motorized wheelchairs, and scooters for those with disabilities." See "Traffic Safety Facts: Pedestrians," *National Highway Traffic Safety Administration* (Washington, DC: US Department of Transportation, 2018).

14. "Pedestrian Traffic Fatalities by State: 2022 Preliminary Data, January–June," *Governors Highway Safety Association*, June 2023. https://www.ghsa.org/resources/Pedestrians23

15. Devon E. Lefler and Hampton C. Gabler, "The Fatality and Injury Risk of Light Truck Impacts with Pedestrians in the United States," *Accident Analysis and Prevention* 36, no. 2 (2004): 295–304.

16. Susan Hogan et al., "Driveway Danger: Kids Being Injured and Killed in 'Frontover' SUV Blind Zone Incidents," *NBC Washington*, July 28, 2022. https://www.nbcwashington.com/investigations/driveway-danger-kids-being-injured-and-killed-in-frontover-suv-blind-zone-incidents/3119237/

17. Yang and Bandivadekar, "2017 Global Update."

18. "Inventory of Greenhouse Gas Emissions and Sinks: 1990–2017," *US Environmental Protection Agency*, 2019. https://www.epa.gov/ghgemissions/inventory-us-greenhouse-gas-emissions-and-sinks-1990-2017

19. Alan Hess, *Googie Redux: Ultramodern Roadside Architecture* (San Francisco: Chronicle Books, 2004).

20. Bill Vlasic, "Trump, Easing Emissions Rule, Vows to Expand Auto Jobs," *New York Times*, March 15, 2017. https://www.nytimes.com/2017/03/15/business/trump-auto-industry-emissions-rules.html

21. See Lauer, "Driven to Extremes."

22. John Urry, "Inhabiting the Car," *Sociological Review* 54, no. 1 (2006): 17–31.

23. Oliver Milman, "How SUVs Conquered the World—at the Expense of Its Climate," *Guardian*, September 3, 2020. https://www.theguardian.com/us-news/2020/sep/01/suv-conquered-america-climate-change-emissions

24. Michael Laris and Luz Lazo, "Cities Are Making Covid-Era Street Changes Permanent. Some Are Facing Pushback," *Washington Post*, June 26, 2021. https://www.washingtonpost.com/transportation/2021/06/26/covid-street-closures/

25. Cadillac, *Discover the Next-Generation 2021 Escalade.*

26 "57. Test Driving the 2021 Cadillac Escalade with Andrew Hawkins," *The War on Cars.* https://thewaroncars.org/episode-57-test-driving-the-2021-cadillac-escalade-with-andrew-hawkins-final-web-transcript/

27. "73. Third Anniversary Mailbag," *The War on Cars,* November 22, 2021. https://thewaroncars.org/2021/11/22/third-anniversary-mailbag/

28. Christine Hauser and Judith Levitt, "Together, Alone: The Car as Shelter in the Pandemic," *New York Times,* May 23, 2020. https://www.nytimes.com/2020/05/23/us/drive-by-graduation-baby-shower-drive-in-coronavirus.html

29. Daniel Miller and Russ Mitchell, "Could Your Car Keep You Safe from COVID-19?" *Los Angeles Times,* October 13, 2020. https://www.latimes.com/business/story/2020-10-13/la-coronavirus-car-protection

30. "43. Victory?" *The War on Cars,* May 22, 2020. https://thewaroncars.org/2020/05/22/victory/

31. This trajectory also has an important class basis, as noted by this recent report: "Impact of the COVID-19 Pandemic on Subway Ridership in New York City," *Office of the New York State Controller.* https://www.osc.state.ny.us/reports/osdc/impact-covid-19-pandemic-subway-ridership-new-york-city

32. "Parents have a way of imagining the worst, especially when your distracted teenager has the car," the narrator of a 2019 Subaru Forester ad observes. The ad, titled "A Parent's Imagination," presents a series of dark comedic moments in which parents imagine their teenage drivers remaining completely nonchalant and phone focused as their vehicles spiral completely out of control. Every scenario presented by the advertisement, however, depicts possible threats to the driver that the vehicle guards against, rather than any danger that young, distracted drivers and their large vehicles may pose to others on the road. See https://adsofbrands.net/en/ads/subaru-forester-a-parent-s-imagination/10080

33. Joey Capparella, "Honda Fit Discontinued for the U.S., Despite New Global Model," *Car and Driver,* July 17, 2020. https://www.caranddriver.com/news/a33337398/honda-fit-discontinued-for-the-us-despite-new-global-model/

34. Andrea Vesentini, "Together and Apart: Encapsulation and the Automobile," in *Indoor America: The Interior Landscape of Postwar Suburbia* (Charlottesville: University of Virginia Press, 2018), 19–53; italics in original.

Chapter 5

1. The original post has been deleted by the user: https://www.reddit.com/r/PublicFreakout/comments/gu3lnw/truck_rolls_coal_through_protesters_in_michigan/

2. Facebook comments posted about the incident: https://www.facebook.com
/uppermichiganssource/posts/walking-as-a-group-protesters-blocked-traffic
-in-one-lane-there-was-no-law-enfor/10163586554080640/

3. Tim Elfrink, "Cop Suspended over 'All Lives Splatter' Meme Posted After Seattle Protester Killed by Driver," *Washington Post,* July 9, 2020. https://www.wash
ingtonpost.com/nation/2020/07/09/summer-taylor-detective-meme-suspended/

4. David Weigel, "Rolling Coal," *Slate,* July 3, 2014. https://slate.com/news-and
-politics/2014/07/rolling-coal-conservatives-who-show-their-annoyance-with
-liberals-obama-and-the-epa-by-blowing-black-smoke-from-their-trucks.html

5. "Rolling Coal on People Compilation: New 2017," *YouTube.* https://www.
youtube.com/watch?v=6fvIuOTYAn4

6. Kat Webb, "Diesel Activism: Truck Drivers Turn Counterprotesters by 'Rolling Coal,'" *Herald Journal,* June 17, 2020. https://www.hjnews.com/news/local/
diesel-activism-truck-drivers-turn-counterprotesters-by-rolling-coal/article_
df413b52-e6af-5533-be39-768e5db50875.html

7. "About Diesel Fuels," *US Environmental Protection Agency.* https://www.epa
.gov/diesel-fuel-standards/about-diesel-fuels

8. "Diesel Engines and Public Health," *Union of Concerned Scientists,* July 15,
2005 (updated February 11, 2022). https://www.ucsusa.org/resources/diesel
-engines-public-health

9. "UN Health Agency Re-Classifies Diesel Engine Exhaust as 'Carcinogenic to
Humans,'" *United Nations,* June 12, 2012. https://news.un.org/en/story/2012/06/412
932

10. Clifford Atiyeh, "Everything You Need to Know About the VW Diesel-
Emissions Scandal," *Car and Driver,* December 4, 2019. https://www.caranddriver
.com/news/a15339250/everything-you-need-to-know-about-the-vw-diesel-emis
sions-scandal/

11 The source for the quote is no longer accessible at the original link: https://
www.vocativ.com/culture/society/dicks-pick-trucks-meme-rollin-coal/

12. "Granger Smith and Earl Dibbles Jr—Diesel (Official Music Video)," *You-
Tube.* https://www.youtube.com/watch?v=g4k1qp7MiJ4

13. Cara Daggett, "Petro-Masculinity: Fossil Fuels and Authoritarian Desire,"
Millennium Journal of International Studies 47, no. 1 (2018): 25–44.

14. Nate Powell, "About Face," *Popula,* February 24, 2019. https://popula.com/
2019/02/24/about-face/

15. Numerous other observers have noted the prevalence of "death's head" imagery in American law enforcement, even in the official response to Black Lives
Matter critiques of police violence. See, for example, Benjamin Linzy, "The Badge

and the Skull: Cops, Militants, and a Punisher Fetish," *Activist History Review*, June 22, 2022. https://activisthistory.com/2020/06/22/the-badge-and-the-skull -cops-militants-and-a-punisher-fetish/

16. Steve Viscelli, *The Big Rig: Trucking and the Decline of the American Dream* (Oakland: University of California Press, 2016), 207.

17. See the chapter "The Big Rig: Running the Contractor Confidence Game," 105–139, in Viscelli's *Big Rig*.

18. For a critical account of the social and racial fantasies that organize American trucking, and close attention to minority and queer trucking communities that complicate normative pictures of the industry, see Anne Balay, *Semi Queer: Inside the World of Gay, Trans, and Black Truck Drivers* (Chapel Hill: University of North Carolina Press, 2018).

19. Kenneth Niemeyer, "'Rolling Coal' to Blow a Thick Cloud of Exhaust Like Video of a Busy Texas Restaurant Shows Is Legal in Most States," *Business Insider*, October 21, 2021. https://www.insider.com/rolling-coal-exhaust-clouds-legal-in -most-states-2021-10

20. Bruce Finley, "Diesel Drivers Who Are 'Rolling Coal' in Colorado: Tune Up or Pay Up," *Denver Post*, May 22, 2017. https://www.denverpost.com/2017/05/22/colo rado-rolling-coal-fines/

21. "Colorado Revised Statutes," *Office of Legislative Legal Services, Colorado General Assembly.* https://leg.colorado.gov/agencies/office-legislative-legal-ser vices/colorado-revised-statutes

22. Young men who admitted to outbursts of road rage spoke similarly of having been wronged previously by those subject to their aggression. See Deborah Lupton, "Road Rage: Drivers' Understandings and Experiences," *Journal of Sociology* 38, no. 3 (2002): 275–290.

23. John Urry, "Inhabiting the Car," *Sociological Review* 54, no. 1 (2006): 17–31.

24. James C. Cobb, "How the Pickup Truck Carried the American South into the Future," *Zocalo Public Square*, July 2, 2018. https://www.zocalopublicsquare.org/ 2018/07/02/pickup-truck-carried-american-south-future/ideas/essay/

25. Lewin Day, "Coal-Rolling Teen That Hit Cyclists Charged with Six Felonies," *The Drive*, November 8, 2021. https://www.thedrive.com/news/43060/coal-rolling -teen-that-hit-cyclists-charged-with-six-felonies

26. "Rolling Coal on Protesters Compilation (BlackLivesMatter, Trump Haters, Tree Huggers)," *YouTube*. https://www.youtube.com/watch?v=rYPMbLO4pAY

27. Josh Cain, "Driver Seen Speeding away from Demonstration with Protester on Hood in Pasadena," *Pasadena Star-News*, May 31, 2020. https://www.pasadena

starnews.com/2020/05/31/driver-seen-speeding-away-from-demonstration
-with-protester-on-hood-in-pasadena-arrested/

28. Paulo Acoba, "Brazen Jerk Films Himself Rolling Coal over Spring Hill Protesters, Meant to 'Spark Conversation,'" *Tire Meets Road*, June 4, 2020. https://tire
meetsroad.com/2020/06/04/jerk-films-himself-rolling-coal-truck-over-spring
-hill-protesters-spark-conversation/

29. Kianna Gardner, "Hundreds Converge on Kalispell for Protest," *Daily Inter
Lake*, June 7, 2020. https://dailyinterlake.com/news/2020/jun/07/hundreds-con
verge-on-kalispell-for-protest-6/

30. Webb, "Diesel Activism."

31. Ruth Wilson Gilmore, *Golden Gulag: Prisons, Surplus, Crisis, and Opposition in Globalizing California* (Berkeley: University of California Press, 2007).

32. Post on Facebook by Natasha Owens, June 20, 2020. https://www.facebook
.com/natasha.owens/videos/10158269227593334/

33. Nicole Vulcan, "Hundreds Gather, Largely Masked, for a Black Lives Matter
Rally in Downtown Bend," *Bend Source*, May 30, 2020. https://www.bendsource.
com/bend/hundreds-gather-largely-masked-for-a-black-lives-matter-rally-in
-downtown-bend/Content?oid=12584807

34. Case report from the Bend Police Department, accessed via a public records request.

35. "Charges Filed in Rally 'Rolling Coal' Incident," *My Central Oregon*, July 29,
2020. https://www.mycentraloregon.com/2020/07/29/charges-filed-in-rally-rol
ling-coal-incident/

36. Ben Michaelis, whose Decency Project provided a framework for the
encounter.

37. Jack Hirsh, "Hummel Leads Way for New Central Oregon Decency Project,"
KTVZ News, October 16, 2020. https://ktvz.com/news/2020/10/16/hummel-leads
-way-for-new-central-oregon-decency-project/

Chapter 6

1. Earl Swift, *The Big Roads: The Untold Story of the Engineers, Visionaries, and
Trailblazers Who Created the American Superhighways* (New York: Mariner
Books, 2012), 3.

2. From the Dyer Historical Society archives.

3. Lincoln Highway Association, *The Lincoln Highway: The Story of a Crusade
That Made Transportation History* (New York: Dodd, Mead and Co., 1935, 207).

4. Mark Baumer, "My Hundredth Day on the Road," *Medium*, January 21, 2017.
https://notgoingtomakeit.com/my-hundredth-day-on-the-road-96727770ae16

5. Angie Schmitt, *Right of Way: Race, Class, and the Silent Epidemic of Pedestrian Deaths in America* (Washington, DC: Island Press, 2020), 48–49.

6. Schmitt, *Right of Way*, 5.

7. Tori Telfer, "This Guy Is Walking Across America Barefoot to Protest Climate Change," *Vice*, December 2, 2016. https://www.vice.com/en/article/xdmv73/poznaj -poete-ktory-chce-przejsc-boso-cale-usa-by-uratowac-ziemie

8. Mark Baumer, "That Time I Walked to West Virginia," *Medium*, December 2, 2016. https://notgoingtomakeit.com/that-time-i-walked-to-west-virginia-bare foot-41ffd0389d27

9. Mark Baumer, *I Am a Road* (independently published, 2016), 151.

10. Mark Baumer, "Walking Across America on My Birthday," *Medium*, December 20, 2016. https://notgoingtomakeit.com/walking-barefoot-across-america-on -my-birthday-e49c8568410b

11. Mark Baumer, "We're Forking over the Earth," *YouTube*. https://www. youtube.com/watch?v=udm5H7tvyFw

12. "Marching Forth for Mark," *Jim Baumer Experience*, March 3, 2017. http:// jimbaumerexperience.com/marching-forth-for-mark/

13. Anna Heyward, "The Tragic Death of Mark Baumer, A Prolific Poet and Environmental Activist for the Social-Media Age," *New Yorker*, January 26, 2017. https://www.newyorker.com/books/page-turner/the-tragic-death-of-mark -baumer-a-prolific-poet-and-environmental-activist-for-the-social-media -age

14. Compelling in this regard is the documentary by Julie Sokolow, *Barefoot: The Mark Baumer Story* (1091 Pictures, 2019).

15. Baumer, "My Hundredth Day on the Road."

16. National Association of City Transportation Officials, "Why the US Gives Monster SUVs Five-Star Safety Ratings and What You Can Do About It," May 24, 2022. https://nacto.org/2022/05/24/why-the-u-s-gives-monster-suvs-five-star -safety-ratings-and-what-you-can-do-about-it/

17. Andrew J. Hawkins, "The US Government Finally Realizes That Cars Kill People Outside the Vehicle, Too," *The Verge*, March 3, 2022. https://www.theverge .com/2022/3/3/22960262/nhtsa-ncap-five-star-safety-rating-adas-proposal

18. Mark Baumer, "I Saw a Lot of Dead Raccoons," *Medium*, November 29, 2016. https://notgoingtomakeit.com/i-saw-a-lot-of-dead-raccoons-2357111f6d49

19. Linda Kleindienst, "Chiles' Journey of 1,000 Miles," *Tallahassee Magazine*, November 1, 2012. https://www.tallahasseemagazine.com/chiles-journey-of-1000 -miles/

20. State Library of Florida: Campaign Literature Collection, 1970-CHILES-01.

21. National Complete Streets Coalition, *Dangerous by Design* (Washington, DC: Smart Growth America, 2021).

22. Florida Department of Highway Safety and Motor Vehicles, *Traffic Crash Facts: Annual Report 2016.*

23. Eric D. Lawrence, Nathan Bomey, and Kristi Tanner, "Death on Foot: America's Love of SUVs Is Killing Pedestrians," *Detroit Free Press*, June 28, 2018. https://www.freep.com/story/money/cars/2018/06/28/suvs-killing-americas-pedestrians/646139002/

24 David L. Prytherch, "Reimagining the Physical/Social Infrastructure of the American Street: Policy and Design for Mobility Justice and Conviviality," *Urban Geography* 43, no. 5 (2022): 1–25.

25. Prytherch, "Reimagining," 19.

26. Prytherch, "Reimagining," 3.

27. Prytherch, "Reimagining," 6.

28. Mark Baumer, "Trying to Think of a Title That Will Save the Planet," *Medium*, January 6, 2017. https://notgoingtomakeit.com/trying-to-think-of-a-title-that-will-save-the-planet-2d8782ee825c

29. Mark Baumer, "Someone Walked Barefoot with Me," *Medium*, November 7. 2016. https://notgoingtomakeit.com/someone-walked-barefoot-with-me-9fdab cao3a25

30. I am deeply indebted to both Jim and Mary Baumer for the generous spirit of our exchanges.

31. Baumer, "My Hundredth Day on the Road."

32 Smart Growth America, "Complete Streets Policies." https://smartgrowth america.org/program/national-complete-streets-coalition/policy-atlas/

33. Adele Peters, "The Pandemic Pushed Cities to Take Back Their Streets from Cars. Will They Keep Them in 2021?" *Fast Company*, December 31, 2020. https://www.fastcompany.com/90586138/the-pandemic-pushed-cities-to-take-back-their-streets-from-cars-will-they-keep-them-in-2021

34. Jorge O. Elorza, Mayor of Providence, "Letter to Green and Complete Streets Advisory Council Members," August 15, 2022. https://www.providenceri .gov/wp-content/uploads/2022/03/Elorza-Vision-Zero-commitment-8-15-22.pdf

35 Available at https://web.archive.org/web/20170224195322/http://www .transportprovidence.org/2017/02/part-2-mark-baumer-reflection-us-90.html

36. City of Providence, "An Ordinance Amending Chapter 23 'Streets, Sidewalks and Public Places' of the Providence Code of Ordinances to Add Article VII 'Green and Complete Streets," 2020. https://pvdstreets.org/wp-content/uploads/2020/12/201203-Green-and-Complete-Streets-.pdf

37. Rob Doss, "Keep Students Safe When Walking to School," *Gainesville Sun*, January 12, 2021. https://www.gainesville.com/story/opinion/2021/01/12/rob-doss -keep-students-safe-when-walking-school/6585890002/

38. The financial information firm ValuePenguin recently identified Florida's stretch of US 90 as the twenty-eighth most dangerous road in the United States, based on 2015–2019 road fatality data from the Fatality Analysis Reporting System of the National Traffic and Highway Safety Administration. See Andrew Hurst, "The Deadliest Roads in the U.S.," *ValuePenguin*, June 28, 2021. https://www.value penguin.com/most-dangerous-roads-america

39. Annie Blanks, "Lofty Plan Aiming to Make U.S. 90 Easier to Walk, Bike," *Pensacola News Journal*, March 24, 2021. https://www.proquest.com/newspapers /lofty-plan-aiming-make-u-s-90-easier-walk-bike/docview/2504237907/se-2

40. "Cervantes Getting 4 Pedestrian Crosswalks: Safety Features Enacted After Woman, Baby Killed," *Pensacola News Journal*, October 15, 2022. https:// www.proquest.com/newspapers/cervantes-getting-4-pedestrian-crosswalks/ docview/2724790199/se-2

41. Colin Warren-Hicks, "'Slow Ride' Rolling Strong: Hundreds Cruise Pensac- ola on Bikes 7 Years After First Ride," *Pensacola News Journal*, June 17, 2022. https: //www.proquest.com/newspapers/slow-ride-rolling-strong/docview/2677282265 /se-2

42. Angie Schmitt, "Will Florida's New Approach to Urban Streets Reduce Its Traffic Carnage?" *StreetsBlog USA*, October 3, 2017. https://usa.streetsblog.org/ 2017/10/03/will-floridas-new-approach-to-urban-streets-reduce-its-traffic-car nage/

Chapter 7

1. Natalie Allison, "Shelbyville Was the Second Largest White Nationalist Rally in a Decade, Experts Say," *The Tennessean*, November 1, 2017. https://www.tennes sean.com/story/news/2017/11/01/white-lives-matter-shelbyville-rally-attendance -white-nationalist/819784001/

2. "Shelbyville Q&A," *Occidental Dissent*, October 4, 2017. https://occidentaldis sent.com/2017/10/04/shelbyville-qa/

3. Barbara Sutton, "Fashion of Fear: Securing the Body in an Unequal Global World," in *Bodies Without Borders*, edited by Erynn Masi de Casanova and Afshan Jafar (London: Palgrave Macmillan, 2016), 80.

4. "Under Armour has strategically embedded its brand within the overtly nationalistic and militarized climate of the post-9/11 U.S.," Gavin Weedon notes in

"'I Will. Protect This House': Under Armour, Corporate Nationalism and Post–9/11 Cultural Politics," *Sociology of Sport Journal* 29 (2012): 265–282.

5. Susan Sontag, *AIDS and Its Metaphors* (New York: Farrar, Straus and Giroux, 1989), 8.

6. Southern Poverty Law Center, "League of the South." https://www.splcenter .org/fighting-hate/extremist-files/group/league-south. See also Brett Barnett, "League of the South's Internet Rhetoric: Neo-Confederate Community-Building Online," *Journal of Hate Studies* 13, no. 1 (2016): 151–174.

7. Michael Hill, "In Defense of Our Blood," *League of the South.* https:// leagueofthesouth.com/in-defense-of-our-blood/

8. For a report on the French genesis of this specific language of racial replacement, see Thomas Chatterton Williams, "The French Origins of 'You Will Not Replace Us,'" *New Yorker*, November 27, 2017. https://www.newyorker.com/magazine /2017/12/04/the-french-origins-of-you-will-not-replace-us

9. Kathleen Belew, *Bring the War Home: The White Power Movement and Paramilitary America* (Cambridge, MA: Harvard University Press, 2018), 7.

10. Belew, *Bring the War Home*, 170.

11. Kenneth T. MacLeish, *Making War at Fort Hood: Life and Uncertainty in a Military Community* (Princeton: Princeton University Press, 2013), 69.

12. Southern Poverty Law Center, "Matthew Heimbach." https://www.splcenter .org/fighting-hate/extremist-files/individual/matthew-heimbach

13. Alan Yuhas, "Man Accused of Assaulting Woman at Trump Rally Says Trump Inspired Him," *The Guardian*, April 15, 2017. https://www.theguardian. com/us-news/2017/apr/15/trump-campaign-rally-lawsuit-assault-kentucky

14. Klaus Theweleit, *Male Fantasies: Volume 2: Psychoanalyzing the White Terror* (Minneapolis: University of Minnesota Press, 1989), 159.

15. Theweleit, *Male Fantasies*, 84.

16. Sutton, "Fashion of Fear," 80.

17. Michael Edison Hayden et al., "'Unite the Right' Five Years Later: Where Are They Now?" *Southern Poverty Law Center*, August 11, 2022. https://www.splcenter .org/hatewatch/2022/08/11/unite-right-5-years-later-where-are-they-now

18. See George Michael, "David Lane and the Fourteen Words," *Totalitarian Movements and Political Religions* 10, no. 1 (2009): 43–61.

19. Jennifer Maas, "John Oliver Uses Tucker Carlson's Own Words to Define 'White Supremacist' For Him," *Yahoo*, March 15, 2021. https://www.yahoo.com/ video/john-oliver-uses-tucker-carlson-144627335.html

Chapter 8

1. Administration of Donald J. Trump, "Memorandum on Securing the Southern Border of the United States," April 4, 2018. https://www.govinfo.gov/content/pkg/DCPD-201800218/pdf/DCPD-201800218.pdf /

2 Fred Lucas, "Trump's Idea of Using Military Resources for Border Wall Isn't Unprecedented," *Daily Signal*, April 2, 2018. https://www.dailysignal.com/2018/04/02/trumps-idea-of-using-military-resources-for-border-wall-isnt-unprecedented/

3. Emily Martin, "Toward an Anthropology of Immunology: The Body as Nation State," *Medical Anthropology Quarterly* 4, no. 4 (1990): 410–426.

4. Post on X (Twitter) by Donald J. Trump, December 31, 2018. https://x.com/realdonaldtrump/status/1079731279032172545

5 Michael Shannon, "Perfect Time for Trump to Fight the Other Alien Invasion," *The Ledger*, March 30, 2020. https://www.theledger.com/story/news/coronavirus/2020/03/30/shannon-perfect-time-for-trump-to-fight-other-alien-invasion/1439875007/

6. Ibrahim Abubakar et al., "The UCL-Lancet Commission on Migration and Health: The Health of a World on the Move," *Lancet* 392 (2018): 2606–2654.

7. Divya Manoharan and Hope Frye, "Biden Must End Mandatory Expulsion on the Border," *Foreign Policy*, May 14, 2021. https://foreignpolicy.com/2021/05/14/biden-title-42-immigration-border-covid/

8. Lawrence Gostin and Eric Friedman, "Title 42 Exclusions of Asylum Seekers — A Misuse of Public Health Powers," *JAMA Health Forum* 4, no. 1 (2023): e230078.

9. Augusta Chronicle, *Painting with a Broad Brush: The Cartoons of Rick McKee* (Vancouver: Pediment Publishing, 2015).

10. In a widely publicized letter to the Centers for Disease Control and Prevention in July 2014, just a few weeks before the publication of Rick McKee's cartoon, Georgia Congressman Phil Gingrey suggested that "reports of illegal migrants carrying deadly disease such as swine flu, dengue fever, Ebola virus, and tuberculosis are particularly concerning."

11. Drawn by cartoonist Friedrich Graetz and published in *Puck* on July 18, 1883.

12. Alan M. Kraut, *Silent Travelers: Genes, Germs, and the Immigrant Menace* (Baltimore: Johns Hopkins University Press, 1995), 255.

13. K. David Patterson, "Yellow Fever Epidemics and Mortality in the United States, 1693–1905," *Social Science and Medicine* 34, no. 8 (1992): 855–865.

14. Kraut, *Silent Travelers*, 26.

15 L. A. Dugas, "Prevention of Yellow Fever," *Southern Medical and Surgical Journal* (October 1856): 638–641.

16. Dugas, "Prevention of Yellow Fever," 638.

17. Committee to Inquire into the Origin and Causes Which Gave Rise to the Late Epidemic in Augusta, "A Report on the Origin and Cause of the Late Epidemic in Augusta, GA" (Augusta: Browne, Cushney and M'Cafferty, 1839).

18. Diane Harvey, "The 'Terri,' Augusta's Black Enclave," *Richmond County History* 5, no. 2 (1973): 60–75.

19. Molly Caldwell Crosby, *The American Plague: The Untold Story of Yellow Fever, the Epidemic That Shaped Our History* (New York: Berkley, 2006), 11.

20. Phinizy Spalding, *The History of the Medical College of Georgia* (Athens: University of Georgia Press, 2011), 26.

21. W. L. Felder, "Observations on the Yellow Fever Epidemic of 1854, in Augusta, Ga," *Southern Medical and Surgical Journal* (October 1855): 601.

22. Mel Robbins, "Fear-bola Hits Epidemic Proportions," *CNN*, October 15, 2014. https://www.cnn.com/2014/10/15/opinion/robbins-ebola-fear/index.html

23. Dan Diamond, "Ebola Comes to America; First U.S. Case Just Diagnosed in Dallas," *Forbes*, September 30, 2014. https://www.forbes.com/sites/dandiamond/2014/09/30/ebola-comes-to-america-cdc-confirms-first-case-of-ebola-diagnosed-in-united-states/

24. Shannon Blakey et al., "Tracing 'Fearbola': Psychological Predictors of Anxious Responding to the Threat of Ebola," *Cognitive Therapy and Research* 39, no. 6 (2015): 816–825, quote at 823.

25. Doug Stutsman, "Coughing Man Causes Ebola Scare at Tag Office," *Augusta Chronicle*, October 10, 2014.

26. Talkback, *Aiken Standard*, November 1, 2014, 3A.

27. Michael Shaw, "Obola: Visual Attacks on Obama Pick Up Where Kenya/Muslim Slurs Left Off," *Reading the Pictures*, October 19, 2014. https://www.readingthepictures.org/2014/10/obola-visual-attacks-on-obama-pick-up-right-where-kenyamuslim-slurs-left-off/

28. Post on X (Twitter) by Donald J. Trump, August 2, 2014. https://twitter.com/realdonaldtrump/status/495531002505494528

29. Emily Yates-Doerr, "Why Are So Many Guatemalans Migrating to the U.S.?," *Sapiens*, October 25, 2018. https://www.sapiens.org/culture/guatemala-migrants-united-states/

30. Eula Biss, *On Immunity: An Inoculation* (New York: Graywolf Press, 2014), 20.

31. Biss, *On Immunity*, 20.

Chapter 9

1. Archival materials from the Hagley Museum & Library, Wilmington, Delaware. The image of Mr. Teflon is from the *Journal of Teflon*, July 1961, Plastics Department, E. I. du Pont de Nemours & Company, Hagley Museum & Library, Wilmington, DE 19807.

2. Archival materials from the Hagley Museum & Library, Wilmington, Delaware.

3. Archival materials from the Hagley Museum & Library, Wilmington, Delaware.

4. Joseph Masco, *The Theater of Operations: National Security Affect from the Cold War to the War on Terror* (Durham: Duke University Press, 2014).

5. Archival materials from the Hagley Museum & Library, Wilmington, Delaware.

6. E. I. du Pont de Nemours & Company, Cavalcade of America Commercials Reel No.1, Audiovisual Collections and Digital Initiatives, Hagley Museum & Library, Wilmington, Delaware.

7. Anna McCarthy, *The Citizen Machine: Governing by Television in 1950s America* (New York: New Press, 2010).

8. National Public Radio, "Beer, Drinking Water and Fish: Tiny Plastic Is Everywhere," *All Things Considered*, August 20, 2018.

9. David Q. Andrews and Olga V. Naidenko, "Population-Wide Exposure to Per- and Polyfluoroalkyl Substances from Drinking Water in the United States," *Environmental Science and Technology Letters* 7, no. 12 (2020): 931–936.

10. "Global Danger: Wildlife at Risk from PFAS Exposure," *Environmental Working Group*, September 26, 2023. https://www.ewg.org/interactive-maps/pfas_in_wildlife/map/

11. Michelle Murphy, "What Can't a Body Do?" *Catalyst*, 2016. https://catalyst journal.org/index.php/catalyst/article/view/28791/html_8

12. Murphy, "What Can't a Body Do?"

13. I am grateful to both Phil Leonard and Corinne Eldred of the Hoosick Township Historical Society for sharing many stories and materials regarding the industrial history of Hoosick Falls.

14. For some of this history, see Tracy Frisch, "An Industrial Chemical Poisoned Their Water, Now Upstate New Yorkers Want to Know What Replaced It," *In These Times*, October 3, 2017. https://inthesetimes.com/article/drinking-water-contam ination-perfluorooctanoic-acid-hoosick-falls-new-york

15. "EPA Proposes Bold New Limits for Tackling 'Forever Chemicals' in Drinking Water," *Environmental Working Group*, March 14, 2023. https://www.ewg.org/

news-insights/news-release/2023/03/epa-proposes-bold-new-limits-tackling -forever-chemicals-drinking

16. For full documentation of hazardous waste sites identified in Hoosick Falls, government agreements with responsible companies, and remedial work under-way, see https://dec.ny.gov/environmental-protection/site-cleanup/regional-re mediation-project-information/region-4/hoosick-falls-area

17. David Bond, *Negative Ecologies: Fossil Fuels and the Discovery of the Envi-ronment* (Berkeley: University of California Press, 2022), 146.

18. Casey Seiler, "PFOA Photos: Hoosick Falls Residents Make Plea on Twitter," *Albany Times Union*, June 11, 2016.

19. See also Liza Gross, "These Everyday Toxins May Be Hurting Pregnant Women and Their Babies," *New York Times*, September 23, 2020. https://www.ny times.com/2020/09/23/parenting/pregnancy/pfas-toxins-chemicals.html

20. Penelope Overton, "PFAS Found in Almost 1,000 Products Sold in Maine, So Far," *Portland Press Herald*, January 3, 2024. https://www.pressherald.com/2024 /01/03/pfas-found-in-almost-1000-maine-products-so-far/

21. James Salzman, *Drinking Water: A History* (New York: Abrams Press, 2012).

22. Marina Bolotnikova, "The Spiritual Bankruptcy of Bottled Water," *Vox*, July 12, 2021. https://www.vox.com/the-goods/2021/7/12/22554546/bottled-water-mich igan-waste-flint-plastic

23. Kendra Pierre-Louis, "We Don't Trust Drinking Fountains Anymore, and That's Bad for Our Health," *Washington Post*, July 2, 2015. https://www.washington post.com/opinions/we-dont-trust-drinking-fountains-anymore-and-thats-bad -for-our-health/2015/07/02/24eca9bc-15f0-11e5-9ddc-e3353542100c_story.html

24. See Peter H. Gleick, *Bottled and Sold: The Story Behind Our Obsession with Bottled Water* (Washington, DC: Island Press, 2010).

25. Olivia Leach, "Rep. Maloney: 'Historic Investment' to Help Newburgh Get the Lead Out," *Spectrum News 1*, January 24, 2022. https://spectrumlocalnews .com/nys/hudson-valley/news/2022/01/24/federal-funding-to-help-newburgh -get-the-lead-out-

26. Riverkeeper, "Contamination of the Drinking Water Reservoir and Water-shed of the City of Newburgh: A Case Study and a Call for Comprehensive Water Source Protection," July 2016. https://www.nysenate.gov/sites/default/files/hf_riv erkeeper_part_2_written_only.pdf

27. Arielle Duhaime-Ross, "The Military Contaminated the City of Newburgh's Water — But Their Cleanup Is 'Lagging,'" *Vice*, January 20, 2017. https://www.vice .com/en/article/8xmz4x/the-military-contaminated-the-city-of-newburghs -water

28. Alexander C. Kaufman, "The Tainted Water Crisis in Upstate New York That Andrew Cuomo Can't Shake," *Huffington Post*, March 9, 2018. https://www.huffpost .com/entry/newburgh-water-pfos_n_5aa0368ce4b0e9381c14d4f7

29. Sharon Lerner, "The U.S. Military Is Spending Millions to Replace Toxic Firefighting Foam with Toxic Firefighting Foam," *The Intercept*, February 10, 2018. https://theintercept.com/2018/02/10/firefighting-foam-afff-pfos-pfoa-epa/

30. Lana Bellamy, "CDC Releases Newburgh PFAS Blood Results," *Middletown Times Herald-Record*, May 29, 2021.

31. Jared Wesley Singer, "Newburgh Clean Water Project," *Sanctuary for Independent Media*, June 22, 2020. https://www.mediasanctuary.org/stories/2020/new burgh-clean-water-project/

32. The Restorative Center was founded in Newburgh by attorney Shailly Agnihotri in 2015. For more on the Newburgh Model of restorative justice, see https: //www.therestorativecenter.org

33. Erin Bell, "Newburgh and Hoosick Falls PFAS Health Study," *The Engagement Ring*, University of Albany, June 10, 2022. https://the-engagement-ring. simplecast.com/episodes/dr-erin-bell-zr6w19pi

34. Lana Bellamy, "How One New York Woman's Brush with Lead Poisoning Inspired Quest for Change," *Middletown Times Herald-Record*, June 13, 2022.

35. Burton-Hill has testified on these issues to the New York State Senate.

36. Restoration Advisory Committee, *Newburgh Clean Water Project*. https:// newburghcleanwaterproject.org/stewart-ang-restoration-advisory-committee/

37. Michael Randall, "All in the Name of Clean Water," *Middletown Times Herald-Record*, July 28, 2019.

38. See John Cronin and Robert F. Kennedy Jr., *The Riverkeepers: Two Activists Fight to Reclaim our Environment as a Basic Human Right* (New York Scribner, 1997).

Chapter 10

1. The Daily Show, "Trump Won't Wear Mask as U.S. Nears 'Pearl Harbor' Moment," *YouTube*, April 6, 2020. https://www.youtube.com/watch?v=BuuD84Yi5eY

2. Ross Douthat, "The Coronavirus and the Conservative Mind," *New York Times*, March 31, 2020.

3. Cuneyt Dil, "West Virginia Promises Campaign to Reach Vaccine Hesitant," *AP News*, April 23, 2021. https://apnews.com/article/health-west-virginia-corona virus-82c713f7f719e5f2904813b61ffd0e4f

4. Eli J. Finkel et al., "Political Sectarianism in America," *Science* 370, no. 6516 (2020): 533–536. https://www.science.org/doi/10.1126/science.abe1715

5. As John Ehrenreich observes in *The Making of a Pandemic: Social, Political,*

and Psychological Reflections on Covid-19 (New York: Springer, 2022), "minimizing the risks of COVID-19, rejecting masks and objecting to vaccination, and refusing to social distance have become a moral issue, embedded in individual and group identity. These beliefs are no more up for "discussion" than religious beliefs or love of family" (115).

6. Jacob Wallace, Paul Goldsmith-Pinkham, and Jason L. Schwartz, "Excess Death Rates for Republicans and Democrats During the COVID-19 Pandemic," Working Paper 30512, *National Bureau of Economic Research*, September 2022. https://www.nber.org/papers/w30512

7. Becky Sullivan, "U.S. COVID Deaths Are Rising Again. Experts Call It a 'Pandemic of the Unvaccinated,'" *AP News*, July 16, 2021. https://www.npr.org/2021/07/16/1017002907/u-s-covid-deaths-are-rising-again-experts-call-it-a-pandemic-of-the-unvaccinated

8. Thomas Paine, "Common Sense," in *The Complete Writings of Thomas Paine*, edited by Philip S. Foner (New York: Citadel Press, 1945), 17.

9. For another account, see Ross Douthat, "Libertarians in the Age of Trump," *New York Times*, July 21, 2018. https://www.nytimes.com/2018/07/21/opinion/sunday/libertarians-in-the-age-of-trump.html

10 Peter Diamandis and Steven Kotler, *Abundance: The Future Is Better Than You Think* (New York: Free Press, 2012).

11. Eli Pariser, *The Filter Bubble: How the New Personalized Web Is Changing What We Read and How We Think* (New York: Penguin, 2012), 15.

12. On this point, also see Siva Vaidhyanathan, *Antisocial Media: How Facebook Disconnects Us and Undermines Democracy* (New York: Oxford University Press, 2018).

13. John Naughton, "How the 'Plandemic' Conspiracy Theory Took Hold," *The Guardian*, May 23, 2020. https://www.theguardian.com/commentisfree/2020/may/23/how-the-plandemic-conspiracy-theory-took-hold

14. Nicholas Carr, *The Shallows: What the Internet Is Doing to Our Brains* (New York: Norton, 2011), 120.

15. Paul Egan and Kara Berg, "Thousands Converge to Protest Michigan Governor's Stay-Home Order in 'Operation Gridlock,'" *USA Today*, April 16, 2020. https://www.usatoday.com/story/news/nation/2020/04/15/lansing-capitol-protest-michigan-stay-home-order/5139472002/

16. Cassie Da Costa, "White Anti-Quarantine Protestors Have Cruelly Co-opted an Enslaved Black Woman from the 18th Century," *The Daily Beast*, May 22, 2020. https://www.thedailybeast.com/white-anti-quarantine-protesters-have-cruelly-co-opted-a-black-18th-century-slave

17. Meagan Flynn, "To Protest Face Masks, Arizona City Councilman Uses George Floyd's Words: 'I Can't Breathe,'" *Washington Post*, June 25, 2020. https://www.washingtonpost.com/nation/2020/06/25/guy-phillips-mask-floyd/

18. Larry Buchanan, Quoctrung Bui, and Jugal K. Patel, "Black Lives Matter May Be the Largest Movement in U.S. History," *New York Times*, July 3, 2020. https://www.nytimes.com/interactive/2020/07/03/us/george-floyd-protests-crowd-size.html

19. Danielle Allen, *Talking to Strangers: Anxieties of Citizenship Since Brown v. Board of Education* (Chicago: University of Chicago Press, 2004), xvi.

20. Allen, *Talking to Strangers*, xxii.

21. Elizabeth Bernstein, "How Can We Reconcile with Each Other When Our Politics Are So Polarized," *Wall Street Journal*, November 24, 2020. https://www.wsj.com/articles/how-we-can-reconcile-with-each-other-when-our-politics-are-so-polarized-11606250555

22. Ayn Rand, *The Fountainhead* (New York: Signet, 1952), 674.

23. Rand, *Fountainhead*, 679.

24. Rand, *Fountainhead*, 698.

25. Rand, *Fountainhead*, 135.

26. Jennifer Burns, *Goddess of the Market: Ayn Rand and the American Right* (New York: Oxford University Press, 2011), 132.

27. Burns, *Goddess of the Market*, 92.

28. Anand Pandian, "What I Learned from an Unlikely Friendship with an Anti-Masker," *The Guardian*, August 19, 2021. https://www.theguardian.com/lifeandstyle/2021/aug/19/anti-masker-unlikely-friendship

29. "Track Covid-19 in the U.S.," *New York Times*, updated March 26, 2024. https://www.nytimes.com/interactive/2023/us/covid-cases.html

Chapter 11

1. David Ng, "Inside Breitbart's Westside L.A. Headquarters, They've Got Plans for Global Expansion," *Los Angeles Times*, November 18, 2016. https://www.latimes.com/business/hollywood/la-fi-ct-breitbart-news-20161116-story.html

2. Andrew Breitbart, *Righteous Indignation: Excuse Me While I Save the World!* (New York: Grand Central Publishing, 2011), 58, 34.

3. Scott Lucas, "How California Gave Us Trumpism," *Politico Magazine*, April 18, 2017. https://www.politico.com/magazine/story/2017/04/how-california-gave-us-trumpism-215038/

4. Breitbart News Daily, "Scott Lucas," April 24, 2017. https://soundcloud.com/breitbart/breitbart-news-daily-scott-lucas-april-24-2017

5. Peter Maass, "Birth of a Radical: White Fear in the White House: Young Bannon Disciple Julia Hahn Is a Case Study in Extremism," *The Intercept*, May 7, 2017. https://theintercept.com/2017/05/07/white-fear-in-the-white-house-young -bannon-disciple-julia-hahn-is-a-case-study-in-extremism/

6. As Sarah Kendzior observed in 2017, "media outlets allow the Midwest to stand in as [Trump's] representative region, which is a convenient way to ignore the prevalence of bigotry in coastal states or among the wealthy and educated. We are still 'flyover country,' only now all our whites are racists and the rest of our population has disappeared." Kendzior, *The View from Flyover Country: Dispatches from the Forgotten America* (New York: Flatiron Books, 2018), 233.

7. Lilliana Mason, *Uncivil Agreement: How Politics Became Our Identity* (Chicago: University of Chicago Press, 2018).

8. Maass, "Birth of a Radical."

9. Nicole Hemmer, *Messengers of the Right: Conservative Media and the Transformation of American Politics* (Philadelphia: University of Pennsylvania Press, 2016), 270–271.

10. Hemmer, *Messengers of the Right*, 264.

11. Hemmer, *Messengers of the Right*, 269.

12. "Supporters of Deported Man Speak Out Against Trump Immigration Policy," *CBS News*, May 4, 2017. https://www.cbsnews.com/news/supporters-of-de ported-man-speak-out-against-trump-immigration-policy/

13. Everett Young, "Why We're Liberal, Why We're Conservative: A Cognitive Theory on the Origins of Ideological Thinking," PhD dissertation, Department of Political Science, Stony Brook University, 2009, 18.

14. Young, "Why We're Liberal, Why We're Conservative," 11.

15. John Jost, *Left and Right: The Psychological Significance of a Political Difference* (New York: Oxford University Press, 2021).

16. Pierre Bouvard, "The State of American In-Car Audio: AM/FM Still King of the Road!" *Westwood One*, November 4, 2015. https://www.westwoodone.com/ blog/2015/11/04/the-state-of-american-in-car-audio-amfm-still-king-of-the -road/

17. Brian Rosenwald, *Talk Radio's America: How an Industry Took over a Political Party That Took over the United States* (Cambridge: Harvard University Press, 2019), 17.

18. William E. Connolly, *Capitalism and Christianity, American Style* (Durham: Duke University Press, 2008).

19. According to Brian Rosenwald, the rise of the Tea Party movement in the 2000s also reflected a similar dynamic of radicalized convictions, in which talk

radio "hosts certainly did channel listener sentiment, but they also drove it" (Rosenwald, *Talk Radio's America*, 186).

20. I write about anthropology as an apprenticeship in uncertainty in *A Possible Anthropology: Methods for Uneasy Times* (Durham: Duke University Press, 2019).

21 Thomas L. Dumm, "Joyce Brown, or Democracy and Homelessness," in *United States* (Ithaca: Cornell University Press, 1994), 155. Far more than a purely metaphorical engagement with the condition of being unhoused, Dumm's chapter thinks between "the material conditions of homelessness" as experienced in American urban environments and "the spiritual possibility of homelessness as the open road, as a possible path of freedom" (163).

Chapter 12

1. Elahe Izadi, "How Local Journalists Proved a Ten-Year-Old's Abortion Wasn't a Hoax," *Washington Post*, July 28, 2022. https://www.washingtonpost.com/media/2022/07/28/ohio-abortion-journalism/

2. Sheryl Gay Stolberg and Ava Sasani, "An Indiana Doctor Speaks Out on Abortion, and Pays a Price," *New York Times*, July 28, 2022. https://www.nytimes.com/2022/07/28/us/politics/abortion-doctor-caitlin-bernard-ohio.html

3. Jennifer Weiss-Wolf, *Periods Gone Public: Taking a Stand for Menstrual Equity* (New York: Arcade Publishing, 2017).

4. Alliance for Period Supplies, "Tampon Tax." https://allianceforperiodsupplies.org/tampon-tax/

5. The Ohio Channel, "Legislative Press Conference: Ending the 'Pink Tax,'" June 22, 2015. https://www.ohiochannel.org/video/press-conference-legislative-ending-the-pink-tax

6. 10TV, "Gov. DeWine Signs Repeal of Ohio's 'Pink Tax,'" November 6, 2019. https://www.10tv.com/article/news/politics/gov-dewine-signs-repeal-ohios-pink-tax-2019-nov/530-be98f2de-2572-4a0c-bfd3-812d0bcc7ca6

7. Here, for example, is advice about building rapport from David McRaney's recent book, *How Minds Change: The Surprising Science of Belief, Opinion, and Persuasion* (New York: Portfolio Books, 2022):

> As you open the dialogue, assure the other party you aren't out to shame them or put them in a position to be ostracized by their peers. Demonstrate your openness and respect, and continuously ask for consent. Don't attack. Tolerate their views, even if you disagree. Listen without interrupting. Attempt to understand their position without replying. And most of all, try to find common ground. An engaged, curious, and compassionate listener is far more persuasive than any fact or figure. (238)

8. Chris Bail, *Breaking the Social Media Prism: How to Make Our Platforms Less Polarizing* (Princeton: Princeton University Press, 2021), 108.

9. Bail, *Breaking the Social Media Prism*, 110.

10. Kaveh Waddell, "The Exhausting Work of Tallying America's Largest Protest," *The Atlantic*, January 23, 2017. https://www.theatlantic.com/technology/archive/2017/01/womens-march-protest-count/514166/

11. Dana R. Fisher, Dawn M. Dow, and Rashawn Ray, "Intersectionality Takes It to the Streets: Mobilizing Across Diverse Interests for the Women's March," *Science Advances* 3, no. 9 (2017). https://www.science.org/doi/10.1126/sciadv.aao1390

12. Reflecting on the "shed walls" slogan, scholar Emilia Sanabria has cautioned that feminist resistance grounded in anatomy "relies on an apolitical understanding of biology blind to race, trans-, queer- and non-reproductive personhood." It may also be the case, however, that committing deliberately to menstrual equity is one way of addressing this danger. See Sanabria, "Shed Walls, Don't Build Them," *Word Press*, February 15, 2017. https://dukeupress.wordpress.com/2017/02/15/shed-walls-dont-build-them/

13. David A. Pizarro and Yoel Inbar, "Explaining the Influence of Disgust on Political Judgment: A Disease-Avoidance Account," in *Social Psychology and Politics*, edited by Joseph Forgas, Klaus Fiedler, and William D. Crano (New York: Routledge, 2015), 165.

14 "Moral intuitions arise automatically and almost instantaneously, long before moral reasoning has a chance to get started, and those first intuitions tend to drive our later reasoning," Jonathan Haidt observes in *The Righteous Mind: Why Good People are Divided by Politics and Religion* (New York: Vintage Books, 2012), xx.

15. Alma Gottlieb, "Menstrual Taboos: Moving Beyond the Curse," in *The Palgrave Handbook of Critical Menstruation Studies*, edited by Chris Bobel et al. (London: Palgrave Macmillan, 2020), 143–162.

16. Gottlieb, "Menstrual Taboos," 153.

17. Nadya Okamoto, *Period Power: A Manifesto for the Menstrual Movement* (New York: Simon & Schuster, 2018), 52–53.

18. TEDx Talks, "We're Going to Solve Period Poverty: Anusha Singh," *YouTube*, February 5, 2021. https://www.youtube.com/watch?v=tqy4yKLcVxc

19. Gabriela Garcia, "Ohio State Senior Garners National Attention in Fight Against Period Poverty," *10TV*, March 24, 2021. https://www.10tv.com/article/news/local/ohio-state-senior-garners-national-attention-in-fight-against-period-poverty/530-de7ab636-e3c9-4616-aabf-755644456205

20. See https://www.loopholescereal.com for further explanation.

21. For a discussion of such political dilemmas, see Chris Bobel and Breanne Fahs, "The Messy Politics of Menstrual Activism," in *The Palgrave Handbook of Critical Menstruation Studies*, edited by Chris Bobel et al. (London: Palgrave Macmillan, 2020), 1001–1018.

22. Hahrie Han, Elizabeth McKenna, and Michelle Oyakawa provide useful perspective on such movement organizing strategies in *Prisms of the People: Power & Organizing in Twenty-First-Century America* (Chicago: University of Chicago Press, 2021), 150:

> Leaders cultivated the constituencies in our study to express a set of characteristics these leaders needed to strategically exert power in dynamic political environments. Having constituencies that leaders know are loyal yet flexible, strongly grounded in their own values but also open to bridging to others, enables leaders to sit at the negotiating table with more tools for wielding power than they otherwise might have.

23. Ohio Senate, "SB 26: Permit Income Tax Deduction for Certain Teacher Expenses," February 5, 2020. https://fastdemocracy.com/bill-search/oh/133/bills/OHB00007915/

24 Kate Clancy, *Period: The Real Story of Menstruation* (Princeton: Princeton University Press, 2023), 183.

25. Gabe Rosenberg, "A Bill Banning Most Abortions Becomes Law in Ohio," *National Public Radio*, April 11, 2019. https://www.npr.org/2019/04/11/712455980/a-bill-banning-most-abortions-becomes-law-in-ohio

26. Danae King, "'Pink Tax' Over, But Advocacy Will Continue," *Columbus Dispatch*, November 8, 2019. https://www.dispatch.com/story/news/politics/state/2019/11/09/pink-tax-over-but/2330077007/

27. Jordan Langs/Moms Helping Moms Foundation, "New Year, Same Old Fight. It's 2022, Yet More Than Half of the Population Is Still Paying the Price for a Natural Bodily Function," *Forbes*, March 3, 2022. https://www.forbes.com/sites/forbeseq/2022/02/01/new-year-same-old-fight-its-2022-yet-more-than-half-of-the-population-is-still-paying-the-price-for-a-natural-bodily-function/?sh=751ee9f52f74

28. See Sophia Rosenfeld, *Common Sense: A Political History* (Cambridge, MA: Harvard University Press, 2011), for essential historical perspective on the way that "common sense" has been harnessed in contemporary American political discourse, especially in conservative circles.

29. Hannah Arendt, *The Human Condition* (Chicago: University of Chicago Press, 1970), 50.

30. Arendt, *The Human Condition*, 58.

31. Astra Taylor, *The Age of Insecurity: Coming Together as Things Fall Apart* (Toronto: House of Anansi Press, 2023), 49.

Conclusion

1. A classic account of this theme was given by Mary Douglas in *Purity and Danger: An Analysis of the Concepts of Pollution and Taboo* (London: Routledge & Kegan Paul, 1966).

2. Prentis Hemphill, "Boundaries Can Be Love," in *Holding Change: The Way of Emergent Strategy Facilitation and Mediation*, by adrienne maree brown (Chico: AK Press, 2021).

3. Wendy Brown, *Walled States, Waning Sovereignty* (New York: Zone Books, 2014), 121.

4. Gloria Anzaldúa, *Borderlands/La Frontera* (San Francisco: Aunt Lute Books, 1987), 195.

5. Viet Thanh Nguyen, "Introduction," in *The Displaced: Refugee Writers on Refugee Lives* (New York: Abrams Press, 2018), 19,

6. The tour was founded on a distinction between such a "view from the shore" and a settler-colonial "view from the boat," a distinction that the educators attributed to the work of the Upstander Project.

7. Allison Kelliher, "Native Americans Have Experienced a Dramatic Decline in Life Expectancy During the COVID-19 Pandemic — But the Drop Has Been in the Making for Generations," *The Conversation*, February 3, 2023. https://theconversa tion.com/native-americans-have-experienced-a-dramatic-decline-in-life-ex pectancy-during-the-covid-19-pandemic-but-the-drop-has-been-in-the-mak ing-for-generations-186729

8. Patty Krawec, *Becoming Kin: An Indigenous Call to Unforgetting the Past and Reimagining Our Future* (Minneapolis: Broadleaf Books, 2022).

9. Patty Krawec, "Ribbon Skirts and Mutual Aid," *Midnight Sun*, May 27, 2023. https://www.midnightsunmag.ca/ribbon-skirts-and-mutual-aid/

10. Baltimore Sun Editorial Board, "Better to Have a Few Rats Than to Be One," *Baltimore Sun*, July 29, 2019. https://www.baltimoresun.com/opinion/editorial/bs -ed-0728-trump-baltimore-20190727-k6ac4yvnpvcczlaexdfglifada-story.html

11. Lawrence T. Brown, *The Black Butterfly: The Harmful Politics of Race and Space in America* (Baltimore: Johns Hopkins University Press, 2021), 7, 63.

12. WJZ News, "20-Year Gap in Life Expectancy Between Richer, Poorer Areas of Baltimore," *CBS News*, July 6, 2017. https://www.cbsnews.com/baltimore/news /life-expectancy-baltimore/

13. See P. Nicole King, Kate Drabinski, and Joshua Clark Davis, eds., *Baltimore Revisited: Stories of Inequality and Resistance in a U.S. City* (New Brunswick: Rutgers University Press, 2019).

14. Both paintings were made by local artist Jessy DeSantis.

15. In the words of organizer Christina Calhoun, as quoted in Rudy Malcom, "Food as a Love Language: Commuity Fridge Gets Upgrade," *Baltimore Fishbowl*, October 29, 2021. https://baltimorefishbowl.com/stories/food-as-a-love-language-community-fridge-gets-upgrade/

16. Julie Scharper, "A Fridge Full of Love," *Johns Hopkins University HUB*, January 28, 2022. https://hub.jhu.edu/2022/01/28/baltimore-community-fridge/

17. Malcom, "Food as a Love Language."

18. Julie Livingston, "To Heal the Body, Heal the Body Politic," *Public Books*, November 19, 2020. https://www.publicbooks.org/to-heal-the-body-heal-the-body-politic/

19. See Chloe Ahmann and Anand Pandian, "The Fight Against Incineration Is a Chance to Right Historic Wrongs," *Baltimore Beat*, June 26, 2024. https://baltimorebeat.com/op-ed-the-fight-against-incineration-is-a-chance-to-right-historic-wrongs/

20. Jeremy Cox, "For Communities of Color, Air Pollution May Heighten Coronavirus Threat," *Bay Journal*, May 4, 2020. https://www.bayjournal.com/news/pollution/for-communities-of-color-air-pollution-may-heighten-coronavirus-threat/article_d557b12e-8978-11ea-90aa-c7b3d7dc8353.html

21. Davarian L. Baldwin, *In the Shadow of the Ivory Tower: How Universities Are Plundering Our Cities* (New York: Bold Type Books, 2021).

22. Abolitionist University Studies is a key inspiration for such efforts. See Abigail Boggs, Eli Meyerhoff, Nick Mitchell, and Zach Schwartz-Weinstein, "Abolitionist University Studies: An Invitation," *Abolition Journal*, August 28, 2019. https://abolitionjournal.org/abolitionist-university-studies-an-invitation/

23. Red Emma's Bookstore Coffeehouse, "Right to the City: Baltimore Activists Talk Back to Anthropology," *YouTube*, November 19, 2021. https://www.youtube.com/watch?v=xj1aSgLpgOs

24. This struggle is documented in a book by one of the organizers of the Red Emma's event, anthropologist Nicole Fabricant: *Fighting to Breathe: Race, Toxicity, and the Rise of Youth Activism in Baltimore* (Berkeley: University of California Press, 2022).

25. See also Chloe Ahmann, *Futures After Progress: Hope and Doubt in Late Industrial Baltimore* (Chicago: University of Chicago Press, 2024), which engages life in the aftermath of concentrated industrial development and pervasive environmental pollution in south Baltimore's Curtis Bay neighborhood in terms of at least "two potential paths — Curtis Bay as cautionary tale or as the spark of something altogether different" (174).

26. "The broad bandwidth of a pluralist ethos is critical," William E. Connolly

writes in *Aspirational Fascism: The Struggle for Multifaceted Democracy Under Trumpism* (Minneapolis: University of Minnesota Press, 2017). "Such an ethos, set both on the affective register of communication and more reflective processes, injects powers of critical responsiveness and resilience into politics" (84).

27. Norman Geras, *The Contract of Mutual Indifference: Political Philosophy After the Holocaust* (New York: Verso Books, 1998).

28. Geras, *Contract of Mutual Indifference*, 15.

29. Geras, *Contract of Mutual Indifference*, 59.

30. Antero Pietila, *Not in My Neighborhood: How Bigotry Shaped a Great American City* (Lanham: Rowman & Littlefield, 2010).

31. Accessed via https://jewishmuseummd.catalogaccess.com/photos/33982

32. Josiah Ryan, "'This Was a Whitelash': Van Jones' Take on the Election Results," *CNN*, November 9, 2016. https://www.cnn.com/2016/11/09/politics/van-jones-results-disappointment-cnntv/index.html

33. Robin D. G. Kelley, *Freedom Dreams: The Black Radical Imagination* (Boston: Beacon Press, 2022), 9–10.

34. For this story and the broader national context, see Jeff Wiltse, *Contested Waters: A Social History of Swimming Pools in America* (Chapel Hill: University of North Carolina Press, 2007).

35. Graham Coreil-Allen, "Struggle and Joy in the Druid Hill Park Memorial Pool," *BmoreArt Magazine*, September 3, 2018. https://bmoreart.com/2018/09/struggle-and-joy-in-the-druid-hill-park-memorial-pool.html

36. Post on Instagram by oureric, August 19, 2020. https://www.instagram.com/p/CEFooO9Daaa/

INDEX

Note: Page numbers in italic type indicate illustrations.

The authorized representative in the EU for product safety and compliance is:
Mare Nostrum Group B.V.
Mauritskade 21D
1091 GC Amsterdam
The Netherlands
Email address: gpsr@mare-nostrum.co.uk

KVK chamber of commerce number: 96249943